Reflections on
History and Historians

Reflections on History and Historians

THEODORE S. HAMEROW

THE UNIVERSITY OF WISCONSIN PRESS

Published 1987

The University of Wisconsin Press
114 North Murray Street
Madison, Wisconsin 53715

The University of Wisconsin Press, Ltd.
1 Gower Street
London WC1E 6HA, England

First printing

Printed in the United States of America

For LC CIP information see the colophon

ISBN 0-299-10930-5

Part of Chapter II appeared in a somewhat different form
in *Reviews in American History*, September 1986.

To all my old graduate students,
who taught me much more than I
ever taught them

Contents

vii

Tables

Preface

It was not my intention in writing this book to deal with the philosophy or methodology of history. Other scholars have done so more thoroughly and effectively than I could. Nor did I seek to describe and analyze the various schools of historiography which have flourished in the past or which are popular at present. I did not even try to write a history of the historical profession, although that comes a little closer to my basic purpose. I sought rather to set down my reflections on what it means to be a historian, on the feel of the discipline, on the experience of scholarship, and on the way of life which higher education represents. After more than thirty years as a practicing historian, I thought that it might be worthwhile to consider the nature of the profession, the transformation which it has undergone, and the direction in which it is moving. In doing so I found that I had to touch on some philosophical and methodological problems, to look at various historiographical schools, and to examine the structure of the discipline, but only as part of a broader attempt to portray what it is like to be a professional historian. Since little has been written on this subject, I hope that my reflections and experiences may prove of some use or interest.

The decision to write this kind of book was reinforced by my belief that history as a field of learning is going through a serious crisis. Its value to society is being questioned; its ability to provide guidance and enlightenment is under challenge. It is gradually being reduced to an academic discipline, still taught in most schools and colleges, but increasingly remote from the vital concerns of the community at large. The lack of employment opportunities for young historians, deplorable though that may be, is only the external manifestation of a deep-seated disorder affecting the intellectual foundations of historical scholarship. It is therefore more important than ever that historians look at the direction their discipline has taken in the last hundred years, at the function which it has come to perform, and at the dilemma which it now faces. They have traditionally gone about the tasks of teaching, researching, and writing without too much reflection on the assumptions or presuppositions on which their scholarly activities rest. That may not have been altogether bad. Doing is by and large more important than theorizing about what is being done. But there are times when even the most spontaneous or instinctive cultural pursuits need to be examined in the light of the purposes they serve and the goals they seek.

In the writing of this book, I have had to rely on a variety of sources and methods. To begin with, I went through a number of statistical and sociological studies dealing with the nature or structure of higher education. I read in addition various books by recent and contemporary scholars regarding the changing nature of historical learning. I looked at the memoirs and reminiscences of many people prominent in the field. And finally I relied on the observations and reflections derived from my own experience as a historian. This is admittedly a hit-and-miss methodology, and there may be those who will object to it for being unscientific and to some extent intuitive. But there are issues and problems, some of them very important, which can be dealt with only by means of a rigorous yet subjective intellectual scrutiny. The historical discipline, facing a grave and unprecedented crisis, has become involved in a fundamental debate regarding its function and goal. Such a debate is bound to reflect not only common fears and disappointments but collective hopes and aspirations. If this book succeeds in some measure in contributing to that debate, in delimiting its scope or sharpening its focus, it will have served its purpose.

Now that the writing is finished, I have the pleasant obligation of acknowledging the help I received from several well-known historians, nearly all of them nonacademics, who kindly agreed to discuss with me their views on history and historians: George Dangerfield, James Thomas Flexner, Paul Horgan, George F. Kennan, David McCullough, Edmund Morris, Arthur Schlesinger, Jr., and Barbara Tuchman. I also want to express my appreciation to a number of administrators from leading philanthropic foundations — the American Council of Learned Societies, the Ford Foundation, the Guggenheim Memorial Foundation, the National Endowment for the Humanities, the Rockefeller Foundation, and the Social Science Research Council — who shared with me their experiences and observations. To encourage them to speak freely, I promised not to reveal their names, so that now I can thank them only as a group. But their comments, illuminating and often quite candid, gave me a better understanding of the way foundations work. Herbert C. Van Deventer, Jr., helped me in preparing the statistical tables. Finally, I owe a debt of gratitude to four of my friends and colleagues in the History Department of the University of Wisconsin–Madison: John M. Cooper, Jr., Jurgen Herbst, Stanley I. Kutler, and Robert C. Nesbit. Not only did they encourage me to believe that the manuscript had some merit, but they tried to help me by pointing out mistakes and weaknesses. If I did not always follow their recommendations or heed their warnings, the fault is mine.

Theodore S. Hamerow
Madison, Wisconsin
June 1986

Reflections on
History and Historians

CHAPTER I

The Crisis in History

The historical profession in America, after some thirty years of rapid change, growth, and diversification, is today troubled by increasing doubts about its purposes and prospects. At the end of a period in which more historians produced more research in more fields than ever before, they stand wondering where the extraordinary boom of the postwar years had led them. It seems ironic that during the long decades of genteel poverty and painful maturation, even during the terrible depression of the 1930s, most of them felt confident about the future of their discipline. They may not have been in agreement about the way in which the past should be perceived and interpreted, but that history was essential for an understanding of the direction and goal of society seemed beyond dispute. Now, after all the bold ventures and exciting experiments in historical investigation of the last generation, they are less certain than ever of the importance of history for the education of the citizen, the conduct of the government, or the guidance of the community. These doubts are so profound and persistent as to suggest a grave crisis, the gravest perhaps since the emergence of history as an organized profession about a hundred years ago. The full dimensions of this crisis are still not clear, but they are visible enough to make possible a tentative examination of its origin and scope.

To be sure, not all historians will agree that the profession is in fact going through a crisis. There may be difficulties, some will argue, there may be strains and tensions, but those are the normal symptoms of a scholarly discipline experiencing growing pains, as it seeks to break out of the constricting mold of traditional approaches and methods. Many branches of learning have gone through such a phase of uncertainty before abandoning outworn orthodoxies for new and exciting truths. The doubts gnawing at historians today are the same as those which troubled astronomers during the transition from the Ptolemaic to the Copernican cosmogony or biologists shifting their thinking from the fixity to the evolution of species. Now we shake our heads in puzzlement at the tenacity with which men in the past resisted the advance of scientific truth, at their shortsightedness in clinging to obsolete theories and erroneous formulas. Will not future generations look back at the doubts of historians in the second half of the twentieth century in the same way in which we look back at the doubts of biologists in the second half of the nineteenth or of astronomers in the second half of the sixteenth century? And will they not wonder, as we wonder, how blind some scholars can be to the glorious opportunities which are beckoning to them?

There are indeed historians who still maintain that the future of the discipline can be regarded with cautious or even confident optimism. Their predictions, however, are usually contingent on some change in focus or improvement in method which alone can avoid the pitfalls besetting history. We must learn to write better; we must become more precise and scientific; we must be bolder in our hypotheses, broader in our interests, deeper in our sympathies, loftier in our aspirations. We should master the techniques of the social sciences, but we should not forget that our roots lie deep in the literary tradition of our civilization. We should learn to count and quantify without severing our ties to the humanities, which remain the foundation of a liberal education. We should learn the lessons of psychology and psychoanalysis for what they can tell us about human behavior without embracing rigid formulas which obscure the role of the historian as a creative artist. We should broaden our intellectual scope to encompass alien societies, popular cultures, and mass mentalities, but we must never forget that our ultimate goal is to synthesize, generalize, and interpret. Exhortations rain down on historians from all directions, each warning of dire consequences if it is ignored, each asserting that by heeding it we can still be saved.

A few of the prognostications are in fact surprisingly cheerful. Michael Kammen, in the introduction to a somewhat self-congratulatory volume prepared under the auspices of the American Historical Association for presentation at the Fifteenth International Congress of Historical Sciences in Bucharest in 1980, maintained that the state of the historical discipline in the United States was essentially sound. There are signs, he wrote, that "Clio's current health is robust." These signs are to be found in "the extraordinary proliferation of societies now affiliated with the American Historical Association," no fewer than sixty-eight of them. There are also the "burgeoning subdisciplines" which, because of the limitations of space, did not receive as much attention in the volume as they deserved, but which are certainly important: for example, "educational history, legal history, ethnohistory, metahistory, military history, environmental history and the histories of science and technology." Many historians now find, moreover, that they have "cross-cutting interests and multiple allegiances in the profession." If it was formerly true that history had many mansions, "it now would seem that History has suburbs and shantytowns, trailer parks and condominiums as well." Kammen did not say which are the suburbs and which the shanty-towns of history, which the trailer parks and which the condominiums. Yet the fact that so many diverse specialties and methodologies coexist within the boundaries of a single discipline suggested to him an undiminished vigor.

Kammen's assessment of the historical profession concluded on an optimistic note: "The final achievement to be noted is attributable to a fundamental shift in the angle of vision of so many historians practicing their craft in the United States today." Previous generations of historians, whether or not they avowed the familiar dictum that history is past politics, tended to deal with the structures of power — administrative, economic, ecclesiastical, social, or intellectual — in times past. The new modes of historical inquiry are likely to describe the human responses to those structures. "One result is a discipline that is more responsive to the pluralistic and increasingly egalitarian society in which it functions. A second result, we hope, will be a more cosmopolitan discipline in a shrinking world — a world that is rapidly discovering just how interdependent its past, present, and future prospects are." The impression which scholars from the rest of the world received or were expected to receive was of history in America emerging from the provincialism of its early interests to a broader and deeper understanding of the past. If the other contributors to Kammen's volume, each writing on his own specialty, felt any concern about fragmentation, insecurity, or unemployment in the profession, they generally managed to suppress it. An international conference is not a suitable place to voice doubts about what historians are doing.[1]

Among themselves, however, they should be willing to speak with greater

1. Michael Kammen, "Introduction: The Historian's Vocation and the State of the Discipline in the United States," in *The Past before Us: Contemporary Historical Writing in the United States*, ed. Michael Kammen (Ithaca, N.Y., and London, 1980), pp. 45-46.

candor. Indeed, the optimism expressed by American scholars in Bucharest probably seemed a little artificial even to their colleagues from abroad. The latter have a pretty good idea of what is happening in this country, partly because they come here often for lectures and conferences, and partly because many of them confront the same problems. The crisis facing historians in America is also facing them in England, France, Germany, and Italy. It has not yet reached the same proportions in all the countries of Western Europe, but in some it has become even more severe than in the United States. We are all in the same boat. Historians in Eastern Europe and those in Asia and Africa have in general been less seriously affected, because there government authorities help determine the relative importance of scholarly disciplines, their decision being based primarily on material or ideological utility. But wherever history has to struggle in a free intellectual marketplace against competing branches of learning for recognition by the academic community and the general public, it is in retreat. The crisis transcends political boundaries and economic circumstances; it is of international scope and probably of long duration.

The most obvious sign of this crisis, though not the most important, is the continuing unemployment among historians. In the United States the great boom beginning in the 1950s and extending to the 1970s has given way to a depression which is unprecedented in the history of the profession. It is clear in retrospect that the frantic growth of the years of prosperity could not continue indefinitely, although at the time we were told and gladly believed that we had entered a period of permanent expansion. There would always be more students, more jobs, more research funds, more salary raises. Those who failed to ride the wave of the future would be left far behind, without government subventions or foundations grants, powerless to increase faculty positions and course offerings, disqualified from organizing scholarly symposia and international conferences. Still, we were not the first to discover that the Roaring Twenties are usually followed by a Black Thursday. To the extent that historians have become more judicious, more cautious, not as sure of their infallibility, less arrogant and smug, the experience may have been salutary. Today's chastened mood after a long wild binge will perhaps make them more sensitive and critical in their scholarship, less self-satisfied, less self-righteous. The uses of adversity can be sweet.

Yet this lesson in humility is being learned at the expense of an entire generation of young scholars who have been decimated. Anyone training graduate students knows what a tragic experience it is to see dedicated and talented men and women go through five, six, or seven years of advanced study only to find, after they get their doctorates, that there is no need for them. Admittedly, those who enter graduate school at the present time to study history are aware of the risks. The more responsible departments inform their candidates for admission that the job opportunities awaiting them are slim. Besides, anyone sufficiently interested in the field to contemplate advanced training cannot be unaware that chances for employment have been dwindling. Our plight has been no secret.

But still they come, gifted young people willing to take great risks to become historians. Their number has diminished considerably, partly because many but not enough departments have reduced admissions, partly because those who have an interest in historical study are increasingly turning to other more remunerative fields. The ones who do undertake graduate work say that they recognize that the prospects are dim, but they are willing to take their chances. Still, when they complete their training and find that their years of preparation have left them with the choice of unemployment or some entirely different line of work, they are bound to feel bitter. And those of us who trained them can only watch their ordeal in silent sorrow.

What makes the crisis even more acute is that it does not affect higher education as a whole, but only some of the fields, especially in the humanities. Here is an important difference between the situation now and that of the 1930s. Then the academic depression facing the historical profession was part of an economic depression which the nation as a whole was experiencing. There were few jobs for historians, but there were also few jobs for engineers, mathematicians, or chemists, for doctors, lawyers, or bankers, for mechanics, draftsmen, or bookkeepers. Those who could not find employment in history did not have to wonder about the value of their discipline, only about the health of their economy and the justice of their society. The crisis was psychologically more bearable because it was more general, more indiscriminate. Its cruelty was blind, haphazard, affecting all pursuits and interests. No one felt singled out for irrelevancy or obsolescence, because everyone had to endure the same hardships. Even in suffering numbers lend strength. But today's historian must wonder why his discipline has experienced such a drastic decline at a time when so many others are thriving or at least holding their own. His crisis, in other words, is internal as well as external; it affects his spirit as much as his pocketbook.

It may be, of course, that this analysis is too gloomy. It may be that we are only going through a temporary depression, a result of intellectual fads and fashions which will eventually give way to a renewed recognition of the value of history. Perhaps job opportunities will improve by the end of the century, as those who were hired in the bloated postwar years finally begin to make way for younger scholars. Perhaps the college curriculum will gradually abandon the cafeteria style of course offerings, in which the appetite of the student is the principal criterion of academic significance, and return to a core of knowledge reflecting our cultural heritage in which history can again play a major role. Perhaps the next generation of young people will rediscover that today is not altogether different from yesterday, and that one cannot be understood without the other. Perhaps.

There are those who argue, as a matter of fact, that even now historians have opportunities for employment which might help alleviate the crisis, but which for one reason or another are ignored. History should leave the classroom and move into the executive suite, the government office, and the union hall. Peter N. Stearns and Joel A. Tarr, co-directors of the program in applied history and social science at Carnegie-Mellon University, concede that "as the size of college-student bodies and the security of college-based jobs have dwindled, the traditional purposes for academics' research and writing have been shaken." But the situation is not hopeless. "A new movement is under way, called public or applied history, to bring history to a nonacademic clientele and to develop uses for serious historical research that depart from the discipline's narcissism." The training provided by the new movement emphasizes skills in data management. "Historians develop a willingness to write narratives for such clients as unions, businesses and government agencies; they work out new programs, such as site preservation and writing of family history, by and for nonacademics; and they apply historical thinking to the making of public policy." Stearns and Tarr express continued confidence in the future of the historical profession, provided we learn to adjust to changing needs and interests: "Something new is required, and it may be forged from a grasp of less-than-new material, from a usable assessment of how the present and future are shaped from the past. The result can revive a key discipline: It can also provide a broader range of data and a surer sense of values to the public-policy arena. A born-again group of historians is busy making sure that our own past can serve these new needs."

Michael Kammen's prescription, though less sweeping, is essentially the same. He suggests that historians turn for help to the same source to which automobile manufacturers, railroad companies, big cities, and other enterprises threatened with bankruptcy turn: the federal government. Washington will provide the jobs which are no longer available on college campuses. More than that, the diversion of historians from the lecture hall to the government bureau will show that their discipline can perform a practical as well as pedagogical function. As he puts it, "insofar as historians do make themselves useful to society and find employment outside of academe, they not only help to counteract the job crisis for new Ph.D.s but help to demonstrate the imperative of a historical perspective as well." Indeed, there are already many scholar-bureaucrats who are proving how valuable history can be in the conduct of public affairs. "The Federal Power Commission has a historian-in-residence who is concerned with environmental matters and historical and archaeological sites. Similarly, full-time historians are now employed by the U.S. Forest Service, the U.S. Energy Research and Development Administration, the Nuclear Regulatory Commission, the U.S. Senate, and the U.S. Food and Drug Administration." Historians who would like to explore the employment opportunities in Washington, Kammen adds in a footnote, should look at a new journal, *The Public Historian*, being published by the Graduate Program in Public Historical Studies of the University of California at Santa Barbara.

A somewhat different strategy is proposed by those who argue that since jobs in traditional history are scarce, the enterprising young scholar should attach himself to some other, more prosperous branch of learning. J. Morgan Kousser of the California Institute of Technology emphasizes the importance of "quantitative social-scientific history," which is "the entrepôt for the products of many disciplines: economics, political science, sociology, demography, geography, and even some segments of anthropology." One does not have to be very astute to see which way the wind is blowing. "Although declining job opportunities and the consequent cuts in the quantity and probably the quality of history graduate students have decreased the role of graduate training in fostering the transition to a quantitatively literate profession, the employment situation is better in social science departments." Not only that, "the number of professionals interested in historical social science should continue to grow, regardless of trends in the number of historians." Kousser summarizes his argument in the language of some nineteenth-century Indian Brahmin or Chinese mandarin urging his countrymen to adjust to the white man's imperialism: "The social-scientific merchants have developed not only an extensive trade, but a large demand within the historical community for their valuable products and a comprador class to look after their interests in the new territory. Isolationism would be ill advised even if it were possible. Can the average citizens of the increasingly colonized country afford to remain semiliterate in the traders' language?" The answer is that we must learn to accept what we cannot change.[2]

How much comfort will unemployed young historians derive from all this advice? Not a great deal, probably. The prospect of developing skills in data management for such clients as unions, businesses, and government agencies is not likely to appeal to scholars interested in the development of medieval scholasticism or the coming of the French Revolution, in the Great Awakening or Jacksonian democracy, in Mogul India or Manchu China. Mastering the techniques of quantitative social-scientific history will not come easily to those who would really like to work in political, diplomatic, military, cultural, or intellectual history. For them the transition from campus to business office or from a humanistic to a scientific approach can be accomplished only by the sacrifice of precisely those values and interests which attracted them to historical learning in the first place. The nine-to-five routine of a white-collar job leaves little time for independent research, so that those who accept it renounce in effect the hope of scholarly achievement. Most important, the number of positions waiting for historians in the Federal Power Commission, the Forest Service, the Energy Research and Development Administration, the Nuclear Regulatory Commission, the Senate, and the Food and Drug Administration is both limited and diminishing. Business firms and trade unions have only a few openings for historians. And the material rewards of social-science history have been dwindling so fast that by now they hardly exceed those of humanistic history.

There thus appears to be no solution to the job crisis beyond the inexorable forces of the marketplace, which are drastically reducing the number of young historians being trained in America. In the course of the next decade or two a balance will probably be reestablished between supply and demand, but at a level far below what it had been at the height of the boom. Somber though this prognosis may be, it is surely better than the wishful illusions in which too many historians have been indulging.

The most serious aspect of the crisis, however, is not the employment situation, which will gradually become stabilized, but the decline in the importance which society assigns to historical scholarship. Until recently his-

---

2. *New York Times,* June 7, 1980; M. Kammen, "Introduction," pp. 44–45; J. Morgan Kousser, "Quantitative Social-Scientific History," in *Past before Us,* ed. M. Kammen, pp. 455–56.

tory had been regarded as central to the education which a well-informed citizen should acquire. Its prominent place in the school curriculum reflected a belief that it held the key to an understanding of the past and a vision of the future. Only if we knew from where we had come — this was the basic assumption — could we know where we were going. We accepted, too eagerly perhaps, George Santayana's warning in *The Life of Reason* that "those who cannot remember the past are condemned to repeat it." We cited it over and over again because we found it reassuring, because it seemed to imply that if we did remember the past, we would not be condemned to repeat its mistakes. History could serve as the guide of society toward our collective destiny. That was a heavy responsibility for historians to assume, but they assumed it willingly, because it enhanced their sense of importance. They felt themselves to be sages and prophets. Those among them who had doubts whether they could actually live up to such lofty expectations managed to suppress them. For how could they be expected to practice humility amid the deference — which they did nothing to discourage — of those who looked to them for understanding, wisdom, and direction? The temptation to play the seer was simply too great.

A gradual disenchantment set in, however, during the postwar years. It is still not entirely clear why it occurred, but the role of historical knowledge as a guide to the future came to be challenged by new disciplines which held out the promise of better answers than history could offer to the perplexities of our time. Economics, political science, sociology, anthropology, and psychology appeared more precise, scientific, reliable, and reassuring than history had proved to be. They were able to devise solutions to the problems of inflation and unemployment, political strife and electioneering, poverty and crime, behavior and morality, private anxiety and collective malaise. History by contrast began to seem ambiguous, indecisive, unable to inspire the sense of infallibility which society had come to expect of scholarship. Government subsidies and foundation grants, those visible symbols of esteem in the competitive world of learning, gradually shifted away from history toward other disciplines, which — to be quite candid about it — historians had looked down upon as upstarts. Here surely was a confirmation of the Biblical warning that pride goes before destruction.

Yet the rise of the social sciences on the scale of academic prestige at the expense of history was not a result simply of more vigorous entrepreneurship and greater marketing skill. In a more fundamental way it reflected a general perception, right or wrong, that the past had ceased to be a guide to the future. The changes in the world following the Second World War seemed so vast that the lessons of history, even if we could be sure what they were, would not prepare us for them. We had to turn for help to other branches of learning which, employing methods of a scientific rather than historical order, could grapple more successfully with the complexities of the age in which we live. Social scientists have largely supplanted historians as the augurs of society. Our positions are now reversed, and it is we who look with concern and a touch of envy at the more prosperous state of our academic rivals. To be sure, their place in the sun may not last even as long as ours did. There is already evidence that the social sciences will not prove much more successful than history in solving the world's ills. Their remedies and prescriptions, derived ostensibly from objective scientific investigation, appear to rest on hunch and guesswork almost as much as those which historians used to recommend. There is growing recognition that scholarship can offer no guarantees for the solution of social problems, and that the community will have to continue to rely to a large extent on hit-and-miss experimentation, common sense, and blind luck.

We have thus been forced to the conclusion that the importance of history is essentially intrinsic; it lies in the interest in the past which human beings instinctively feel as part of their humanity, and not in its relevance to the problems of a particular society or age. We have had to recognize that history in this sense is "irrelevant," and this recognition is what accounts ultimately for its eclipse in the constellation of academic disciplines. In his examination of historical learning at the present time, the philosopher Hans Meyerhoff describes the dilemma facing us: "Our age has witnessed the climax of difficulties that took shape in the nineteenth century; and a modern historicism must find its way out of a distressing and quixotic situation." There may still be those who see in history the most exhilarating testimony to the creative vigor and splendid variety of the human spirit, but it is doubtful whether many of us subscribe to a bold reaffirmation of historicism. "For most people the contemporary situation seems to be much more depressing. . . . It seems to present a gigantic jigsaw puzzle for which there is no solution." Thus the conquest of the distant frontiers of historical knowledge has also coincided with an increasing awareness of the meaninglessness of history. And this awareness has in turn led to a decline in the appetite for historical knowledge. "There is a deep craving for an escape from the nightmare of history into a mode of existence beyond history: art, mythology, religion, or apathy."

To Meyerhoff this disenchantment is the natural result of the dilemmas besetting modern man to which history can no longer offer satisfactory answers. The world has become too complex to be understood by a process of historical analysis, he maintains:

Who can still make sense out of history either as a theoretical system or in its impact upon the life of the individual. For most people the succession of events in history is so rapid, paradoxical, and unintelligible, the powers that guide them so elusive, irrational, and uncontrollable that they feel lost in this world of history which they did not make. The only alternatives they seem to face are either to abdicate and leave history to the historians or to escape, as many historians choose to do, from the burdens of history into a faith beyond history.

To our society, then, the methodology of historical scholarship appears inadequate for an understanding of the world in which we live. The brave phrases about history being our guide to the future, about knowing whence we have come so that we may know whither we are going, about those who cannot remember the past being condemned to repeat it, all sound a little hollow now. The promises historians made, to others as well as themselves, that they could steer a safe course for mankind amid the perils of an uncharted future seem naive and clearly unfulfillable. Here and there they may still be able to offer a piece of good advice, a sound analysis, a sharp insight, a constructive suggestion. But they can no longer pose as the guides and prophets of our age. No one would believe them, even if they tried.[3]

It is this growing sense of fallibility which helps explain the decision of many historians in the postwar period to seek the assistance of other disciplines, especially the social sciences. These disciplines had lived in a state of uneasy coexistence with history for a long time, each side regarding the other with outward cordiality but covert suspicion. To the social scientists, historians appeared unmethodical, imprecise, and sometimes patronizing. To the historians, social scientists seemed preoccupied with concepts, principles, and definitions; they seemed more interested in theory than practice, appearance than reality. Once in a while some scholar would try to cross the boundary between historical and social-scientific scholarship, but he was an exception, almost an oddity. By and large historians and social scientists

3. Hans Meyerhoff, "History and Philosophy: An Introduction," in *The Philosophy of History in Our Time*, ed. Hans Meyerhoff (Garden City, N.Y., 1959), pp. 22–23.

went their separate ways, neither feeling much need to collaborate with the other. Only after the mid-century did this academic isolationism begin to diminish, due primarily to the efforts of historians, not social scientists. It was the historians who came to feel that economists, statisticians, political scientists, sociologists, anthropologists, and psychologists could enrich and fortify their discipline, not the other way around. While some of the social sciences — sociology and political science, for example — did develop a growing interest in historical problems, the main current of influence flowed in the other direction. It might be an exaggeration to say that the relationship between the social sciences and history became that of patron and client; it might be closer to the truth to speak of a partnership between them. But history was undeniably the junior partner.

The reason for the sudden attention paid by historians to the insights and techniques of the social scientists lies in the first place in their recognition of the vulnerability of their own discipline. As they saw history ceasing to be regarded as essential for an understanding of our society, they began to seek, consciously or unconsciously, to regain their sense of mastery through a change of emphasis and methodology. This is in no way to deny that the social sciences do in fact have a great deal to give to the historian. They can teach him to be more persuasive in some of his conclusions, more precise in some of his generalizations, more understanding in some of his perceptions. Quantification can be very useful in dealing with certain kinds of historical problems, sociology in dealing with others, psychology with still others. There are valid objective reasons for broadening the historian's horizon with the help of insights borrowed from other disciplines. But the sudden rush to the social sciences of so many historians at the same time after such a long period of indifference suggests a widespread feeling that the traditional *modus operandi* of their craft is no longer adequate. It represents an attempt to transcend the limitations and ambiguities of historical knowledge by new categories of analysis. It reflects a determination to alter the nature of historical investigation by scientific or quasi-scientific techniques. It seeks to make history get outside its own skin, so to speak.

The result has been a revolution in historical scholarship greater than any since its beginning more than two thousand years ago. Historians have increasingly turned away from the traditional narrative form describing political, diplomatic, military, economic, constitutional, and cultural events and processes toward problems which in the past were the preserve of the social scientists. They have begun to develop subspecialties and subdisciplines which can best be described as historical statistics, historical demography, historical sociology, historical anthropology, and historical psychology or psychohistory. They have shifted their attention more and more to the quantitative analysis of voting patterns and social backgrounds, to changes in birth, marriage, and death rates, to folkways and mores, to popular cultures and collective mentalities, to the structure of the community and the composition of the family, and to the countless details of everyday life as it was lived by the inarticulate masses whom traditional history had largely ignored. Scholarly organizations and learned journals began to appear devoted exclusively to one or another of these new subdivisions of history. The government and the foundations expressed by their financial grants approval of what they regarded as "cross-fertilization," a word dear to the hearts of those bestowing academic subsidies. And the social scientists themselves encouraged by means of symposia, colloquia, and interdisciplinary conferences the conversion of those who had in the past been not only unbelievers but competitors.

What effect has this transformation had on the conditions and prospects of historical scholarship in America? Although it has been going on for a generation or more, there is still no agreement regarding its result. At first the pendulum seemed to swing in favor of those who greeted the new history as a way out of the wilderness, as the only escape from decline, neglect, and irrelevance. Now it appears to be moving in the other direction, toward a recognition that the new history is encountering some of the same difficulties which had beset the old. While its supporters continue to predict ultimate victory, their initial confidence and enthusiasm have begun to evaporate. This is not to say that the outcome is clear, but the contest no longer appears as one-sided as in its early stages. In one corner are the historians who feel that out of the innovation and experimentation in which they are engaged will emerge a new historical discipline, stronger, broader, more scientific, more usable, more relevant. In the other are those who maintain that the crisis in history is the result of forces so profound that no amount of tinkering with technique or content can alter their effect. While it is too early to tell which side is right, the promise of the new history does not shine as brightly as it once did.

Its supporters, however, continue to defend their position with a variety of arguments and logics. Some declare that the historians really have no choice, that either we will save our discipline with the aid of the social sciences or we will go down. We may not all be fond of our new allies, but they are the only ones we have. Take the views of Geoffrey Barraclough, who wrote extensively on the problems of history and historical learning. In a book published in 1955, he seemed to endorse the position of those who assert that the decline of history is irreversible. We are assailed by a sense of uncertainty, he wrote, because we feel that we stand on the threshold of a new age to which previous experience offers no sure guide. "One result of this new situation is that history itself is losing, if it has not already lost, the hold which it once exercised over the best minds as a key to present living." At a time when the crisis was still in its early stages, when funds and students were still plentiful, Barraclough was already foreseeing a future collapse.

Yet more than twenty years later, in a long article which he contributed to a volume dealing with research in the "social and human sciences," Barraclough appeared to have changed his mind. There is hope after all, he now argued, there are opportunities which can save us, if we recognize and seize them:

> Only history can provide the insight we need for a full understanding of the working of social processes and social institutions in time. But it must be a history approached in a scientific spirit and infused with a social purpose. Recent developments have brought such a history within our grasp: it is for the new generation to take it and put it to good use. We live today in a society which requires positive returns from its investment not only in capital equipment but in expensively trained manpower, which expects the social scientist to frame working hypotheses by which we can harness nature to our purposes and transform our environment. The historian is not exempt from this demand. In the short run he may perhaps continue comfortably enough in the old ways. But in the long run he will be judged — and history will be judged with him — by the contribution he makes, in co-operation with other related disciplines, in using his knowledge of the past for the shaping of the future.

The meaning was clear. Historians must provide society with "positive returns" on its "investment" in the form of guidelines to the future developed in collaboration with the social scientists. If they succeed, all will be well. If not, they will pay the penalty which investors usually impose on those to whom they have entrusted their money in the unfulfilled expectation of making a profit.[4]

4. Geoffrey Barraclough, *History in a Changing World* (Oxford, 1955), p. 1; idem, "History," in *Main Trends of Research in the Social and Human Sciences*, part 2, volume 1, ed. Jacques Havet (The Hague, Paris, and New York, 1978), p. 443.

Most defenders of the new history, however, support their position with arguments of principle rather than expediency. To them the important thing is not whether society finds what they are doing useful. What matters is that they are breaking down the walls within which history has been imprisoned; they are uncovering new fields of historical investigation the existence of which earlier generations had not even imagined. They are pioneers and pathfinders. They are broadening, deepening, refining, and clarifying the range of their discipline. Their writings reflect a sense of discovery, an exuberance derived from the feeling that they stand on the threshold of a golden age of historical learning.

There is the article, for example, which the sociologist Edward Shils of the University of Chicago published in 1966 concerning the emergence of an entirely different kind of historical learning. We are seeing in the United States the first signs of "a scholarly amalgamation of history and the social sciences," he wrote, at a time when scholars have ceased to regard it as legitimate to confine themselves within the boundaries of their own society, and historians are beginning to free themselves from the bonds of historicism. The result, which we can see at present only in a very incipient state, is "a scholarly comparative social science and a comparative history." It is the beginning of a true *"science humaine."*

Or listen to the talk which H. Stuart Hughes, who has written brilliantly on the history of ideas, gave at a colloquium series of the Harvard Center for Cognitive Studies, later published in a collection of his essays. New approaches to an old discipline have taught us, he asserted, that if we turned the conventional prism of historical vision only a little, "a whole new world of possibilities would come into view." They have released us from bondage to a type of study which had narrowed the aim of history to the systematic exploitation of documentary materials. As Hughes portrayed the exciting intellectual vistas before us, his tone began to rise. "I think it is quite possible that the study of history today is entering a period of rapid change and advance such as characterized the science of physics in the first three decades of the twentieth century." This advance is proceeding on a number of fronts simultaneously. The social historians are incorporating into their thought the stream of speculation on class and status and on the relation of economic activities to the cultural "superstructure" which descends from Karl Marx and Max Weber. In the fields of economic and political history alike, imaginative scholars are experimenting with applications of quantitative method and the calculus of probabilities. Most important, "on the boundary where the concerns of anthropology, biology, the humanities, and psychology meet and blend, the historian is at last beginning to broaden his definition of human motivation and of psycho-physical change."

The most eloquent, plausible, and persuasive defense of the new history, however, came from Lawrence Stone, whose massive study of the English aristocracy from the accession of Elizabeth I to the outbreak of the Civil War is a standard work in the field. For him the importance of the new history lies not in its methods and techniques. As a matter of fact, he maintains, the intelligent reading public, eager to learn about the latest discoveries of historical scholarship, is repelled by "indigestible statistical tables, dry analytical argument, and jargon-ridden phrases." As a result, structural, analytical, and quantitative historians have been increasingly talking only to one another. Their findings have been published in learned journals and monographs which only libraries feel a need to buy. What makes the new history important is that it is examining in the past the same problems and issues which demography, sociology, anthropology, and psychology are examining in the present:

> The questions being asked by the "new historians" are, after all, those which preoccupy us all today: the nature of power, authority and charismatic leadership; the relation of political institutions to underlying social patterns and value systems; attitudes to youth, old age, disease and death; sex, marriage and concubinage; health, contraception and abortion; work, leisure and conspicuous consumption; the relationship of religion, science and magic as explanatory models of reality; the strength and direction of the emotions of love, fear, lust, and hate; the impact of literacy and education upon people's lives and ways of looking at the world; the relative importance attached to different social groupings, such as the family, kin, community, nation, class and race; the strength and meaning of ritual, symbol and custom as ways of binding a community together; moral and philosophical approaches to crime and punishment; patterns of deference and outbursts of egalitarianism; structural conflicts between status groups or classes; the means, possibilities and limitations of social mobility; the nature and significance of popular protest and millenarian hopes; the shifting ecological balance between man and nature; the causes and effects of disease. All these are burning issues at the moment and are concerned with the masses rather than the élite. They are more "relevant" to our own lives than the doings of dead kings, presidents and generals.

This is the authentic voice of today's new history, in its mature stage, slightly disillusioned after three decades of experimenting with quantitative, structural, and analytical approaches, but still hopeful that it can save the discipline by broadening its scope and democratizing its content.[5]

There is still a third group of historians who remain optimistic: those who deny that there is a crisis to begin with. There may be problems, some of them quite serious, they concede, but these are only temporary difficulties which can be overcome with courage and determination. The state of history remains essentially sound; indeed, evidence suggests that it is or at least that it may be improving. No more than a few such optimists are left at the present time, but only yesterday they sounded cheerful and confident amid the gathering gloom. What made their confidence all the more reassuring or puzzling was that among them could be found highly gifted and perceptive historians, historians of sound judgment and sharp insight. Surely, their optimism had to be more than wishful thinking.

Consider the opinion of John L. Snell, whose promising career as a student of German history was cut short by an untimely death. In a book which appeared in 1962 dealing with the training of historians in the United States, he suggested that historical scholarship might soon regain the eminent position in the world of learning which it had occupied in the past. During the eighteenth century, he recalled, when much less history was being published than today, about a fourth of all the books in private libraries in France were histories. Can history in America at the present hope for so large a measure of acceptance? To Snell the answer was that a rediscovery of literary art and a renewal of the capacity for generalization can make history a more vital cultural force than it has been in this century. And even more heartening, "the admonitions of the last decade allow one to hope that both are underway."

The views of John Higham, a leading authority on American intellectual history, were equally encouraging. In a work published in 1965, he sounded as sanguine as Snell. Since the Second World War relations between professional historians and the reading public have gradually moved into a new and more hopeful phase. The sharp intellectual cleavage between them which characterized the 1920s and 1930s has diminished, as the social grievances of the academic community have lessened. Considerable public interest in

5. Edward Shils, "Seeing It Whole," *Times Literary Supplement*, July 28, 1966, p. 648; H. Stuart Hughes, *History as Art and as Science: Twin Vistas on the Past* (New York, Evanston, Ill., and London, 1964), pp. 20–21; Lawrence Stone, "The Revival of Narrative: Reflections on a New Old History," *Past & Present* 85 (1979): 15.

the past persists, and what is more important, much of that interest exists now on a higher plane. The spectacular and florid types of historical literature which once flourished, the historical novel and the romantic biography, have greatly declined. Nor do sweeping surveys any longer meet our cultural needs. Instead, a better educated public is, with greater self-assurance, buying substantial histories of a war, an age, or a single episode. This advance in sophistication has brought part of the reading public within reach of professional historians, while many of the latter in turn are welcoming the chance to be heard without demeaning themselves.

All signs thus point toward a revitalization of historical learning, Higham concluded. "Changes in American society and culture since World War II have somewhat revived the prestige and influence of the humanistic scholar and diminished the alienation between the professional historian and the American public." A new basis has gradually emerged for a richer historical culture. "We are now in a position to observe a parallel development on the level of theory: a revival of confidence in historical knowledge." The restoration of intellectual self-respect which has taken place since 1945 has not in any simple way resulted from an improvement in the social status of historians, for the intellectual transformation began before a new social adjustment became apparent. Indeed, the former contributed to the latter. "But emancipation from skeptical and derivative theories of history might not have gone very far if the historian's morale and his position in American culture had not hearteningly improved." All in all, we can look forward to the future with hope, confident that time is our ally.[6]

Today that analysis seems shallow, for the decline of self-assurance among historians during the last decade has been sharp and rapid. It was easy, perhaps even reasonable, to be optimistic during the affluent 1960s, when exciting new contributions to the study of history teemed, when subspecialties proliferated and subdisciplines multiplied. History was like Africa in the second half of the nineteenth century, a dark continent, circumnavigated but to a large extent unknown, now suddenly being explored, delimited, partitioned, and annexed. There was a scramble to establish priority of discovery, to stake out the first claim. Many historians were caught up in the headlong race of academic imperialism, not sure of what they might find,

6. Dexter Perkins and John L. Snell, *The Education of Historians in the United States* (New York, San Francisco, Toronto, and London, 1962), p. 172; John Higham, Leonard Krieger, and Felix Gilbert, *History* (Englewood Cliffs, N.J., 1965), pp. 82, 132.

but convinced that it would be humiliating to be left behind. For those who lagged would be labeled hacks, dullards, old fogies, and sticks-in-the-mud. In the midst of this intellectual gold rush, optimism seemed justified. But by the end of the 1970s the unknown continent had been explored; the excitement of an age of discovery had given way to a feeling of powerlessness in the face of shrinking opportunities. An era of somber reflection and soul-searching had begun.

Yet even during the roaring sixties there were writers warning against overconfidence in historical learning. At the same time that Snell was finding in a rediscovery of literary art and a renewal of the capacity for generalization the key to a revitalization of history, at the same time that Higham was insisting that the historian's morale and his position in American culture had hearteningly improved, J. H. Plumb, a British scholar whose writings dealt with history and historians on both sides of the Atlantic, was suggesting that the assumptions which had traditionally served to justify the study of the past were now largely eroded. In an essay on "The Historian's Dilemma" published in 1964, he declared that Edward Albee's *Who's Afraid of Virginia Woolf?*, a play of unrelenting rage and anguish in an academic setting, implies that history is without meaning, power, or hope. "Among the professional historians the idea of progress is out. Ninety percent, perhaps, prefer Mr. Albee's view, that the subject they practise is meaningless in any ultimate sense." Here lies a tragic paradox, he continued. Our century has witnessed the brilliant conquest of the distant frontiers of historical knowledge, "yet fewer and fewer historians believe that their art has any social purpose: any function as a coordinator of human endeavour or human thought." While around him scholars were scurrying to find El Dorado, Plumb remained full of forebodings.

Whether 90 per cent of all professional historians in the early 1960s shared the view that history had become meaningless may be doubtful, but it is clear that even then there was an undercurrent of anxiety among them concerning the direction in which their discipline was moving. Two decades later the optimism of the postwar years had been largely superseded by a growing feeling of depression. Here and there some writer would still maintain that history can be saved with the aid of the government, the business community, the trade unions, the social sciences, the techniques of quantification, the insights of psychoanalysis, the discovery of new fields of investigation, or the laws of economics which decree that every depression is sooner or later followed by a new prosperity. But more and more historians were beginning to sense that the profession had entered a period of crisis different from any it had previously experienced. It was not just a question of waiting until the market improved, until demand caught up with supply. The justification of historical learning was being questioned; the foundation of historical knowledge was in danger. The crisis was not one of jobs and funds; it was a crisis of confidence.

Its intensity was even reflected in the volume on *The Past Before Us* which was presented in 1980 to the Fifteenth International Congress of Historical Sciences. In the introduction Michael Kammen had spoken hopefully of the advances which historical learning in America had made during the previous decade. But the tone of the concluding essay, on the teaching of history, by Hazel Whitman Hertzberg, professor of history and education at the Teachers College of Columbia University, was entirely different. She spoke of the gravity of the crisis we face, "a crisis not only for historians but also for the American people." For a century now historians have had the formal teaching of the past in their keeping, since it was in the classroom that most Americans confronted the glories and follies of their own past and the past of humankind. Put aside for the moment the question of how fundamental historical consciousness is to the future of our society, she argued, how destructive the consequences if only stray bits and pieces of history fall haphazardly into people's minds, how harmful the results of a national historical lobotomy. It is clear nevertheless that "at the close of the 1970s history's position in the classrooms and curricula of American schools and colleges was based essentially on the dwindling capital created by earlier generations of historians."

In her opinion, institutional inertia had been history's curricular protector as well as its insidious enemy. Even the research function of history could not flourish indefinitely, if the educational base on which it rested continued to crumble. Yet the revival of the teaching of history, so vital to society, so essential to the historical profession, had only begun. What the teaching of history needed, Hertzberg concluded, were theories, historical analyses, and unifying ideas sufficiently powerful to recreate a sense of purpose, sufficiently broad to encompass all who teach and learn history, sufficiently applicable to reshape the curriculum and inform the teaching, and sufficiently persuasive to convince students as well as the public that history in the schools and colleges is worth studying. Such developments, however, required profound changes in the structure and direction of the profession. "Whether American historians would so commit themselves to the study and practice of teaching was . . . a question that could not yet be answered."

There were those, however, who felt that it could be answered. They felt that the sense of superfluity and dispensability which was spreading through the profession made a renewed commitment to the study and practice of teaching appear unlikely. To them this was an inescapable conclusion, harsh but preferable to self-deception. The most poignant statement of their doctrine of renunciation came from David Herbert Donald of Harvard, as he prepared for the opening of a new academic year in the fall of 1977. In an article entitled "Our Irrelevant History," which appeared on the "Op-Ed" page of the *New York Times*, he uttered the unutterable. America in the second half of the twentieth century faced problems so complex that the past could offer no guidance for their solution. What, then, could the historian tell undergraduates which might help them in this new and unprecedented age? Perhaps his most useful function would be "to disenthrall them from the spell of history," to help them recognize the irrelevance of the past, to assist them in understanding what Lincoln meant in saying that "the dogmas of the quiet past are inadequate to the stormy present." Perhaps he could also make it easier for some students to face a troubled future by reminding them to what a limited extent human beings control their own destiny. As he began his new set of lectures on American history, Donald declared, he would take his text from Reinhold Niebuhr: "Nothing that is worth doing can be achieved in our lifetime; therefore we must be saved by hope."

Yet the hope by which historians must be saved, according to this argument, sounds almost indistinguishable from hopelessness. It implies a conscious abandonment of the traditional view that history can teach and enlighten us, that it can help us make right decisions and adopt wise policies. Instead, history only shows us how weak and fallible we are, how little influence we have over what happens to us, how helpless we are in the grip of the elemental forces which shape human existence. Here was a doctrine of resignation and existential despair which only the courageous or fatalistic could accept. Most historians decided that it could not or at least that it should not be true, for to believe otherwise would be too distressing.

Donald's *cri de coeur* did send a ripple of uneasiness through the profession. He had peeked behind the veil of the temple; he had questioned an article of faith. His essay was promptly reprinted in the *AHA Newsletter*, followed by two rejoinders. The first, from Edward L. Keenan, professor of history and dean of the Harvard Graduate School of Arts and Sciences,

gently chided "dear David" for losing faith in the value of his discipline.
"I, too, struggle each semester with uncertainty about the worth of 'facts'
in the classroom, and even, when the hour is late, with darker doubts about
the worthiness of my activity in general. I, too, despair for the young historians who can find no jobs, and for the Republic that provides them none."
Still, the most important means of production and the most crucial resources
of society are human resources, the resources embodied in a highly trained,
inventive, and responsive citizenry. We still have them, even in our present
travail, in an abundance that is the child of our abundance. Some of these
resources, our students, are entrusted for a time to our care. We must struggle against our doubts to teach them to see the past in a context in which
they can discover "not only that history is relevant, but that they are."

The second rejoinder, from Blanche Wiesen Cook, associate professor of
history at John Jay College of Criminal Justice, CUNY, was less gentle. It
opened with the declaration that Donald's lament for history would be "poignant," if it were not so "wrong-headed." It then went on to explain that
history as it has been taught in the past, the history whose irrelevance he
had acknowledged, largely ignored the poor, the exploited, the oppressed.
Indeed, many of the lessons taught by professional historians are not merely
irrelevant but dangerous, because they are not and never were true. Only
people are capable of progress, not the vagaries of "hope." People can control their own destiny. History is a record of the continual struggle to do
so, and of the frequent and gallant triumphs which people have achieved.
We must create a human destiny marked not by control but by security and
dignity. We live in revolutionary times, and revolution is a process, not an
event. Finally, the peroration: "If we aspire to teach history we must avoid
the temptation to become antiquarians. During World War II, the great
French historian Marc Bloch, a victim of the holocaust, wrote of the difference. Antiquarians revere buildings and institutions. They romanticize the
past. Historians are citizens of the present who love life."

The profession in general, however, read Donald's article in silence, em-
barrassed by his *credo quia absurdum*. It was so clearly indiscreet, so obviously inexpedient, suitable perhaps for discussion on the campus, but
hardly on the pages of a widely read newspaper. Too close to the truth to
be peremptorily rejected, it was too painful to be readily accepted. It became part of the private agony of a discipline going through a period of
decline.

But the most systematic statement of the pessimistic position regarding the future of history appeared in a collection of essays by Donald's colleague at Harvard, Oscar Handlin, published in 1979 under the defiant title *Truth in History*. Handlin like Donald believes that the profession is in the grip of a crisis from which there appears to be no escape. The golden age is behind us; ahead stretches the dreary prospect of isolation, superfluity, and atrophy. But whereas to Donald this decline is a result of the irresistible forces of the time in which we live, to Handlin it is a retribution for our weaknesses and transgressions, particularly our surrender to faddism and modishness. The fault is not in our stars but in ourselves. We ourselves undermined a vital discipline, we perverted its function, we destroyed its cohesion. No one has criticized the new history more harshly than Handlin for its reliance on the social sciences, its penchant for quantification, and its endless hunt for novelty. His *J'accuse* against the efforts of the historical profession to remain "relevant" is expressed in language so trenchant and uncompromising that it must be quoted, not summarized:

> In the frenzied effort to cope, prospective teachers struggled to sharpen performing and teaching skills — to innovate. A few aging radicals still threatened to tear the world down, but the most common response was assertively to promise that the subject would equip citizens with the nostrums to dissolve current and future problems. "Perhaps," a professor wistfully wrote, "the criteria for organizing introductory courses in history may emerge from present-day ecological interest." Ecology, which treated "the shape of things, both in the beginning and in an approaching end," offered "a new and attractive alternative to the remnants of the traditional histories."
>
> The effort to float with that particular fashion was doomed to futility, as were earlier frantic scratchings for substance, in femininity, ethnicity, and population. The obvious practical rewards students valued were not within the power of departments of history to bestow. The study of the past was not pre-anything; it did not promise ready entry into a lucrative profession; it did not offer direct access to positions of prestige or authority. Nor would sleek audiovisuals stir the interest of an audience reared since childhood on TV offerings. Stuck with a product not easy to sell, the historians and their professional organizations tumbled into a scramble for customers which for earnestness would have gladdened the heart of any PR man, and for awkwardness would have saddened his sense of technical competence.
>
> A pity. The misdirected search for clients obscured the genuine values of the discipline. History could not compete for attention on any terms but its own. Other, more flexible departments of knowledge could always outbid it in a marketplace geared to relevances. In the rivalry for audiences likely to

be attracted by quick cures for the ills of personality or society or pulled by entertaining images on a screen, the historian was at a hopeless disadvantage. What remained, therefore, was the plea from unemployment, a plea more likely to evoke sympathy than support, because all too often it implied that the use of history was to feed historians.

The basic problem, according to Handlin, is that the profession has lost its sense of purpose and direction. It confused popular acceptance with intellectual validity, so that having forfeited the one, it began to have doubts about the other. Standing on uncertain ground, blinded by the urgencies of the academic marketplace, historians neglected the true value of their subject. "The crisis they perceived was but the surface manifestation of a deeper, less readily visible ill that sapped the vitality of the profession." Even the terrible problem of unemployment was the result not of professional oversupply but of inadequate training. For while scores of Ph.D.'s without jobs drifted into other occupations, desirable positions went unfilled because of the lack of scholars qualified to fill them. Handlin did not say where these desirable positions waiting for qualified scholars were to be found, but he was convinced that the crisis of the historical profession was a result of the abandonment of solid, time-tested learning for fads, fashions, tricks, and gimmicks. "Erosion of the basic skills, atrophy of familiarity with the essential procedures, dissipation of the core fund of knowledge left stranded many worthy individuals, who simply did not know what they were doing or why. Only a reversal of the trend could redeem the discipline and lead to our understanding of the true uses of history."

How likely was such a reversal? Not very, Handlin concluded, because we have destroyed the feeling of community which had sustained and nurtured the profession in the past. The historian must now work in isolation, deprived of the support which comes from the knowledge that his research is part of a great collective quest for knowledge. In his youth Handlin had feared "the fate of the dusty little men in dusty little rooms, who hoarded up the dusty little learning no one valued." He had wanted to believe that a net of connections with what has gone before and what will follow would support his scholarship. But now his fears conjured up a more grotesque image: "a super, super, super market, in which shiny, shiny men stock the endless shelves, indiscriminate, inarticulate, each to his own pitch — with no questions asked about the content of the boxes." He therefore tried now to read and write each book as if it stood entirely alone, following nothing, with nothing to follow, its worth depending entirely on its contents. It was this sense of fragmentation and rootlessness which Handlin found most painful. He continued to look, though without much success, for evidence of a modest upturn, of a slow recovery. "The crisis may pass, and chaos may prove to be the present appearance of new forms sturdier than any of their predecessors. The historian may nurse that much hope. But he must not confuse wish with reality, and he cannot pretend to be one of a community that no longer exists." The discipline had suffered a terrible loss which could not be made good for a long time to come.[7]

The tone of pessimism concerning the future of history is so clear and persistent — not only in the writings of Plumb, Hertzberg, Donald, and Handlin, but in discussions on campuses all across the country — that it is difficult to escape the conclusion that the profession is indeed going through an unprecedented crisis of which falling enrollments and shrinking jobs are only outward manifestations. The complaints about the erosion of the discipline, about its loss of purpose, lack of direction, and decline of confidence, all suggest that the crisis is intellectual rather than economic in nature. They suggest that history may have reached a turning point, one of the most important in its evolution as a branch of learning, as important as the one reached a little more than a hundred years ago when it first became an academic pursuit. We may be witnessing the conclusion of that process; we may be witnessing the decline of history as an organized occupation and its return to a less institutionalized and professionalized form of cultural endeavor.

There is no need to make this sound too apocalyptic. It certainly does not imply that history is about to disappear from the college curriculum, the way theology or rhetoric disappeared. But it does seem that history as an academic discipline is approaching the position reached by the classics sixty years ago or by philosophy forty years ago, that is, branches of knowledge, once regarded as essential, which are still included among the course offerings of any respectable college as evidence of a commitment to higher learning, but no longer with a wide appeal to students and teachers. Such disciplines gradually come to perform a ceremonial rather than practical function in the academic community, a little like the caps and gowns worn

7. J. H. Plumb, "The Historian's Dilemma," in *Crisis in the Humanities*, ed. J. H. Plumb (Baltimore, 1964), pp. 25–26; Hazel Whitman Hertzberg, "The Teaching of History," in *Past before Us*, ed. M. Kammen, pp. 503–54; *New York Times*, September 8, 1977; *AHA Newsletter*, December 1977, pp. 4–6; Oscar Handlin, *Truth in History* (Cambridge, Mass., and London, 1979), pp. vii–ix, 22–23.

in commencement processions. History is beginning to move in this direction, and while it still has a long way to go before it reaches the exoticism of Greek and Latin, the similarity to the process by which the classics arrived at their present situation is too close for complacency.

Indeed, the decline of history in higher education appears to be part of the decline of the disciplines with which it had been combined during the nineteenth century to form the "humanities," the mainstay of a "liberal education." At that time the chief justification for the inclusion of history in the college curriculum had been that, like languages, literature, philosophy, and religion, it familiarized the mind of the student with the collective wisdom of our civilization. Such disciplines did not have a utilitarian purpose; they did not provide training for any particular pursuit or occupation. Their importance lay precisely in their impracticality, in their uselessness for making a living. In an age of exuberant industrialization and rugged individualism, they represented a conspicuous consumption of learning, just as mansions and servants represented a conspicuous consumption of wealth. The man who attended the university was demonstrating that he did not have to work with his hands or drudge in a countinghouse or salesroom. Perhaps he would eventually prepare himself for one of the learned professions; perhaps he would choose the life of a gentleman of leisure. But in any case, he would not support himself by any of the lower forms of employment. The education he received was as much a badge of distinction as the clothing he wore or the vocabulary he used.

Those who accepted this system of higher education did not dwell on its social and psychological function. They were as a rule not even aware of it. If it had been mentioned to them, they would no doubt have rejected the idea indignantly. To them the learning taught in colleges and universities stood above race and class, wealth and birth. Its purpose was to refine and improve human nature, to mold a temper of mind and a quality of character. The academic community had the responsibility of nourishing cultural and intellectual individualism, just as the civil community fostered political and economic individualism. The goal was self-understanding and self-improvement, for the perfection of society can be achieved only through the perfection of the individual. This ideal of learning was advanced by many writers during the nineteenth century, in Europe as well as America, but no one spoke of it more eloquently or persuasively than John Stuart Mill in 1867 in his inaugural address as rector of the University of Saint Andrews:

Universities are not intended to teach the knowledge required to fit men for some special mode of gaining their livelihood. Their object is not to make skillful lawyers, or physicians, or engineers, but capable and cultivated human beings. . . . Men are men before they are lawyers, or physicians, or merchants, or manufacturers; and if you make them capable and sensible men, they will make themselves capable and sensible lawyers or physicians. What professional men should carry away with them from an University, is not professional knowledge, but that which should direct the use of their professional knowledge, and bring the light of general culture to illuminate the technicalities of a special pursuit. Men may be competent lawyers without general education, but it depends on general education to make them philosophic lawyers —who demand, and are capable of apprehending, principles, instead of merely cramming their memory with details. And so of all other useful pursuits, mechanical included. Education makes a man a more intelligent shoemaker, if that be his occupation, but not by teaching him how to make shoes; it does so by the mental exercise it gives, and the habits it impresses.

Here is a classic statement of what was once regarded as the main purpose of higher education.[8]

It may have been a mistake, however, for the humanities to become closely identified with a system of learning which was exclusive and hierarchical in nature. Their complaisance was understandable, to be sure. They had been invited to become the keystone of an educational structure which purported to shape and direct human nature. Who could resist such a tempting opportunity, both noble and remunerative? Yet by accepting the perfection of the individual as the chief justification of their inclusion in the college curriculum, the humanities were running a terrible risk. For the ideal of personal cultural development, suitable to an age of laissez-faire capitalism, could not be sustained in an era of growing social consciousness. At a time when individual enterprise seemed more important for the welfare of the community than collective justice, liberal education had the effect of helping to internalize the problem of class relations, of diverting it from public action to private conscience. Those troubled by the pitilessness of an economy based on unrestrained entrepreneurship were taught that lasting reform cannot be achieved by coercive government regulation but only by intellectual and moral improvement. Thereby the demand for a more equitable organization of the community became divided and weakened.

8. John Stuart Mill, *Inaugural Address Delivered to the University of St. Andrews, Feb. 1st 1867* (London, 1867), pp. 5-7.

Among those who had studied the humanities were slaveholders and mill-owners, militarists and imperialists, jingoists and racists, exploiters, oppressors, profiteers, and hucksters. Their knowledge of Greek and Latin, of philosophy and literature, and even of history appears to have done little to curb their rapacity or soften their harshness. Life and learning were separated and compartmentalized, so that what men learned in school had little effect on how they behaved in the world. Thus, by committing themselves to a system of higher education which, whatever its claim to transcendent truth, served in large part the interests of the dominant classes at a particular stage in the development of society, the humanities took a long chance.

This is not to say that they have had no value other than to help maintain an exclusive organization of learning corresponding to an exclusive organization of wealth and power. The humanities can nourish the spirit and challenge the mind. They have an inherent esthetic and intellectual appeal which many people find irresistible. Those making a serious commitment to them are as a rule more sensitive, tolerant, discerning, and reflective than those devoting themselves exclusively to the business of everyday living. But the question is, How did they acquire their sensitivity, tolerance, discernment, and reflectiveness? Do the humanities make us more humane? Does a liberal education make us more liberal? Himmler, the son of a secondary-school teacher, knew the classics well, but they did not teach him much kindness. Goebbels had studied literature and history at the university without learning generosity or compassion. What the humanities bring to the student is what the student brings to the humanities. If he likes art or music, they may make him more appreciative; if he has a bent for philosophy, they may make him more perceptive; if he is interested in literature, they may make him more knowledgeable; and if he is attracted to history, they may make him more temperate and judicious. But they cannot teach wisdom or virtue; they cannot shape human nature or mold human character. To pretend that they can only invites disappointment and rejection.

This is the heart of the problem which the humanities face today. Having become identified with the individualistic cultural ideals of the past, they appear irrelevant to the collective social aspirations of the present. To put it another way, society in the second half of the twentieth century has become increasingly committed to the achievement of greater justice for disadvantaged groups in the community, for the poor, weak, scorned, and oppressed. Hence the resolve to abolish poverty, end discrimination, emancipate social and ethnic minorities, reverse the process of urban decline, provide greater economic opportunity for women, broaden the availability of education, lighten the burden of exploitation, and reduce the danger of war. These goals are being pursued with the same determination with which a hundred years ago people pursued the production of goods and the accumulation of wealth. The humanities, however, appear to have little to contribute to the quest for collective equity. Society has therefore turned to the social, behavioral, and natural sciences, which promise to provide practical solutions for its problems. Whether they can deliver on those promises remains to be seen, but in its search for greater social and economic equality, the community has come to regard the humanities as peripheral to its central concerns.

The supporters of the humanities do not usually see the problem in this light. They tend to complain that we live in an age of materialism, an age in which the competition for wealth and power has obscured the higher values which sustain the intellect and the spirit. They regard themselves as a small band of defenders of our cultural tradition against the threatening hordes of Babbittry. But such a view is manifestly unfair. Did any age pursue affluence as unremittingly and single-mindedly as the nineteenth century, when the humanities dominated higher education? Students who had read Homer and Cicero, Spinoza and Kant, Shakespeare and Milton, Gibbon and Macaulay went on to become robber barons, land speculators, railroad promoters, stockjobbers, and Wall Street lawyers. Today students often graduate with only a smattering of the humanities obtained in a handful of required courses. They flock to law, medicine, business, and the natural sciences, while the classics, philosophy, languages, literature, and history languish. But when have so many young lawyers been willing to work, at a financial sacrifice, to make justice accessible to the defenseless? When have so many young physicians volunteered to postpone a lucrative practice in order to provide better health care for the poor? When have so many young businessmen acknowledged that their responsibility to the community is as great as that to their stockholders? When have so many young scientists wrestled with their conscience about the social consequences of what they do in the laboratory or the classroom?

The students of today are at least as idealistic as those of yesterday; probably more so. But their idealism is expressed in different ways. They no longer see learning as a means of achieving personal cultural fulfillment but of pursuing collective social justice. Their view is not likely to change in the foreseeable future, so that the dilemma confronting the humanities will in all probability prove of long duration.

The implications of this conclusion for the study of history are serious. If history cannot provide us with a guide to the future, and if it cannot make us wiser citizens or better human beings, what is its purpose? Do we really need to devote much time and effort to its study? Should it even be included among course offerings as one of the central disciplines of a college education? These are questions being quietly asked on the campus at the present time, questions for which there are still no clear answers.

They suggest once again, however, that the crisis in history is deep-seated and long-lasting, a result not of the ups and downs of the economy, but of a change in the form and direction of higher learning. History is not likely to be abandoned by the educational system entirely, but it may well come to be regarded as a token of scholarship and respectability rather than as one of the key offerings of the college curriculum. There are those who maintain that the outlook is not really as gloomy as it seems, that an upturn may be just around the corner. They point to the attempt of a few institutions of higher learning to reintroduce a central core of knowledge composed largely of the traditional humanistic disciplines. But their expectations appear unrealistic. Society's view of what a college education should provide has undergone a profound change in the last generation or two, and the vigorous new fields of study which have emerged recently are not likely to let themselves be forced out of their hard-won place in the sun. All signs indicate that we are witnessing the decline of history as an academic discipline, not its disappearance perhaps, but certainly its eclipse.

Such a conclusion may produce discouragement among those who view history as a branch of learning which can be pursued effectively only in an institution of higher education. But calm reflection suggests — and historians after all are taught to remain detached, to regard all temporal change *sub specie aeternitatis* — that history expresses elemental needs and interests rooted in the very foundations of collective human experience. History is older than colleges and universities; it is older than libraries and archives; it is older than any of the nations on earth. It is as old as society itself. Not only that, history of a very high order was being written and read long before it became an academic discipline. The historian does not need to be part of an organized and institutionalized profession in order to be a creative scholar and artist. Outstanding works of historical learning — brilliant, wise, moving, and exciting — appeared when there were as yet no courses on history, no professorships or fellowships, no journals, conferences, or conventions. Indeed, history through most of its existence, an existence which coincides with that of the organized community, has been an art and science pursued outside institutions of higher education. Some of its most successful practitioners have been and continue to be people who were never trained for an academic career. Their inspiration comes simply from the need felt by all of us to relate the isolated events of our private life to the common heritage, to the collective experience of the society of which we are part.

This is what the British historian W. K. Hancock meant by his emphasis on the direct experience of life rather than the abstract teaching of theory as the most important source of good historical writing. He maintained in his autobiography that the scholar who chooses theory may write a valuable monograph on monopolistic competition or on the trade cycle in West Africa. But even if his statistics go back a hundred years, he will write historical economics, not economic history. The scholar who chooses life, on the other hand, will write history—with theory to support it, one would hope, and perhaps an adjective in front of it—but still history. Historical inquiry, Hancock concluded, "has its deepest impulse in the lust for life."[9]

But if history has its deepest impulse in the lust for life, then it can be practiced by anyone, anywhere, at any time. We are all potential historians, because we all have an instinctive interest in the relationship of past and present. History can be and has been written by journalists, lawyers, businessmen, politicians, and soldiers as effectively as by professional scholars. Thus the decline of the monopoly which higher education has exercised over its study will no doubt result in a material loss, but it may also have a liberating effect. It can free historical learning from the narrowness and pedantry of academic life, from the heavy-handedness of formal scholarship, from the conventionality of an organized profession. It can help revitalize an ancient but still challenging concept of history as an individual and spontaneous expression of human creativity like art, music, or literature.

A recognition of the instinctive and indigenous nature of our interest in what has happened will help us deal with that troublesome question with which historians are constantly assailed: "What is the use of history?" The answer is that history is of no use; it simply is. It is, because the life of the community cannot continue without it. We feel a compelling need to know whence we have come so that we may know where we are. We feel a need

9. W. K. Hancock, *Country and Calling* (London, 1954), p. 213.

to transcend the limits of our short span of years on earth, to see our own existence as part of the common existence of our nation, society, civilization, or of the entire human race. The people who crowd the microfilm reading room of the State Historical Society of Wisconsin, poring over old census reports and obscure local newspapers to find out when their great-great-grandparents came over from the old country; the annual spring parade in the town of Stoughton to celebrate the *Syttende Mai*, the anniversary of the adoption of the Norwegian constitution almost two hundred years ago; the tourists who pay a dollar or two to visit the restored nineteenth-century stone houses of the Cornish settlers on Shakerag Street in the old mining community of Mineral Point; similar evidences of interest in the past which can be observed in every part of this or any other country; all express the human need, unconscious but powerful, to find some connection between what has been, what is, and what will be.

This need has to be met, though not necessarily by the formal study of history. It has in fact been satisfied at various times by other forms of intellectual or artistic explication, by mythology and religion, for instance, by epic poetry and folk tale, by nationalistic chauvinism and racist propaganda. They can all help us see a relationship between now and then, between the actual and the vanished world. It is no doubt better that historians should undertake this important task, because they are taught to search for the truth, unattainable though it may be in any ultimate sense, in a spirit of dispassion and compassion, *sine ira et studio*. But if they fail to undertake it, if they turn their back on those who seek their guidance in order to pursue a recondite professionalism, there will be others more than willing to take their place.

Look at the major book reviews or list of best sellers in any Sunday newspaper. There are almost always some titles dealing with history: life in a village in southern France during the Middle Ages, the calamities which befell Europe in the fourteenth century, the achievements of Peter the Great of Russia, the ordeal of a young nation during the American Civil War, the rise and fall of the Third Reich, and so forth. Is it not clear that popular interest in history has in no way diminished? The question is whether professional historians will be able to satisfy it or whether it will be left increasingly to gifted amateurs who compensate by the vigor of their prose and vividness of their imagination for the technical shortcomings from which their work occasionally suffers. On the answer to this question depends to a large extent the future of historical scholarship in the United States.

The classic expression of the view that history as a branch of learning has its roots in the human need to see the present in the light of the past is the brilliant presidential address which Carl Becker delivered on December 29, 1931, before the meeting of the American Historical Association in Minneapolis. In it he openly acknowledged the social and psychological function which historians perform for the community of which they are part:

> We are thus of that ancient and honorable company of wise men of the tribe, of bards and story-tellers and minstrels, of soothsayers and priests, to whom in successive ages has been entrusted the keeping of useful myths. . . . In the history of history a myth is a once valid but now discarded version of the human story, as our now valid versions will in due course be relegated to the category of discarded myths. With our predecessors, the bards and story-tellers and priests, we have therefore this in common: that it is our function, as it was theirs, not to create, but to preserve and perpetuate the social tradition; to harmonize, as well as ignorance and prejudice permit, the actual and the remembered series of events; to enlarge and enrich the specious present common to us all to the end that "society" (the tribe, the nation, or all mankind) may judge of what it is doing in the light of what it has done and what it hopes to do.
>
> History as the artificial extension of the social memory (and I willingly concede that there are other appropriate ways of apprehending human experience) is an art of long standing, necessarily so since it springs instinctively from the impulse to enlarge the range of immediate experience; and however camouflaged by the disfiguring jargon of science, it is still in essence what it has always been. History in this sense is story, in aim always a true story; a story that employs all the devices of literary art (statement and generalization, narration and description, comparison and comment and analogy) to present the succession of events in the life of man, and from the succession of events thus presented to derive a satisfactory meaning. The history written by historians . . . is thus a convenient blend of truth and fancy, of what we commonly distinguish as "fact" and "interpretation." In primitive times, when tradition is orally transmitted, bards and story-tellers frankly embroider or improvise the facts to heighten the dramatic impact of the story. With the use of written records, history, gradually differentiated from fiction, is understood as the story of events that actually occurred; and with the increase and refinement of knowledge the historian recognizes that his first duty is to be sure of his facts, let their meaning be what it may. Nevertheless, in every age history is taken to be a story of actual events from which a significant meaning may be derived; and in every age the illusion is that the present version is

valid because the related facts are true, whereas former versions are invalid because based upon inaccurate or inadequate facts.[10]

But if this analysis is correct, if the task of the historian is indeed to preserve and perpetuate the social tradition, to harmonize the actual and the remembered series of events, to enable the community to judge what it is doing in the light of what it has done, to satisfy the human impulse to enlarge the range of immediate experience, and to present a succession of events from which a satisfactory meaning may be derived, then it follows that the crisis which we are facing today is not a crisis in history but in a particular form of history, the form which it assumed during the nineteenth century when it first became an academic discipline and organized profession. Its passing could help break the grip of the doctoral degree and the professorial chair on the study of history. It could help history emerge from the sheltering campus, which has served as its nursery, hothouse, crutch, stronghold, and prison. And it could help mitigate the pedantry, competitiveness, narcissism, overspecialization, and one-upmanship which are the common consequences of professionalization, but which demean the spirit of intellectual inquiry.

The crisis, in other words, may lead not only to disappointments and hardships, but to challenges and opportunities. It may end the monopoly exercised by holders of the Ph.D., and once again attract to historical learning people with a range of experiences broader than those acquired in the university classroom and the scholarly conference. Perhaps there will once again be among the historians of the future gentlemen-scholars like Prescott and Parkman, Brahmins thirsting for knowledge about the past; or philosophers like Voltaire and Hume; or writers like Carlyle and Macaulay; or journalists like Claude G. Bowers and Douglas Southall Freeman; or politicians like Theodore Roosevelt and Albert J. Beveridge; or military and naval officers like William Napier and Alfred T. Mahan; or perhaps even poets like Schiller and Carl Sandburg. And why not? The Greeks believed that history was inspired by the muse no less than poetry, music, dance, drama, or eloquence. Why then should not writers and thinkers and people in public life help break down the barriers between study and experience, between imagination and reality? Their participation can only strengthen a branch

10. Carl Becker, "Everyman His Own Historian," *American Historical Review* 37 (1931–32): 231–32.

of learning which has for too long been drifting away from the arts, the letters, and the world of practical affairs.

But the history of the future must not yield to the temptations of pride and ambition; it must not overestimate its own capacity. It should always remember, as it confronts the bewildering complexities of the collective experience of mankind, how imperfect is human understanding. The past remains obscured by countless details as well as crucial omissions, by ambiguities, mysteries, imponderables, and riddles. It is the lot of the historian to grapple with questions for which there never is and never can be a final answer. This is what John Lothrop Motley was saying when he declared in 1868 in his address on historical progress that "there is no such thing as human history. Nothing can be more profoundly, sadly true. The annals of mankind have never been written; never can be written; nor would it be within human capacity to read them if they were written. We have a leaf or two torn from the great book of human fate as it flutters in the storm-winds ever sweeping across the earth. We decipher them as we best can with purblind eyes, and endeavor to learn their mystery as we float along to the abyss." Behind even the greatest triumphs of historical scholarship lurks an uneasy feeling of inadequacy and incompleteness.[11]

This does not mean that history cannot shed a feeble light on the darkness concealing the future. The illumination which it provides may be weak, but it is the only one we have. Historical study, pursued with intelligence and blessed with a little luck, can help guide our steps toward tomorrow. It may even make some of us wiser or better human beings, although it appears to have little effect on the conduct of most people. But above all, history bears witness to the infinite diversity, fascinating yet intimidating, of what all of us, the living and the dead, have experienced during the lifetime of the human race. Almost twenty-five hundred years ago Herodotus, the father of history, opened his account of the Persian Wars with the statement that his purpose was "that the things wrought of men be not blotted out by time, neither works great and marvellous performed of Greeks and barbarians be without fame." This remains our chief task. We can still wrestle with the enigmas of the future, never forgetting how fallible is our judgment. We can still try to subdue old Adam, always remembering how power-

11. John Lothrop Motley, *Historic Progress and American Democracy: An Address Delivered before the New-York Historical Society, at Their Sixty-Fourth Anniversary, December 16, 1868* (New York, 1869), p. 3.

ful are the forces of evil. But most important, let us attest to what happened in the past, so that the things done by men and women shall not be blotted out by time, and the works great and marvelous performed by us and by others shall not be without fame. This is and always will be a noble pursuit.[12]

12. *Herodotus*, trans. J. Enoch Powell (2 vols., Oxford, 1949), I, 1.

CHAPTER II

The Professionalization of
Historical Learning

The transformation of the study of history from an avocation into a profession was part of a general process of institutionalization which scholarship underwent in the nineteenth century. Until then historians had been amateurs in the strict sense of the word, men who wrote about the past out of sheer love of the subject. Their chief occupation was in some other field. Thucydides was a military leader in the Peloponnesian War who, after his exile from Athens, decided to write about the conflict in which he had been a participant. Einhard was counselor and architect at the court of Charlemagne before becoming the emperor's biographer. To Voltaire the writing of history was only one campaign in a lifelong war for the intellectual emancipation of mankind. Macaulay published his massive celebration of the Glorious Revolution as part of a broad literary output which included critical essays, political commentaries, biographical studies, and popular verse. Even Parkman, who devoted his entire life to the study of history, did so not out of professional commitment but as a labor of love.

For about two thousand years history continued to be written in a haphazard hit-and-miss fashion, intermingling scholarship with theological speculation, philosophic reflection, moral uplift, and national pride. The lack of a systematic methodology and autonomous purpose, however, was in no way incompatible with the creation of important works of historical learning. Indeed, it often encouraged a broad outlook and sharp insight. Gibbon's *Decline and Fall* or Carlyle's *French Revolution* continue to attract readers, more than many later works of greater scholarship but lesser brilliance, although their point of view now appears outdated. What draws us to such books is the grandeur of their theme, the passion of their conviction, or the vividness of their style.

The institutionalization of history, that is, its metamorphosis from a branch of literature, theology, or philosophy into a profession with a purpose, method, and spirit uniquely its own, was the result of the reorganization of education which began in Europe during the period of the French Revolution and the Napoleonic Wars. But indirectly it reflected the growing affluence of society resulting from the rationalization of economic activity. The curriculum of the university in the preindustrial era had of necessity been meager, since the financial resources of the community could support advanced training in no more than a handful of disciplines: law, medicine, theology, philosophy, and mathematics. History was taught in institutions of higher education only as the auxiliary of other subjects, as legal history in the faculty of law, as ecclesiastical history in the faculty of theology, or as universal history in the faculty of philosophy. Its function was to illustrate, with examples drawn from the past, truths derived deductively by the more important disciplines, moral and philosophical rather than historical in nature. In the course of the nineteenth century, however, the increase in wealth made it possible to broaden the curriculum to include subjects which had developed outside the classroom. Among those which appeared for the first time as regular course offerings were the natural sciences, the social sciences, modern languages, and history. Only now did the university begin to approximate what it had always claimed to be: a center of learning in which all major fields of knowledge were pursued and taught.

The transformation of historical study into an academic discipline meant that for the first time it became capable of professionalization. There was now a body of men, initially small but growing rapidly, who earned their livelihood by teaching and writing history. They shared the same intellectual interests, engaged in the same scholarly activities, occupied the same social positions, and faced the same economic problems. Their new sense of collective identity soon led to the formation of a professional organization whose function was to define a common standard of occupational conduct. The vehicle by which this standard was publicized and reinforced was the professional journal and the professional meeting. These became the chief instruments for the institutionalization of a branch of learning which had traditionally been pursued in a spirit of cultural laissez-faire. The *Historische Zeitschrift* was founded in Germany in 1859, the *Revue historique* in France in 1876, the *Rivista storica italiana* in Italy in 1884, and the *English Historical Review* in Great Britain in 1886. The tendency toward cartelization, a central feature of economic development in the nineteenth century, became apparent also in the scholarly life of the age.

In America the rise of a historical profession took place about a generation later than in Europe. The writing of history, to be sure, had begun soon after the establishment of the British colonies in the New World. As Higham has pointed out, the first historians in this country were Puritan divines, to whom the past was a chronicle of God's inscrutable will. These clergymen-historians, however, were gradually displaced in the course of the eighteenth century by gentlemen-historians, patricians whose wealth provided leisure for a scholarly examination of the past without any underlying commitment to religious orthodoxy. The tradition of the independent man of learning, of the gifted amateur studying history to improve his mind rather than to earn a living, persisted long after the emergence of the professional historian. As late as 1884, when the American Historical Association was organized, there were in the four hundred institutions of higher education in the United States no more than fifteen professors and five assistant professors teaching history exclusively, although many more combined it with political science, political economy, literature, philosophy, philology, geology, natural history, and modern languages. By the time the *American Historical Review* was founded in 1895, however, there were about a hundred full-time college teachers of history — almost half of whom had studied at a German university — and the number was increasing steadily. Thus the professionalization of history meant a gradual transformation of the historian from a gentleman-scholar into a teacher-scholar, who earned the support he received by the instruction he provided.[1]

This transformation had a profound effect on the study of history. It meant that historians as a group could for the first time count on established financial and intellectual rewards for their work. They no longer had to depend on private income, outside employment, a wealthy patron, or the favor of the reading public. It became possible for them to pursue their discipline secure in the knowledge that they would receive adequate compensation. Being a historian ceased to be a high-risk venture like being a writer, composer, or painter. It became an organized occupation with a clearly defined standard of conduct, procedure, method, and reward. History could now be studied with greater independence, with less regard for the tastes of publishers or readers. It became possible to do research of a more specialized

---

1. J. Higham, L. Krieger, and F. Gilbert, *History,* pp. 3–4, 323–24, 330; J. Franklin Jameson, "The American Historical Association, 1844–1909," *American Historical Review* 15 (1909–10): 2; idem, "The American Historical Review, 1895–1920," ibid., 26 (1920–21): 2.

nature, research of interest to other scholars rather than the public at large. Greater specialization in turn meant greater technical competence and methodological rigor. The nineteenth century, when history was first professionalized, has thus come to be regarded as the golden age of historical scholarship.

But the great advances which institutionalization made possible exacted a price. The transition from amateur scholar-writer to professional scholar-teacher meant that the worth of the historian began to be measured not only by what he achieved through his research, but also by how he performed in the classroom. The distinction between the scholarly and the pedagogical function became a problem for the historian for the first time. In Europe the issue did not prove as serious as in America, because there the system of higher education regarded the professor as first and foremost an authority in some field of scholarship who was expected to impart his expertise to students, but only as an activity incidental to his main concern, the expansion of knowledge. In the United States, however, the prevailing view of the historian's proper role became more ambiguous.

The public was prepared to acknowledge that in some fields, primarily the learned professions, where a high degree of technical competence is essential for admission into an occupation providing a comfortable and prestigious livelihood, the scholarly reputation of the professor was more important than his pedagogical skill. No one asked whether a prize-winning chemical engineer was eloquent and charming in the classroom. No one complained because a famous heart surgeon mumbled or stuttered while explaining the correct operating-room procedure to his students. Was Einstein a good teacher? Were Freud's lectures well organized? Did Oliver Wendell Holmes write legibly on the blackboard? Such questions seemed beside the point. Most people agreed that what a master of physics, psychoanalysis, or jurisprudence had to say was of such benefit to those he instructed that it did not matter how he said it.

But historians were less fortunate. Together with their colleagues in the liberal arts, they were expected to sharpen the student's intellect and refine his sensibility, not prepare him for a profession. And to this end, the public scrutinized their teaching skills much more carefully. Were they warm, sympathetic, lively, and appealing? Did undergraduates enjoy taking their courses? How did their enrollments hold up? Did they have good rapport with students outside the classroom? These were questions which few historians could afford to ignore. The relative importance attached to teaching and scholarship varied from college to college, depending on status and purpose but the two functions are essentially independent and sometimes incompatible.

There was a third role which the historian assumed when he became part of a system of higher education, that of campus politician. He was now a member of a highly structured community in which academics representing a broad diversity of disciplines and interests interacted in the daily operation of the institution they served. He had to establish a network of subtle, tacit relationships with the chairman, dean, chancellor, and president. He found himself allied with or competing against other scholars and departments. He had to deal regularly with the promotion committee, the curriculum committee, the research committee, and the budget committee. As a member of the faculty senate, he sought to maintain high standards for students, defend the rights of professors, enlarge the number of history courses, and rebuke the administration for acts of highhandedness. He engaged in a form of politics.

The skills necessary for the effective performance of this function were different from those required in research or instruction, but they could be at least as rewarding. Those who possessed them often achieved an important position on campus regardless of their success as scholars or teachers. They soon acquired a reputation among their colleagues as natural leaders. They were asked to chair important faculty committees; they headed task forces studying problems confronting the college; they prepared reports and drafted regulations. They could even rise from the ranks and become deans, provosts, vice-presidents, or presidents. Generally they disclaimed any ambition to leave the professoriate; sometimes they expressed a slight disdain for the bureaucrats who ran the school. But very few of them turned down the opportunity to become part of the administration. The rewards of the campus politician in salary, power, and prestige, even of the campus politician who never made it to a deanship, were by and large greater than those of the scholar or teacher.

There is still another function which the historian has come to perform as a result of professionalization, that of academic entrepreneur. Like the campus politician, to whom he is psychologically and methodologically related, the entrepreneur derives importance from his interaction with other people in higher education rather than from the investigation of scholarly data or from the instruction of college students. But the range of his activity extends far beyond the campus. His talent lies in dealing with philanthropic foundations, government bureaus, professional organizations, university presses, commercial publishers, and learned journals. He achieves prominence not as a scholar but as an organizer, coordinator, and administrator of scholarship. He is generally recognized in the profession as a leader in applying the "interdisciplinary approach" to history. He is acknowledged to be at the "cutting edge" of his field. He has gained a reputation as an expert in the art of "grantsmanship." He has attained the highest goal of the go-getter in higher education: "visibility."

The success of the academic entrepreneur is measured by the funds he obtains from private or public sources, the collaborative volumes he edits, the editorial boards on which he serves, and the honorific or influential positions he holds in professional societies. The contribution he makes to learning may be lasting or ephemeral; there may not even be any. That does not matter. His importance derives not from the way he analyzes historical records but from the way he deals with people. While his colleagues watch his rise with surprise and secret envy, the administration admires him as a mover and shaker. He is held up as a model which the more stodgy members of the faculty would do well to follow. To be sure, skillful entrepreneurship is as rare in academic life as in the business world, but it is widely sought and respected as essential in the bureaucratization of learning.

The transformation which history has undergone in the last hundred years is not unique. The second half of the nineteenth century was a period during which the structure of scholarship in every discipline became altered. After the founding of the American Philological Association in 1869, at least 70 learned societies came into existence in the course of the next decade and 121 more in the next. No fewer than 15 major scholarly organizations were established between 1876 and 1905, one every two years on an average: the American Chemical Society in 1876, the Modern Language Association of America in 1883, the American Historical Association in 1884, the American Economic Association in 1885, the Geological Society of America and the American Mathematical Society in 1888, the American Academy of Political and Social Science in 1889, the American Psychological Association in 1892, the American Astronomical Society and the American Physical Society in 1899, the American Philosophical Association in 1901, the American Society of Zoologists and the American Anthropological Association in 1902, the American Political Science Association in 1903, and the American Sociological Society in 1905.

The founding of a scholarly organization, moreover, was as a rule soon followed or sometimes preceded by the founding of a professional journal: the *American Journal of Mathematics* in 1878; the *American Journal of Philology* in 1880; the *Publications of the Modern Language Association of America* in 1884; the *Modern Language Notes*, the *Quarterly Journal of Economics*, and the *Political Science Quarterly* in 1886; the *Botanical Gazette* in 1887, the *American Anthropologist* in 1888; the *Journal of Political Economy*, the *Philosophical Review*, and the *School Review* in 1892; the *Physical Review* and the *Journal of Geology* in 1893; the *Psychological Review* in 1894; the *American Journal of Sociology* and the *American Historical Review* in 1895; and the *American Journal of Physiology* in 1898. The pattern of professionalization which historical study followed was thus repeated in virtually every other scholarly discipline in America at about the same time.[2]

There was, however, a significant difference. Of all the branches of learning, none had had a longer or more fruitful existence as an independent intellectual pursuit than history. Some had become part of the university curriculum almost immediately after their emergence as distinct fields of scholarship; for example, the social sciences, modern languages, literature, and linguistics. Others, such as the natural sciences, were assimilated by higher education after only a century or two of free and autonomous development. Still others, like philosophy and the classics, formed a part of the course offerings of the universities from the time of their founding during the late Middle Ages. Only history, mathematics, and astronomy remained separate and sovereign disciplines for more than two thousand years before becoming institutionalized as academic subjects. For history, then, even more than for other fields of study, the transition from avocation to profession meant a basic change in structure and spirit.

Those who brought this change about did not foresee all the consequences to which it would lead. To them professionalization signified above all a more coherent and scholarly discipline. Impressed by the achievements of the natural sciences during the nineteenth century, they sought to apply equally rigorous methods of examination and evaluation to the study of the past. They found a field of learning which was part literature, part philosophy, part homiletics, and part fairy tale. Speculation, conjecture, and myth were so intermingled with research, analysis, and interpretation that

2. J. Higham, L. Krieger, and F. Gilbert, *History*, p. 8; Bernard Berelson, *Graduate Education in the United States* (New York, Toronto, and London, 1960), pp. 14–15.

it was hard to tell where one ended and the other began. Those who read history were sometimes seriously interested in understanding the formative experiences of their society, but more often all they sought was entertainment, comfort, or uplift. The founders of the historical profession in America, therefore, wanted the historian to become less of a storyteller and more of a scientist. They wanted to establish a recognized standard of scholarship, a standard which would improve the quality of learning and extend the range of knowledge. They hoped that through organization they would enable history to realize more fully its potential as the guide of mankind.

Some of them sensed that professionalization might inhibit the free play of talent, the spontaneous exuberance which had been a hallmark of the great masters of the craft. But that was a price they were prepared to pay. J. Franklin Jameson, one of the founders of the American Historical Association and later the first editor of the *American Historical Review*, wrote in 1891 that while no one could predict the advent of genius, it appeared unlikely that the roll of the classical historians would be greatly increased in the immediate future, or that the next generation would in this respect abound in eminent names. He conceded that, in the words of the Swiss writer Henri Frédéric Amiel, "the era of mediocrity in all things is commencing. Equality begets uniformity, and we divest ourselves of the bad by sacrificing the eminent, the remarkable, the extraordinary." This was also likely to be the case for a long time with historical writing in America.

Yet it should not in the main be a cause of regret, Jameson argued. "If there is not produced among us any work of supereminent genius, there will surely be a large amount of good second-class work done; that is, of work of the second class in respect to purely literary qualities. Now it is the spread of throughly good second-class work — second-class in this sense — that our science most needs at present; for it sorely needs that improvement in technical process, that superior finish of workmanship, which a large number of works of talent can do more to foster than a few works of literary genius." Historians should be prepared to sacrifice the dramatic sweep and moral import of their discipline for greater scholarly precision.

Even this was a concession which not all American historians were willing to make. Why should not a better organization of history lead to a better history? Why should not the new sense of collective purpose produce clearer understanding and profounder appreciation of the past? Charles M. Andrews, a distinguished historian of colonial America, recalled later that "these years from 1880 to 1900 were a time of great awakening in the American historical world, as effective in its way as was the corresponding awakening already taking place in the field of the natural sciences. It was a time of exhilaration and almost religious fervor among the younger scholars, who saw new spheres of opportunity opening before them and entered on the quest with the zeal of explorers making new discoveries or of crusaders advancing to new conquests." Narratives and descriptions, chronicles and annals, the representative types of historical writing of earlier days, became less important, while such subjects as institutions and constitutions, legal and social organizations, economic theory and public law, administration and government assumed greater significance. In the end Clio proved to be "not the scullion in the kitchen of political science, but the mistress of the whole house." Here was "a true renaissance, in which the conception and treatment of history, under the inspiring leadership of men who saw visions and dreamed dreams, rose above the level of mere schoolmastering and became creative. This was the springtime of the historical movement in America."

At the end of that springtime, twenty years after the founding of the American Historical Association, Woodrow Wilson, who had recently become president of Princeton, expressed confidence that the results of professionalization would live up to the expectations of those who had brought it about. As a scholar who had taught the subject in the early years of his academic career, he delivered on September 20, 1904, an address dealing with "The Variety and Unity of History" before the Division of Historical Science of the International Congress of Arts and Science of the Universal Exposition in St. Louis. In a bold, ringing affirmation, he declares: "We have seen the dawn and the early morning hours of a new age in the writing of history, and the morning is now broadening about us into day. When that day is full we shall see that minute research and broad synthesis are not hostile but friendly methods, coöperating toward a common end which neither can reach alone."

No piece of history is true when set apart, divorced and isolated from the other pieces, Wilson went on. It is always part of an intricately various whole, and it must be put in its proper place in the total scheme of events to be seen in its true color and meaning. Yet it must also be studied and understood individually, if the whole is not to be weakened by its imperfection. Whole and part are thus "of one warp and woof." We are now in a position to recognize this, and we can therefore achieve harmony with regard to the principles and objectives which we shall hold most dear in the pursuit of our several tasks. Upon reflection and after a little explanation of the terms we use, we shall all agree, the address concluded, that what we seek in history is the manifestation and development of the human spirit, whether we seek it in precedents or in processes.[3]

The optimism of scholars like Wilson who had witnessed the early stages of professionalization rested on the assumption that history was a cumulative science similar to physics or chemistry, where small increments of knowledge in a wide variety of special fields gradually lead to comprehensive explanations. The amassing of data could thus be justified as the precondition for a general advance of the discipline. According to this assumption, archival materials and specialized monographs are the building blocks out of which a properly trained scholar can construct a more solid edifice of learning. The historians of the past had used indiscriminately whatever materials lay at hand — documents, traditions, rumors, allegations, apologias, and fictions — disguising with literary glitter or narrative skill the structural weaknesses of their work. But that would change now. They polished meretricious phrase, gilded prejudice, and glib generalization would be stripped away by careful, precise craftsmanship establishing facts and correcting errors. Then, some time in the future, the task of synthesis could begin anew, but on a broader foundation and with a sturdier methodology. Art and science would cease to be incompatible elements in the study of history, the strength of one compensating for the weakness of the other. They would instead become complementary, enriching and reinforcing each other, making possible a higher unity in which form and content fused to constitute the indissoluble essence of fruitful scholarship. Such was the vision of the advocates of professionalization.

Its realization, however, proved more difficult than had been anticipated. It was one thing to talk about the brave new history which would provide a deeper understanding of the past; it was another to write it. The higher synthesis which the systematization of learning was supposed to make possible continued to recede into the future, while the laborious spadework necessary for its attainment went on and on. This is not to deny that a great deal of important research was accomplished around the turn of the cen-

3. J. Franklin Jameson, *The History of Historical Writing in America* (Boston and New York, 1891), pp. 132–33; Charles M. Andrews, "These Forty Years," *American Historical Review* 30 (1924–25): 233–34, 236; *The Papers of Woodrow Wilson*, ed. Arthur S. Link (51 vols. to date, Princeton, N.J., 1966–), IV, 472–73.

tury, probably more than ever before. New historical records were discovered and explored, monographic studies and learned articles accumulated, doctoral dissertations proliferated and professional conferences multiplied. But the expectation that specialized scholarly activity would prepare the way for sweeping narrative and broad interpretation remained unfulfilled. What was supposed to be preliminary began to look more and more permanent. It gradually became apparent that professionalization led logically to specialization, to an expertness which was exhaustive in intensity but narrow in scope. It tended to inhibit an examination of the broad historical framework of society, dividing the past instead into a number of semiautonomous subdivisions, a little like medieval baronies, each guarded jealously by its feudal aristocracy against intruders from the outside. The historian who tried to cross the boundaries of these fiefdoms ran the risk of critical attack for naiveté or unfamiliarity with "the latest scholarship." Thus while the building blocks for historical synthesis were growing into a huge pile, the determination to arrange them into some symmetrical shape dissolved in the face of academic feudalism and scholarly specialization.

This was a source of growing disappointment to the men who had hoped that professionalization would make possible a more vital form of scholarship. They came to recognize that the key to the writing of good history is not method but talent, not the letter but the spirit, not the materials but the historians using the materials. As this realization grew on them, they began to sound impatient, almost bitter. When would the accumulation of data and its analysis finally end and the stage of synthesis start? As early as 1910 Edward Channing, author of a voluminous *History of the United States*, was complaining: "Nowadays the size of the output and not the quality of the production is what attracts attention. The standardization of education, not the making of scholars, is the cry. Let anyone turn the matter over in his own mind and see if he cannot count the really first-class works of American historical writers within the last twenty-five years, on his fingers; and yet conceive of the number of persons engaged in historical pursuits and the number of books constantly published under the guise of history!"

Had the sport been worth the candle? The question was asked again and again, as the hopes aroused by professionalization faded. In 1920 the executive council of the American Historical Association, responding to the "general protest of a large portion of the public against the heaviness of style characteristic of much of the history now being written," appointed a committee to study the problem. Its report, which appeared six years later, dealt not only with style and exposition, but with the general direction of historical scholarship in the United States. William C. Abbott of Harvard maintained that if any tendency had developed more than another, it would seem to the pessimist to be "the printing of documents by the ton and the publication of monographs by the score." To him this was as much a sign of academic staleness as the insistence on education instead of scholarship or the neglect of history as a form of literature. He conceded that in the last few years there had been a revival of universal, if not cosmic, history, but from the pens of untrained or half-trained historians. There had been a tremendous amount of attention paid to the history of the progress of the human mind from philosophic historians or historical philosophers. There had been an increase in the number and content of textbooks, taken by publishers, by the public, and perhaps even by their authors as serious history. And yet — here Abbott used words almost identical with Channing's sixteen years before — "the number of fingers required to count the really notable writers of history has not increased."

Another member of the committee, John Spencer Bassett of Smith College, dwelt on the decline in the influence and esteem enjoyed by the historian in America. There could surely be no difference of opinion that such a decline had occurred, he began. "Fifty years ago historians like Bancroft and Prescott stood side by side with the great poets at the top of the world of letters. . . . They lived like proconsuls over provinces of literary expression." But today the historian's position is less eminent. "He is no longer to be compared with the lordly proconsul, but rather to the hard-working centurion, whose labors held together the military units on which rested the Roman authority in the provinces. He is, perhaps, a more genuine writer of truth and more industrious; but he is not at the top of the world as formerly." Why had his fortunes declined? The answer seemed to lie in the difficulty of combining good writing with good scholarship, of uniting the creative and the analytical elements in the study of history. "The craftsmanship of the historian is a subject of great importance and not often enough considered. Perhaps it is necessary for some minds to have settled the question of the possibility of having good style in good histories. Can writers devoted to research and filled with the scientific spirit be true to their purposes, and at the same time write history that has the charm of literature? And if that can be done, what suggestions can be made of a practical nature for helping the young historian to write in such a manner?" Those were crucial questions, Bassett believed, because the future of the discipline depended on the ability to present the findings of historical scholarship in the idiom of literary art.

Even Jameson, who in 1891 had declared that what history needed above all was "the spread of good second-class work," decided thirty years later that that was not enough. The time had come to talk once again about first-class work. In an address which he delivered on June 15, 1923, at the University of Michigan, he compared the historical work of the preceding half century to that of "the Benedictines and other giants of erudition" who had flourished between 1650 and 1750. The scholars of the recent period had added enormously to the mass of published raw material for the historian's work, he explained. Volumes upon volumes of records and documents and correspondence had been printed for the use of the scholar which had not been available to his predecessors. Critical dissection of the sources had been carried out with thoroughness and rigor. A greater acuteness in estimating their value had been developed, bringing with it greater detachment of view and fairness of mind. Archaeological discoveries, studies of primitive man, and the advance of comparative philology had given a new perspective to ancient history, while in modern history a broader knowledge of religion, law, economics, morals, and the structure of society had extended the domain of learning into horizons far beyond those of previous generations. Yet the period had been only preparatory, for while it had produced good historians, in the main their modest function had been, in Bacon's phrase, "to tune the instruments of the Muses, that they may play that have better hands."

After such an age of accumulation, sifting, and criticism of the materials, "the natural next development is into an age of generalization, of synthesis, of history more largely governed and informed by general ideas." This was the course of progress after the period of the Benedictines; this was likely to be its course now. When masses of good materials have been accumulated and prepared for use, why not proceed to use them for large ends? "Why not turn from the exact copying of words and punctuation marks, the scrutiny of texts, the dissection of documents, to the higher purposes which all these processes are meant to serve?" Indeed, there were already signs that scholarship was moving in this direction, taking a new interest in general ideas. Consider the acclaim bestowed on the bold new ventures into universal history by H. G. Wells and Hendrik Van Loon. One might sometimes wish that their judgment were more balanced or their prose more restrained, "but histories that are read do more good than histories that are not read." Surely, scholarly research had piled up the raw materials with the intention that they should be used by historians of insight who could make the public listen. For what other purpose had we tuned the instruments of the Muses? "By all means let the concert begin," Jameson concluded.[4]

But the audience is still waiting for the concert to begin. The instruments of the Muses have been tuned and retuned and tuned again. The musicians have been warming up for a long time, studying the score and practicing the difficult passages. Yet so far there has been no concert, nor is there likely to be one. The first generation or two of professional historians was sustained by a belief that the growing mass of primary materials and monographic studies would ultimately help scholarship arrive at a grand synthesis or at least a broader insight into the past. It became impatient or discouraged at times, because the accumulation of small pieces of knowledge seemed to outstrip the capacity to assimilate them. Still, there was always the hope that some day someone would bring history to full fruition, creating a portrayal of the human experience more convincing than any by the old masters of the craft.

The historians of today have largely abandoned this faith. The course of scholarship has made it appear visionary. They are intimidated by the complexity of the past, by the bewildering variety of what mankind has experienced on earth. They despair of being able to bring order out of chaos, and so they make a virtue of discovering and contemplating the profusion of history. Not even the most optimistic among them really believe that all the new methodologies and specialties will in the end become integrated into some great work expressing the underlying unity of historical learning. Like physicists, astronomers, or chemists, they have come to accept the fragmentation of their universe.

To be sure, professionalism cannot be held chiefly responsible for the erosion of their belief, which was in any case inescapable. The institutionalization of learning should be credited rather with helping to raise the level of technical competence by promoting systematic training and establishing a uniform standard of scholarly performance. But the advance has come at

4. J. Franklin Jameson, John Bach McMaster, and Edward Channing, "The Present State of Historical Writing in America," *Proceedings of the American Antiquarian Society*, n.s. 20 (1909–10): 434; Jean Jules Jusserand, Wilbur Cortez Abbott, Charles W. Colby, and John Spencer Bassett, *The Writing of History* (New York, 1926), pp. v–viii, 36–37; J. Franklin Jameson, *The American Historian's Raw Materials* (Ann Arbor, Mich., 1923), pp. 40–42.

the expense of spontaneity and breadth of view; it has encouraged routiniza-tion and conformity. The part-time scholar, who had turned to history when-ever the spirit moved him, and the free-lance historian, ranging across a variety of interests and pursuits, have almost vanished as accredited practi-tioners of the craft. Without the credentials conferred by a doctoral degree and monographic publication, they are regarded with the superiority which the specialist feels toward the general practitioner. They continue to write history, very popular history at times, better history in many cases than the members of the guild are willing to admit. Just look at the list of new books published by the commercial presses each year to see what a large number of historical works are being written outside the profession. Such works lack the cachet of academic respectability, however, which only a Ph.D., professorial rank, and specialized research can bestow. They are gen-erally dismissed by the professionals as journalism, vulgarization, or semifiction.

A rough measure of the decline of the free-lance historians is provided by the change in status of the winners of the Pulitzer Prize in history, a prize which seeks to reward not only original research and scholarly expertise, but narrative skill and interpretive insight. In the 1920s there were 4 non-professionals among the winners, that is, historians who did not earn their livelihood by teaching in an institution of higher learning. There were 3 in the 1930s, 5 in the 1940s, 5 in the 1950s, 3 in the 1960s, and 2 in the 1970s. The pattern reinforces the impression that the reign of the amateurs, who dominated the discipline for two thousand years, has now come to an end.

This is not to deny that they continue to do what they have always done, frequently with considerable success. They interpret for the community the relationship between past and present experience. In this sense their func-tion is not different from that of the professionals, although as a rule they have a broader appeal and a wider audience. While the level of their scholar-ship is often lower — even if not as low as their critics claim — they generally display a greater talent for communicating the excitement and vitality of history. They will therefore go on writing their books; their number may even increase, as academic historians move farther away from popular tastes and interests. But their status will continue to decline, they will be increas-ingly barred from the guild, and the gulf between amateur and professional will grow wider. The exclusion of the free-lance historians from a branch of learning in which they predominated for such a long time will no doubt encourage scholarly rigor, but it will also deprive the discipline of a spontaneity and enthusiasm which it badly needs.

The victory of the professionals, however, has not been easy. The battle raged for close to a hundred years before the issue was decided. While the professionals accused the amateurs of sacrificing scholarship for melodrama, the amateurs charged the professionals with a deadly pedestrianism which destroyed the human dimension of history. Those on one side looked down on the others as gossipmongers and sensationalists; the others regarded them in turn as dryasdust pedants and schoolmasters. In 1904 Theodore Roosevelt, a successful amateur historian who had written on *The Naval War of 1812*, *Thomas Hart Benton*, *Gouverneur Morris*, *Oliver Cromwell*, and *The Winning of the West*, took time out from the burdens of the presidency to explain in a private letter why he felt little sympathy with efforts to make history more of a science and less of an art. He criticized writers "who in endeavoring to be moderate and impartial succeed in leaving the impression that there is really no difference between the good and the evil, the great and the small. True impartiality, true justice, is as far as possible removed from the dreadful habit of painting all character drab-colored. . . . The 'impartiality' which would only study the flaws in the character of . . . great and good men and set forth the occasional tricks of virtue in . . . evildoers would be a shame and a mockery."

Warming up to his theme, Roosevelt maintained that those who sought only bloodless objectivity in portraying the past—he meant academic historians—"are doing much damage to the cause of historic writing." He had been waging war with their kind for a number of years. "We have a preposterous little organization called I think the American Historical Association, which, when I was just out of Harvard and very ignorant, I joined. Fortunately I had enough good sense, or obstinacy, or something, to retain a subconscious belief that, inasmuch as books were meant to be read, good books ought to be interesting, and the best books capable in addition of giving one a lift upward in some direction." His attack on professionalization grew increasingly bitter. "After a while it dawned on me that all of the conscientious, industrious, painstaking little pedants, who would have been useful people in a rather small way if they had understood their own limitations, had become because of their conceit distinctly noxious. They solemnly believed that if there were only enough of them, and that if they only collected enough facts of all kinds and sorts, there would cease to be any need hereafter for great writers, great thinkers." It was these diligent mediocrities who were trying to wrest history away from talented but casual free-lance scholars. There was a place, to be sure, a modest place, for hard-working, conscientious, unimaginative historians, Roosevelt conceded. "Each of them was a good-enough day laborer, trundling his barrowful of bricks and worthy of his hire; as long as they saw themselves as they were they were worthy of all respect; but when they imagined that by their activity they rendered the work of an architect unnecessary they became both absurd and mischievous."

And then all the accumulated resentment of the amateur toward the usurping professionals came pouring out: "Unfortunately with us it is these small men who do most of the historic teaching in the colleges. They have done much real harm in preventing the development of students who might have a large grasp of what history should really be." The revolt of the technicians against the superficiality and unreliability of many of the popularizers may have been justified, but "they have grown into the opposite and equally noxious belief that research is all in all, that accumulation of facts is everything, and that the ideal history of the future will consist not even of the work of one huge pedant but of a multitude of articles by a multitude of small pedants." They have failed to recognize that all they are doing is gathering bricks and stones. Whether their work will amount to anything worthwhile depends on whether "some great master builder" will arrive who can go over their material, reject the bulk, and out of what is left "fashion some edifice of majesty and beauty instinct with the truth that both charms and teaches." A thousand academic drudges with their noses to the grindstone, turning out scholarship by the ton, will not begin to add to the wisdom of mankind what another Macaulay would add. "The great historian must of course have the scientific spirit which gives the power of research, which enables one to marshal and weigh the facts; but unless his finished work is literature of a very high type small will be his claim to greatness."[5]

The struggle between amateurs and professionals dragged on until after the Second World War. It was not always waged with the acrimony of a Roosevelt, who was so exuberantly unrestrained in both his dislikes and enthusiasms. The opposing sides were generally more moderate and gentlemanly; sometimes they even seemed to reach an uneasy accommodation. Roosevelt himself revealed that his bark was worse than his bite. What he

5. *The Letters of Theodore Roosevelt*, ed. Elting E. Morrison (8 vols., Cambridge, Mass., 1951–54), III, 707–8.

really wanted was not rejection of the academic historians but acceptance by them. In 1912, only eight years after he had spoken with disdain about "a preposterous little organization called I think the American Historical Association," he agreed to serve as its president, delivering a vigorous yet conciliatory address on "History as Literature." The reconciliation, however, reflected the power of vanity rather than a change in attitude. To Roosevelt it represented an official recognition of his status as a serious scholar, while the academic historians found satisfaction in counting a former President of the United States among their colleagues. Beneath the surface the old animosities remained.

The free-lancers made their last major stand in the late 1930s and early 1940s. Until then many of them still occupied a respected position within the historical discipline. They were on the defensive, but their retreat was orderly, and at times they could still launch a counterattack. Their most eloquent spokesman during that period was Allan Nevins, a prolific scholar whose academic career at Columbia did not begin until he was almost forty, after many years as a successful journalist. Although he had changed sides in the midst of the battle, his heart was always with the amateurs. He never felt at home among the academics, to many of whom history meant above all technique, research, and analysis. They in turn often looked with suspicion on the newspaperman turned professor, without a Ph.D., who ground out books with embarrassing regularity, subordinating methodology to creativity. Behind his back, and sometimes to his face, they would criticize his work for being shallow or unsophisticated. He responded by waging a long rearguard action against the advance of professionalization. Isolated in a discipline which was gradually turning from the humanities to the social sciences, he spent his life defying the rising tide.

As early as 1938, in his *Gateway to History*, a work on the nature of historical knowledge emphasizing the dramatic and inspirational aspects of the past, Nevins complained that what had once been a branch of literature has now become a branch of learning, "and in that field the only passports are diligence and accuracy, which are too often synonymous with plodding dullness." The artisans have multiplied far more rapidly than the artists. Too many historical works have been printed, sold or not sold, and placed on library shelves to gather dust. A multitude of books, "chiefly petty in scope and pettier in aim," flows from the presses only to be forgotten. "The very size of the shallow stream, the brawling clamor it wakes in reviews, its brackish taste when sampled, repel many readers from history altogether."

Nothing would do more to encourage the reading of historical works than some reform by which fewer people would take up the pen, and these few would do so later in life or at least not until they were intellectually mature and fully trained. Nevins was no doubt thinking of himself.

A year later, in an article published in the *Saturday Review of Literature*, he identified more closely the culprit responsible for undermining the position of history in cultural life. It is "the pedant," whose "touch is death," who helps spread the impression that history is synonymous with stolid, heavy writing. He warps and debilitates the young talent still interested in historical study, exerting a steady pressure in the direction of his own deadly ponderosity. "History in his opinion should be the possession of a Germanic-minded few, a little knot of *Gelehrten* squeezing out monographs and counting footnotes." The pedant, though he benumbs all interest in history, holds learned societies and institutions of higher education in the iron grip of the Old Man of the Sea, supported by professorial chairs, philanthropic foundations, scholarly associations, university funds, and research fellowships. It is against this entrenched professionalism that the war of true history will have to be "most determined and implacable."

Nevins went on to paint a mordant portrait of the quintessential academic, a composite of many of his colleagues among the professional historians:

He has never written, or at least never published, a real book. Perhaps he was guilty in his so-called youth of printing a doctoral dissertation, but of that he has repented. He regards the man who writes books as self-convicted of superficiality; as not a "true scholar." At long intervals he prints an unreadable paper in some learned periodical. He may once in a decade excrete a slender, highly specialized, and to everybody concerned quite exhausting monograph. Apart from this his literary production is confined to an occasional spiteful review of some real historian. Fellow-pedants then gather in little knots and cackle: "Did you see what a fall Professor Dryasdust took out of Beard's [or Nevins's] latest book?" or "Did you see how Dryasdust made mincemeat out of Claude G. Bowers?" By this device — for morose jealousy of intellectual superiors is another hallmark of his type — our pedant labors to create the impression that if he were not too scholarly to rush into print, his own books would make Beard and Bowers look small. He adds to this impression by talking . . . of the great *opus* on which he is engaged as the decades drag by; an *opus* never quite finished. By long persistence on these lines a perfectly terrifying reputation for erudition and authority is built up. The cost in effort is almost zero; the return in the esteem of his fellows is enormous.

Even today this type will not seem unfamiliar to those who know something about academic life.

Nevins considered it a tragedy that the pedants controlled the study of history. They teach gifted students, he charged, to look for petty monographic subjects; they drill them in their own plodding discipline of footnotes and bibliography; they destroy the "vital spark." They try to reduce professional societies founded with broad and generous aims, like the American Historical Association, to strictly academic and narrowly "learned" bodies. They try to fasten their deadly grip on the journals of history, and often they succeed. "As the most execrable specimens of literary criticism in print can be found in the *Journal of the Modern Language Association,* so the worst examples of how history should never be written can be discovered in past files of the *American Historical Review.*"

The result of all this is evident. By whom is the real history being written today? Nevins asked. To an overwhelming extent by the men and women farthest removed from the withering touch of the "academic glossologists." The larger number by far of our best historical writers are to be found outside the colleges and universities. We must admit that higher education is simply not setting the pace, and yet the academic world offers the leisure, the facilities, and the special knowledge which theoretically should make it the pulsing heart of historical work. The trouble is that the best writers of history are essentially individualistic; they have no time to think about societies, reviews, funds, and the other "appliances of scholarship." Most of them have never attended a session of the American Historical Association. They never think of rights, privileges, and petty possessions, while the pedants have nothing else to think about. "And thus the pedantic school maintains and even extends a grip that has been disastrous to history in the past and will continue to be disastrous in the future."

Nevins's attack on the professionalization of history was not some abstract critique of the direction in which the discipline was moving. It was a profoundly personal statement, a cry of pain by an outsider beating at the walls of an increasingly institutionalized and bureaucratized field of knowledge. He never became reconciled to the narrowness and rigidity of academic scholarship. In 1959, after his retirement from Columbia, when, nearing the age of seventy, he was finally elected president of the American Historical Association, his address at the annual dinner dealt once more with the subject with which he had wrestled throughout his career as a scholar. Why do historians no longer speak of instructing the nation? Why do so few aspire to a general democratic public? The answer was complex, but the central explanation had to be the diversion of history into scientific channels, and the resultant widening gap between history which is broadly acceptable and history which is academically acceptable.

"In proportion as history took a scientific coloration, employed mechanistic or evolutionary terms, and abandoned its old preoccupation with individual act and motive, it lost much of its serviceability to democratic needs." Its significance to the ordinary citizen began to pale, for it tended to place people and communities in a position in which they were controlled by inexorable, impersonal forces, in which man lost the power to decide or move. The new history was given a special position by the rise of graduate instruction which emphasized abstract ideas and detailed research. "It became more original, but more confusing; more expert, but grayer and grimmer." The reading public turned away from such a history toward what it preferred, toward "the popular writers who remained faithful to a human, romantic, and stylistically appealing type of presentation." This was what the community found usable.

The outcome was easily predictable. Historical study lost much of its appeal, so that even well-read men and women began to feel that history must be either authoritative and boring or interesting and untrustworthy. The academic historians in general did little to allay this suspicion. They confirmed it rather by writing dull books and abusing bright ones. And the general public, faced with the choice, never hesitated. "It took the book which emphasized human motive and action almost every time."

To Nevins in the twilight of his career the task of the historian today was the same as thirty years before, when he first began to write about what he considered the greatest of all epics, the experience of the American people. History must return to its roots in the storytelling and literary tradition of society. It must begin to explain once again to ordinary men and women how the past became the present; it must present the experiences of those who had made the long and difficult journey. To fail to do so, to allow history to withdraw into an arid professionalism, would lead to isolation and the gradual decline of what had been a vital part of the cultural heritage. Historical learning could still be saved from the pedants and academics; but there was no time to lose. The rescue had to begin at once, if talent and imagination were to prevail over mandarindom and scholasticism.[6]

6. Allan Nevins, The Gateway to History (Boston, 1938), p. 14; idem, "What's The Matter

Nevins intended his presidential address to be a battle cry, but to those who heard him it sounded more like a dirge at the passing of the age of free-lance scholars. He was now the last of the great autodidacts who still occupied an important position within the discipline. The others had all been cast out, branded as journalists and popularizers, still attracting readers and earning royalties, but denied the cachet of scholarly respectability. Their decline had begun before the First World War with the transformation of history into an academic subject, the formation of a professional organization, and the establishment of an official journal. It had accelerated during the interwar period, as graduate schools started to turn out more and more Ph.D.'s, as specialties increased, as learned periodicals and scholarly societies multiplied, and as the gap between the trained technicians and the self-taught storytellers grew wider. The final victory of the professionals came in the decade following the Second World War, when the academic boom swept away the last remnants of the amateur tradition. At the time Nevins addressed the American Historical Association in 1959, the battle was already over.

By then the preponderance of the professionals had become so great that they were able to overwhelm the opposition by the sheer weight of numbers. The thousands of men and women who attended graduate school in the years after 1945 became eager recruits in the campaign for professionalization. Trained in increasingly sophisticated techniques of research and analysis, they scorned the free-lance historians, who had little more to offer than talent and style. As historical scholarship drew closer to the social sciences; as it started experimenting with quantification, demography, psychohistory, popular culture, and collective mentality; as it explored regions and civilizations which had been largely ignored in the prewar period, the hit-or-miss amateurs began to seem hopelessly antediluvian. There was still a large audience eager to hear what they had to say. There was still fame to be won and money to be made by writing history for the popular market. But to the professionals such prizes appeared less and less attractive. Enjoying an assured income as teachers in institutions of higher education, they no longer had to compete in the cultural marketplace for the patronage of the general public. The approbation which they now sought was not that of the readers of best sellers, but that of other professionals, who were less impressed by style and wit than by technical virtuosity.

---

with History?" *Saturday Review of Literature*, February 4, 1939, pp. 4, 16; idem, "Not Capulets, Not Montagus," *American Historical Review* 65 (1959–60): 256–57.

The triumph of professionalization was hastened by the various philanthropic and cultural foundations which began to play an increasingly important role in academic life during the postwar period. Most of them were established after 1939, but many arose between the two world wars, and a few had come into existence before 1914. Of those which have become most important for historians, the Rockefeller Foundation was founded in 1913, the American Council of Learned Societies in 1919, the Social Science Research Council in 1923, the Guggenheim Memorial Foundation in 1925, the Ford Foundation in 1936, and the National Endowment for the Humanities in 1965. To be sure, these foundations differ considerably in their structure and their source of income. The Rockefeller, Guggenheim, and Ford have at their disposal gifts and bequests made by some of the richest families in America. The ACLS and SSRC are basically middlemen, distributive agencies obtaining funds from other philanthropic organizations and disbursing them among scholars in the humanities and the social sciences. The NEH is a public institution established by the federal government and dependent for its resources on the national budget. All of them, however, whatever their differences in organization or financing, are committed to the encouragement of scholarship, supporting a variety of research projects which might otherwise remain impracticable.

This objective has involved the foundations in the evaluation and direction of academic activities. How could it be otherwise? Having to decide which scholar to support and which to turn down, which project to encourage and which to reject, they were of necessity forced to establish criteria, explicit or implicit, of what learning is or should be. The mere fact that the foundations had vast wealth to distribute gave them, whether they sought it or not, great influence over scholarly values and objectives. If they had limited themselves to making lump-sum grants to colleges and universities for broadly defined purposes, leaving the distribution to school administrators, they might have escaped the responsibility of determining in which direction research should move. But since they decided to choose the areas, interests, projects, and scholars receiving their philanthropy, they were drawn into the process which shapes higher learning. They became a major force in the cultural life of America.

The influence which the foundations could exercise over education was recognized by some observers from the very beginning. As early as 1909 Jacob Gould Schurman, president of Cornell and member of the board of trustees of the Carnegie Foundation for the Advancement of Teaching, warned that "the very ambition of such a corporation to reform educational abuses is itself a source of danger. Men are not constituted educational reformers by having millions to spend. And, indeed, an irresponsible, self-perpetuating board of this sort may become a real menace to the best interests of the higher education." The foundations, having the power to grant or withhold financial support, could become the advisers, partners, or even masters of institutions of learning:

> I cannot but think that they create a new and dangerous situation for the independent and privately endowed universities. Just in proportion as these are supported by those benevolent corporations is their center of gravity thrown outside themselves. It is no longer the case of a rich man giving his money, going his way (eventually dying), and leaving the university free to manage its own affairs. The purse strings are now controlled by an immortal power, which makes it its business to investigate and supervise and which lays down conditions that the university must accept if it is to receive grants of money. An irresponsible, self-perpetuating board, whose business is to dispense money, necessarily tends to look at every question from the pecuniary point of view; it wants its money's worth; it demands immediate and tangible results. Will not its large powers and enormous influence in relation to the institutions dependent upon it tend to develop in it an attitude of patronage and a habit of meddling?[7]

Until the time of the First World War such fears may have seemed exaggerated. The foundations had as yet neither the power nor intention to mold the values of higher learning in America. Even during the interwar period their influence, though increasing, remained subtle and indirect. They were generally willing to accept the judgment of those within the discipline regarding the originality or importance of a proposed project. The grants they made were based by and large on achievement in the case of the senior scholars, or on promise in the case of the junior ones. They did not prescribe the direction which research should take. Yet the foundations were already beginning to play a significant role in determining the nature and scope of scholarly activity. Frederick Paul Keppel, who was president from 1923 to 1941 of one of the best-known, the Carnegie Corporation of New York, recognized that their philanthropy had become more than an aid to

---

7. Jacob Gould Schurman, "Some Problems of Our Universities — State and Endowed," *Transactions and Proceedings of the National Association of State Universities in the United States of America* 7 (1909): 30–31.

learning; it had become a measure of value, a badge of distinction. "One must consider not merely the foundation itself and its place at the bar of public opinion, but also the effect on those who either make application for help or may reasonably expect help to be offered. Foundation decisions seem to be serving more and more as a measuring rod of merit, to a degree alarming to those who are familiar with their very human limitations. Either affirmative or negative action by a foundation may have an influence upon other possible contributors much more powerful than it should."

Since grants were now becoming so important, those who sought them tended almost unconsciously to pursue the kinds of research which they thought would meet with the approval of foundation administrators. The latter were thus acquiring, not necessarily by design, the power to shape higher learning. It was a power, Keppel conceded, which they did not always use wisely:

> It must, alas, be admitted that there is a good deal of bunk connected with this whole question of research and scholarship. The foundations must accept their share of the blame. Without the least intention of doing so, they have over-stimulated certain fields, they have spoiled certain individuals, for your man of scholarship is a human, often a very human being. They have, I fear, been the chief offenders in forcing the techniques of research which developed in the natural sciences, where experimentation is relatively simple, where verification is usually possible, where controls are available, into the social sciences and the humanities, where conditions are very different.

It was becoming clear that the encouragement and support of scholarship could not be separated from the evaluation and supervision of scholarship.

The most critical assessment of the role which philanthropy was beginning to play in academic life came from Harold J. Laski, the British political scientist, who in 1928 published a mordant article in *Harper's* on "Foundations, Universities, and Research." His point was that the power of the foundations to grant or deny financial aid was having a profound effect on the structure of higher education. The trustees of a university, he maintained, expect the president to appoint professors likely to attract endowments from the foundations. The president then looks for professors who can produce the kind of research in which the foundations are interested. And the professors in turn search for graduate students who can help them provide the basis for the "ultimate generalizations." There are endless committees to coordinate or correlate or integrate. And there are the foundation executives, people who do no research themselves, but who judge whether others are suitable for it. They are widely traveled and gracious, but firm in manner, "as befits men who have vast benefactions to dispense." There are interim reports, special reports, confidential reports, and final reports. There are programs for the development of every theme, surveys for the dissection of every problem, industrial, racial, national, or international. There are experimental centers, statistical centers, and analytical centers. "More energy, I venture to believe, has gone this last five years into the systematization of research in this field than in any previous generation of intellectual effort."

The result, according to Laski, is that the faculty of a university comes to be dominated by the "executive" type of professor, who is busy putting its goods on display in the shopwindow. The school with a large grant received attention in the press. Its president comes to be regarded as a man who can get things done. "The enthusiasm for quantity — the most insidious of all academic diseases — grows by what it feeds on." Those who cannot further the new tendencies, finding themselves without influence, are naturally discouraged. People in academic life are too often judged by their output, so that they are tempted to spend their time not in reflection on ultimate principles, but in the description of social machinery or the collection of research materials. "It is the business of a university to breed great scholars; and in such an atmosphere great scholars will hardly be bred."

Learning is bound to suffer, Laski concluded. The president of a university who wants his school to expand has no alternative but to see it expand in the direction which one or another of the foundations happens to approve. There may be doubt or dissent among the faculty, but what chance does doubt or dissent have against a possible gift of a hundred thousand dollars? And how can the professor whose work fits in with the purpose of the prospective endowment fail to appear more important in the eyes of the president and the trustees than the professor for whose subject or views the foundation has neither interest nor liking? What chance does the professor of an "unendowed" subject have to carry the same weight in his school as the professor of one that is "endowed"? How can he avoid the embarrassment which may come when he is asked to put his own work aside and cooperate in a piece of research which a foundation has adopted and on which the position of his school may depend? What are his chances of promotion if he pursues a path of solitary inquiry in an academic world competing for the crumbs which fall from the foundation's table? Still, "there is not a single point here in which there is the slighest control from, or interference by, the foundation itself." The mere fact that a fund is within reach, however, permeates everything and alters everything. The school develops along the lines which the foundation approves. "The dependence is merely implicit, but it is in fact quite final." The control of philanthropy over learning is in no way diminished because it is indirect.[8]

Laski's article failed to attract the attention it deserved, because at the time it was more of a prophecy than an accurate description of academic life. It could be dismissed as mere guesswork by a morose social critic about the shape of things to come. Only a generation later did it come to be recognized as a sharp analysis of the course on which higher education had embarked. After 1945 the American people, flushed with victory over the forces of aggression and totalitarianism, began to believe that they could deal with their problems at home as effectively as with their opponents abroad. The ills of poverty, ignorance, oppression, exploitation, bigotry, racism, disease, and pollution could all be cured by unremitting exertion, determination, and money. The concept of a "Great Society," free from want and pain, ceased to be an inspiring but unattainable ideal, summoning mankind to a battle in which there could be no ultimate victory. It became rather a practical goal which might be reached in our own lifetime, if only we worked for it hard enough. The result was a heroic effort to enhance the quality of life, an effort aided and sometimes guided by the philanthropic foundations, which finally came into their own. Vastly increased in size and wealth, they were no longer content to assist in cultural and social improvement. They now became the pathfinders and pioneers of fundamental reform, seeking to alter attitudes, institutions, and practices, to transform the very character of the nation. For about twenty-five years public philanthropy was a major force in determining the direction in which the community and its culture would develop.

In the case of higher education, this meant that the foundations ceased to exercise their influence indirectly, using their resources as a means of encouraging certain kinds of scholarly activity. They now defined more openly and precisely what the purposes and techniques of learning should

8. Frederick P. Keppel, *The Foundation: Its Place in American Life* (New York, 1930), p. 50; idem, "American Philanthropy and the Advancement of Learning," *Brown University Papers* 11 (1934): 15–16; Harold J. Laski, "Foundations, Universities, and Research," *Harper's Monthly Magazine* 157 (1928): 296, 299, 301–2.

be. For historians the prescription was above all to broaden the scope of their discipline geographically and methodologically. Substantial sums — "seed money" was the common phrase — awaited scholars and institutions willing to explore areas which had hitherto been largely ignored — Eastern Europe and the Soviet Union, the Far East, South Asia, the world of Islam, Africa, and Latin America — or to experiment with subjects, models, and techniques which were still untried — quantification, social-science history, comparative history, psychohistory, prosopography, literacy, popular culture, mass mentality, nuptiality, sexuality, natality, and mortality. The emphasis was above all on innovation, exploration, and experimentation. The foundations had little patience with old-style biographies, chronological narratives, political studies, or diplomatic monographs, forms of historical writing which they had once tolerated or even encouraged. The professionalization of history was thus accelerated by philanthropic institutions favoring analysis over exposition, method over style, and sometimes originality over common sense. It is doubtful whether Prescott could have received a grant during those years for the Conquest of Mexico or Parkman for his Montcalm and Wolfe.

Jacques Barzun, who had been a university administrator as well as cultural historian, noted in the late 1960s the desire of almost all the foundations for novelty. They are on the lookout for "gaps, needs, talents, and opportunities," he wrote; they are busy proposing "departures, new branches of study, and the reformation of old ones by injections of new men and new plans." The scholar seeking their support "must think of something which has not been done before." The funds which they have disbursed have fostered research and teaching in international affairs as well as work in the "remoter languages," in the improvement of curriculum, and in social research. "On top of this, foundations have distributed large sums in fellowships and training or travel grants, usually through intermediaries, such as the Woodrow Wilson Foundation and the American Council of Learned Societies." Yet their bias has by and large been single-minded in its pursuit of novelty. "It is not unfair to say that foundations were the first to conceive of the university as an instrument." Barzun quoted a leader in private philanthropy as saying that "a grant from us is a piece of venture capital for social change."[9]

9. Jacques Barzun, *The American University: How It Runs, Where It Is Going* (New York, Evanston, Ill., and London, 1968), pp. 148–49.

The result of the sudden availability of substantial sums for historical research was comparable to the effect of wealthy American tourists on the natives of some Caribbean island or Mediterranean fishing village. From one end of the United States to the other historians began to huddle in faculty offices and conference rooms to devise projects which would find favor with the philanthropic moneymen in New York. Rumor had it that the Rockefeller Foundation was prepared to make grants for interdisciplinary or multidisciplinary proposals, but they should be restricted to the twentieth century. The Ford people were supposed to like "underdeveloped" areas in Africa and Asia, although if you had the right approach, you might get something out of them for America or even Western Europe. Comparative history was all the rage with NEH, provided it involved parallels between Western and Eastern civilizations. The SSRC was strong on collaboration between historians and sociologists; economists and political scientists might also help a project, but the big thing was "cross-fertilization" between history and sociology. And so it went during that gold rush when philanthropy was calling the tune for scholarship.

Those who guided the process of innovation were primarily middle-level foundation executives, men and women who established the criteria of what research should be, who helped decide which proposals measured up to those criteria, and who determined how much money should be allotted to the successful ones. Most had started out in higher education, though their careers had as a rule been respectable rather than distinguished. They might have had a book, perhaps even two, a few articles, some administrative experience in a college department or scholarly association, but they were typically not among the big shots of the profession. Their importance came after they entered the service of the foundations, not before. Whatever their convictions while still college teachers, often their new unspoken assumption was that cultural endowments should not merely support but shape scholarship. From the vantage point of philanthropy, above academic self-seeking and professional bias, they were in the best position to see which direction learning should follow.

This is not to suggest that the foundations used their resources to impose on the historical profession standards and values which it accepted only under financial coercion. Their decisions were as a rule reached in consultation with recognized scholars in the field through "peer review." That is, historians meeting in committees with foundation administrators helped make almost every determination regarding general policy as well as specific projects. But the key to this process was the choice of historians to serve on the committees. To a considerable extent, those selected were scholars favorable to experimentation, especially with the methodology of the social sciences. The old-fashioned chroniclers and storytellers were almost never invited; they had simply ceased to be regarded as serious historians. The writers of biography might still appear on a consulting panel, but not very often. Those with specialties in straight political, diplomatic, or military history were also regarded in general as less than prime candidates. The scholars most likely to be asked to advise the foundations were those in the newer fields: quantification, demography, economic history, social history, urban history, comparative history, ethnic history, and women's history. They were in the great majority capable people; often they were highly gifted. But their predilections were unmistakably for novelty, which was one reason why foundation administrators, eager to pioneer, sought their opinion and endorsement. Each side knew what the other wanted, and since they wanted the same thing, their collaboration proved highly effective.

The outcome was predictable. The inner tendencies of history toward specialization and professionalization were reinforced by external pressures. The transformation of the discipline intensified and accelerated. But there were dangers in this hothouse cultivation of novelty in scholarship. J. H. Hexter, whose writings on history are usually wise and always charming, has pointed out that since higher learning began to receive large subventions from public and private philanthropy, there have been serious inducements to historians to claim that their field, while different from the natural sciences, is a science nevertheless. For support has overwhelmingly gone to those disciplines which call themselves sciences: physical sciences, life sciences, earth sciences, social sciences, behavioral sciences, or administrative sciences. While history has received only crumbs, many of those crumbs have landed on the plates of historians who proclaim themselves social scientists. Conversely, when historians refuse to describe their discipline as a science, they risk relative poverty. That is because, "as Mr. William Sutton once so sagely remarked of banks, science 'is where the money is.'" Yet it may help historians resist the temptation to claim that history is a science if they recall "(1) that Willie was a safecracker, (2) that his observation was his response to the question, 'Why do you rob banks, Willie?' (3) that in the end Willie was caught up with and sent to jail." Historians, unlike safecrackers, will not be sent to jail for wanting to be where the money is, but their vision may be distorted and their judgment warped.

This is the gist of the criticism which has been directed against the foundations. By rewarding those who conformed to their idea of what scholarship should be, they encouraged a form of intellectual dishonesty, a game of "grantsmanship," in which success depended not on the inherent merit of a research project, but on the ability of an applicant to tell those reviewing his application what they want to hear. The result was bound to be a subtle corruption of standards and ideals. In his popular sociological study of *The Organization Man*, William H. Whyte, Jr., touched on this point. "Almost as important as the actual pattern of foundation giving is the academic's *idea* of how the foundations want to give." Most social scientists believe that the best way for them to get support is through a large project which is tailored to foundation interests. "Foundations can complain that this is an unjustified stereotype. Stereotype or not, however, it has a way of conjuring up its own reality."

There are exceptions, White conceded, but they do not alter the "over-all climate," that is, the effect of foundation giving on people in the middle, on the nine out of ten who are neither lonely geniuses nor confirmed team operators. "Which side of his work is a man to emphasize? Which of the many problems that can interest him will he choose? What he thinks the foundation wants will have more influence than he cares to think." Through the grapevine the social scientist hears how so-and-so got a large grant with one approach, while someone else with another approach did not. Writing up the prospectus in the right way thus becomes all-important. "One man I know," a social scientist reported, "has been working away at a prospectus for a year now. Every time he rewrites it, he gets further away from his original idea. I don't think he himself realizes how much he has gotten into plain merchandising." The bureaucratization of learning, moreover, "compounds the younger men's already great interest in the externals of research rather than the content of it. In social science, particularly, methodology is being made the route to prestige."

Scholars could of course refuse to play the game of "grantsmanship," but that required considerable will power and conviction. For foundation grants brought with them more than money; they brought prestige. They were a valuable item to be added to the curriculum vitae, a trophy to be mounted on the wall. They received mention in the local press and the professional newsletter; they earned the praise of the dean and the chancellor. Scholars might have been able to conduct their research without them, by relying on their own resources or those of the school where they taught. But they could never gain the "visibility," the sense of importance and distinction which a grant conferred. With it they received the assurance that what they were doing was right, and to receive that assurance, they revised what they were doing and how they were doing it.

This effect of philanthropy on scholarship has not gone unnoticed. The foundations have been criticized for fostering the illusion that learning is whatever they choose to support, and conversely, that whatever they do not choose to support cannot be learning. But not enough has been said about the effect of philanthropy on scholars, on the men and women whose behavior has been affected by the quest for support, who have become or have tried to become academic entrepreneurs, organizers, and operators. Yet as early as 1930, William Harvey Allen, in his critical assessment of the philanthropic activities of John D. Rockefeller, put his finger on the problem:

> Big giving's influence upon social conduct is far more subtle than most people realize. The basic menace of foundations is not their size, although size aggravates the menace. Nor is it the lust of power and fallibility of foundation agents. The basic menace is the attitude of the rest of us toward foundations which are created to give away money. We want some of the money. We want some of the power which the money gives. We want the smiles and favors of agents controlling such huge power to help or withhold help. It is what we are willing to do for foundation money not what foundations want or ask us to do that makes foundation giving a social and governmental menace.
>
> We tend to be like Polonius, rotten Denmark's prime minister; for Hamlet's good will we gladly say the cloud is camel-shaped or weasel-shaped or like a whale.
>
> We stop believing what foundations don't like; we do our best to believe what and to like whom foundation agents believe and like.

Perhaps this view is exaggerated, but it is widely shared. Surveys of more than 60,000 professors in 24 disciplines, conducted during the late 1960s and early 1970s, showed that 37 per cent of all respondents agreed with the proposition that "research grants [are] corrupting to institutions and men that get them." History with 46 per cent was near the top, exceeded only by philosophy with 54 and English with 48. The percentage for electrical engineering, curiously enough, was also 46. Then came political science with 45, anthropology and sociology with 43 apiece, and botany and zoology, chemistry, fine arts, and mechanical engineering, each with 37. The disciplines below the average were civil engineering, economics, mathematics, and psychology with 36. At the bottom of the list were law with 35 per cent, education with 34, agriculture and business with 33 each, medicine with 32, physics with 30, bacteriology and physiology each with 29, and finally biochemistry with 28.

The figures reveal that between a quarter and a half of the scholars in every discipline were critical of the foundations, with disaffection greatest in the humanities and the social sciences, and least in the natural sciences and the professions. Some of it can no doubt be dismissed as the disgruntlement of malcontents and losers, of those who have been unable to get ahead and blame the system for their own shortcomings. But some of it reflects the perception of sensitive men and women who feel a serious concern about what philanthropy has been doing to learning.[10]

There is admittedly a danger in blaming the foundations for all the ills of scholarship. While it is clear that their activities represented more than cultural benovolence or intellectual almsgiving, they cannot be held primarily responsible for the bureaucratization and fragmentation of learning. The complete picture of the role they have played—and it is still much too early for that—will have to be painted in many colors and shades. To begin with, all of the tendencies in history which philanthropy encouraged originated within the discipline itself. The foundations merely hastened their development, thereby, however, aggravating the frictions which a process of far-reaching change entails. Without them the confrontation between amateurs and professionals might not have become so uncompromising; the innovations in subject matter and methodology might have seemed less threatening; the gulf between the scholar and the intelligent reading public might not have grown so wide. In short, the transformation of history, which was no doubt bound to come, would have been slower and less painful. By accelerating it, the foundations made it more disruptive, but they did not initiate it. The change would have taken place in any case.

Philanthropy, moreover, has furthered the expansion and enrichment of historical learning. To be sure, the almost exclusive emphasis on America and Western Europe which characterized the discipline before the Second World War would inevitably have given way to a more comprehensive view of the human experience. As our political and economic contacts with the

10. J. H. Hexter, *The History Primer* (New York and London, 1971), p. 287; William H. Whyte, Jr., *The Organization Man* (New York, 1956), pp. 226, 234–35; William H. Allen, *Rockefeller: Giant, Dwarf, Symbol* (New York, 1930), pp. 504–5; Everett Carll Ladd, Jr. and Seymour Martin Lipset, *The Divided Academy: Professors and Politics* (New York, 1975), p. 360.

peoples of the non-Western world increased, our awareness of their cultural and historical heritage was also sure to increase. But the foundations helped enlarge the scope and sharpen the focus of history. More than that, they promoted a broadening of the techniques as well as the dimensions of the discipline. They encouraged historians not only to investigate regions and civilizations which were geographically new, but materials and techniques which were methodologically new. The results were mixed. Too much too soon set off a scramble for the financial and psychological rewards of scholarly innovation. Yet many of the changes were unavoidable and in the long run beneficial. Historical learning could not go on relying almost entirely on documentary materials to be analyzed and summarized in narrative form. A diversification had to come.

The role of the foundations in bringing it about is well-known. But there is another important though less tangible influence which they have exercised over history. They have helped change the ethos of the discipline. The professionalization which philanthropy furthered put an end to the reign of the amateurs. In place of their spontaneous exuberance came a sense of regulated togetherness, a feeling of collective participation in the study of a sharply delimited field of knowledge. The free-lance historians had been individualists, aware that there were others who shared their interests, but motivated primarily by a compelling private curiosity about the past. The professionals are always conscious that they are part of a common scholarly enterprise, members of a distinct occupational group identified by shared activities and objectives.

The best analytical description of the ritualistic function of such a group has come from sociology rather than history. Talcott Parsons and Gerald M. Platt suggest that in the academic social system the key structure at the professional level is the dual one of membership in a college or university faculty and membership in one or more associations devoted to subject matter fields. In a scholarly profession, they write, "contribution to identity calls attention to features of departments and disciplinary associations which are not strictly part of the cognitive complex, but which serve as institutional mechanisms reinforcing solidarities." To illustrate, the annual school commencement and the annual meeting of the scholarly association fortify the sense of solidarity. "In both cases there is a ritual surfacing of a combination of individual and group achievement and an affirmation not only of its value through recognition but for the solidarity of those who share the same identification." At the annual meeting the communication of research findings may be less important than the symbolic aspects of the occasion, since publication is in general a more effective means of communication. But "giving a paper" symbolizes professional status and the importance attached to the subject of the paper and the achievement, position, or promise of its author. "The culmination of the honorific-ritual aspect of such associations is the election annually of a member to the presidency and the ritual occasion on which he delivers his presidential address." This is a sharp insight into the emotional and psychological satisfactions which professionalism provides, apart from its contributions to the pursuit of knowledge. Parsons and Platt describe here a dimension of the change experienced by history which has not always been recognized.[11]

Its most characteristic expression is the annual meeting at which members of the profession gather, partly to exchange findings and ideas, but also to reinforce their sense of belonging. In his inquiry into the nature of higher learning in America, Howard Mumford Jones spoke of the "wonderful professional opportunities for professional intercourse" which scholars today enjoy. "All the learned professions have their national organizations, the annual meetings of which give the opportunity for exchanging specialized information, learning of experimental work done by colleagues at other institutions, and discussing the present state and future development of the field."

Yet the systematic exchange of knowledge is only the official purpose of scholarly conventions. Even more important are personal contacts established through private meetings in lobbies, lounges, and hotel rooms. Such meetings often deal with ideas or proposals for research, stimulating enthusiasm for the discipline. A solid-state physicist, quoted in Warren Hagstrom's study of the natural scientists, says that "meetings are important. You don't go so much to hear papers as to talk to people. I have read papers at meetings, but the informal aspects are more important. Several meetings are focused on the informal aspects." A mathematician agrees: "Contacts of this sort are extremely valuable; in exchanging ideas you get new ideas yourself. It helps tremendously. I know I was all fired up because of this last conference. It's a little more difficult to have this enthusiasm if you're working by yourself. These conferences certainly tend to generate it." Oscar Handlin still remembers the first convention of the American Historical Association

11. Talcott Parsons and Gerald M. Platt, *The American University* (Cambridge, Mass., 1973), p. 113.

which he attended in 1936, especially "the excitement of the sessions, the exhilaration of talks with men whose names graced the title pages of books I had read. Ideas seemed everywhere in circulation through the corridors . . . ; and I recall to this day the cordiality of older men . . . who made me feel at once involved in a group of shared values and interests. It was to edge into this fellowship that I had joined the Association while still an undergraduate; and this token of fulfillment of the desire to be a historian was ample reward for the costs I could then ill afford."

Still, the dissemination of scholarship, formally or informally, is not the sole function of scholarly meetings. Indeed, their atmosphere is not really conducive to calm reflection on the problems of higher learning. At the sessions where papers are presented there is a constant movement of people in and out of the room. They wave to one another, they gesture, they cough, they whisper, they shuffle their feet. There is an undercurrent of restlessness, a suppressed excitement against which the droning on the platform struggles in vain. No matter. Of the three hundred or so papers which are read at a typical meeting of the American Historical Association, a sizable number are inspired by a desire for personal recognition as much as by original research. They are part of a quest for an appointment, promotion, move, or raise. Besides, all which are good and some which are not will eventually be published in one or another of the professional journals. There they can be read at leisure, with undivided attention, in a more complete and polished form. Why then spend a lot of time listening to papers? Those who attend the sessions most regularly are often people on the periphery of the profession: teachers in denominational or community colleges, many of them priests and nuns; graduate students hoping for a job interview, wallflowers at the big dance; history buffs dedicated to some special period like the Civil War or the Third Reich; and former history majors curious to see how the discipline is doing.

For the pros the real action is in the hotel lobby, which always looks the same. Whether in New York, Washington, Chicago, or San Francisco, there is the same red carpeting, the same restless crowd, the same jovial backslapping, the same steady hum of animated conversation. But the subject of the conversation varies. Sometimes it is research and scholarship. Sometimes it is professional or personal gossip. Sometimes there is simply camaraderie, good-fellowship, high spirits, the buoyancy which comes from a sense of group solidarity. And sometimes there are important business deals: job offers, no longer as plentiful as in the years of prosperity, but still obtainable by those with talent or connections; commercial publishing ventures redolent of royalties and publicity; and the politics of officeholding in the profession, which have to be organized and directed. Even the annual election of the president, "the culmination of the honorific-ritual aspect" of a learned society, requires preparation behind the scenes. The candidate should be an active scholar, to be sure, but he should have other attributes as well. He should be or appear to be an effective leader, experienced organizer, congenial committeeman, sympathetic listener, a "nice guy." In the social sciences as a whole, including history, there is a high but imperfect correlation between scholarly productivity and officeholding in professional organizations. In 1955 21 per cent of those with the highest productivity scores had never held office, while 23 per cent of those with the lowest scores had. This too reveals the conditions and values of professionalism.[12]

A convention of historians thus resembles in important respects a convention of Rotarians, Shriners, or American Legionnaires. The former are more sedate, not as likely to succumb to adolescent exuberance, but the difference is of degree rather than kind. For three days the scholars eat and drink too much; they don't get enough sleep; they keep going on sheer nervous energy. And then, when it's all over, they return home exhausted but fulfilled, like conventioneers from Peoria or Kalamazoo after a long weekend in Las Vegas. Now they can face more readily the everyday routine of the campus: the students, the classes, the committees, the administrators. The scholarly meeting with its intermingling of functions — the dissemination of learning, the affirmation of group identity, the opportunity to socialize, and the conduct of private or official business — manifests important characteristics of the discipline as a whole. It reflects the transformation which history underwent when, after two millennia as an avocation, it became a profession.

12. Howard Mumford Jones, *One Great Society: Humane Learning in the United States* (New York, 1959), p. 238; Warren O. Hagstrom, *The Scientific Community* (New York and London, 1965), pp. 29, 32; O. Handlin, *Truth in History*, p. 3; Paul F. Lazarsfeld and Wagner Thielens, Jr., *The Academic Mind: Social Scientists in a Time of Crisis* (Glencoe, Ill., 1958), p. 9.

CHAPTER III

Becoming a Historian

The institutionalization of scholarship has had the effect of changing the social base of the study of history. Although historians had generally come from a variety of backgrounds, their common characteristic had always been broad learning derived from superior status. Some of them were men who had exercised political power directly or at least observed it firsthand: Joinville at the court of Louis IX, Raleigh as a favorite of Queen Elizabeth, or Clarendon as the minister of Charles II. The history they wrote reflected the outlook of those who had been close to the center of authority. Others were clergymen, often holding important positions, who looked at what had befallen mankind as the manifestation of a divine design: Gregory of Tours, the Venerable Bede, Otto von Freising, or Bossuet. Then there were the politicians and soldiers of antiquity who left their accounts of recent or contemporary events: Herodotus, Thucydides, Xenophon, Polybius, Tacitus, and Procopius. Even after history began to find a mass audience late in the eighteenth century, those who wrote about it usually had enough inherited or acquired wealth to provide them with the leisure needed for systematic study. Gibbon's father was a member of parliament, Macaulay's a governor of Sierra Leone, Prescott's a well-known lawyer, and Parkman's an eminent clergyman. In short, since the writing of history provided as yet neither affluence nor status, those who engaged in it came almost without exception from the well-to-do classes.

That changed after history turned into an occupation. The professionalization of the study of collective human experience meant that being a historian could provide an income and even confer status. It ceased to be an avocation and became a pursuit competing with other pursuits for the rewards of service to the community. Thus institutionalization had the effect of attracting to history people who sought to earn a living as well as to understand the past. This does not mean that the new historians were less dedicated to learning, but now historical scholarship began to include those who formerly would not have been able to afford their scholarly interests. To them the study of what society had experienced meant not only intellectual satisfaction but also economic support and social acceptance. To put it another way, while previously history had been a preserve of patricians who often played an important role in political or religious affairs, now it became an avenue of upward mobility for people of scholarly ability but plebeian origin. There were still many men of wealth who turned to history, usually as amateurs and popularizers, but they were increasingly outnumbered by those who became historians to improve their position as well as to broaden their understanding.

This conclusion is supported by extensive data concerning the social background of American academics during the last fifty years. The figures do not generally distinguish among the various disciplines, but where they do, no significant difference between historians and other scholars emerges. By and large, people employed in higher education tend to come from a middle-class or lower middle-class background; they are typically the children of professionals, often teachers, of small businessmen, managers and farmers, of salesmen, clerks, and other white-collar employees, and sometimes of skilled workers. A survey of college teachers published by the American Association of University Professors in 1938 showed that out of 4,667 responding members, the occupational status of the fathers was 31.8 per cent professionals — 10.6 clergymen, 5.1 teachers, 5.1 physicians, 4.1 lawyers, 3.9 professors, and 3.0 chemists and engineers — 26.6 per cent businessmen, 24.7 farmers, 12.1 manual workers, 1.9 public officials, 1.2 editors and writers, and 1.0 per cent artists and musicians.

Commenting on this data, the sociologist Logan Wilson observed that in many other professions, especially medicine, where doctors are often the sons of doctors, there is more social inheritance of occupation and less recruiting from below the ranks of the middle class. Indeed to Wilson the social composition and economic status of people in academic life accounted not only for "strongly democratic-minded faculties," but also for their "typically plebeian cultural interests" outside their specialty, and for their "generally philistine style of life." It seemed to him that, in comparison with other societies, American academics had more in common with the "new quasi-proletarian intelligentsia" of the Soviet Union than with the "aristocratically inclined university staffs" of Germany before the Nazi era. In making the ascent from their plebeian origins, academic recruits in the United States were more likely to acquire intellectual acuity than social grace. Except in the humanities, he suggested, the training to become a professor may so shape the personality that it is left culturally and artistically undeveloped.

Wilson surmised that those entering academic life were recruited in disproportionate numbers from the "greasy grinds," who had avoided or been denied full participation in "such socializing forms of undergraduate life" as fraternities, clubs, athletics, and other extracurricular activities. Social and family background, while a significant factor in occupational placement, was not as important in higher education as in those professions where personal qualities played a major role. Since graduate work is a more accessible channel for upward mobility than most forms of professional training, he speculated — though this was admittedly hard to prove — that mental superiority is more often coupled with proletarian characteristics among scientists and scholars than among other professionals. "Individual instances of faulty speech, boorish manners, bad dress, and general uncouthness are primarily the results of a system of selection that stresses what a man knows rather than how he appears."[1]

The perception of the scholar as distinguished for intellectual achievement rather than social grace has changed to some extent in the last generation, perhaps because social grace in the old-fashioned sense no longer seems so important. But the class origin and economic background of people in higher education have remained pretty much the same. The most detailed studies of academics — some of them dealing with graduate students, who today are the senior scholars in colleges and universities — were conducted in the late 1950s. They show a pattern similar to that of the late 1930s. On the basis of questionnaires and interviews with 2,451 social scientists in the spring of 1955, for example, Paul F. Lazarsfeld and Wagner Thielens found that more than half of the respondents came from a professional or managerial background. Specifically, 8 per cent of the fathers were teachers, 23 per cent were other professionals, 25 per cent managers, 15 per cent white-collar employees and small businessmen, 13 per cent farmers, and 15 per cent were in manual labor.

Another survey of about 3,000 graduate students, conducted in 1958 by

---

1. Logan Wilson, *The Academic Man: A Study in the Sociology of a Profession* (London, New York, and Toronto, 1942), pp. 19–20. Cf. B. W. Kunkel, "A Survey of College Teachers," *Bulletin of the American Association of University Professors* 24 (1938): 262.

James A. Davis, revealed that "from the viewpoint of the society as a whole, graduate students are disproportionately recruited from higher-class levels, but in absolute terms they come from families of modest economic circumstances, and about one-third work their way through undergraduate college." Their pursuit of a Ph.D., moreover, represented educationally a conspicuous upward mobility, since 40 per cent of their fathers had not even finished high school, and no more than 30 per cent were college graduates. The occupational mobility of the graduate students was less obvious, 70 per cent of them reporting that their fathers held a white-collar job while they had been in high school. Because of age differences among the respondents, precise comparisons are impossible, but in 1950 only 18 per cent of the employed men in the United States were managers or professionals, as opposed to 58 per cent of the fathers of the graduate students.

Finally, Bernard Berelson's book on graduate education, based partly on replies obtained in 1959 from 2,331 recent recipients of the doctorate, concluded that graduate students have become "more heterogeneous in background and social origin," a result of the increase in their number. "There simply were too few of the 'elite' variety to support such a growth." Yet actually the distribution of the fathers' occupations was not very different from twenty years before: 27 per cent professional and executive, 21 per cent small business and technical, 21 clerical, sales, and service, 11 agricultural, 14 skilled, and 6 per cent unskilled.

Berelson noted, moreover, the same difference in social background between academics and other leading professionals which Wilson had observed in the early 1940s. By comparison, he wrote, students of law and medicine tended to come more from the top occupational groups. Between two-thirds and three-fourths — 67 per cent of the medical students and 75 per cent of the law students — were from professional, managerial, or proprietary families, while the proportion for Ph.D. recipients was less than half. He speculated that perhaps lawyers and doctors were better recruiters for their profession than college and university teachers. The three groups were roughly equal in size, yet about 15 per cent of law and medical students had fathers in the same profession, as opposed to no more than about 6 per cent for academics. "Does that fact indicate greater morale in the professions, more nepotism in getting sons and nephews into the professional school in the first place, the prospect of more help in getting set up in practice, the lower salaries of academic people, or perhaps their broader interests?" Whatever the reason, it is clear that until recently higher education recruited its personnel from a lower class base than law or medicine. It may be that the difference has diminished or even disappeared in the last thirty years as a result of the increase in numbers in all the professions. But modest class origins have characterized and continue to characterize those who become college and university teachers.[2]

This conclusion is reinforced by an examination of the level of education attained by the parents, usually the fathers, of those in academic life. In Berelson's study, 13 per cent of the fathers had received advanced training beyond the bachelor's degree, another 13 per cent were college graduates, 12 per cent had attended college without graduating, 17 per cent were high school graduates, 9 per cent had attended high school but had not gotten their diploma, and almost a third, 32 per cent, had not gone beyond elementary school.

This distribution resembles the findings of a report, prepared in 1958–59 for the American Historical Association by the National Opinion Research Center at the University of Chicago, which was based on questionnaires received from 2,842 graduate students. The fathers of 40 per cent of the respondents had failed to complete high school, while 30 per cent had earned a bachelor's degree and 18 per cent a higher degree. A total of 54 per cent, moreover, were in "low prestige" occupations, as opposed to only 19 per cent in "elite" occupations. Modest social circumstances were also suggested by the level of education of the mothers. While 37 per cent had failed to complete high school, a lower proportion than the fathers, only 17 per cent had earned a bachelor's degree and only 5 per cent a higher degree. The report underscored the plebeian origin of many of the respondents by revealing that 32 per cent of them had met half or more of their undergraduate expenses by their own earnings, and for 30 per cent no undergraduate expenses had been met by their parents.

Finally, there is the data, less extensive but derived from a larger sample, concerning more than 60,000 professors who participated in the Carnegie Commission's survey of student and faculty opinion in 1969 and a supplementary inquiry by Everett Carll Ladd and Seymour Martin Lipset in 1972. It shows that the percentage of respondents with college-educated fathers averaged 39, although there were wide variations among the disciplines, rang-

---

2. P. F. Lazarsfeld and W. Thielens, Jr., *Academic Mind*, p. 7; James A. Davis, *Stipends and Spouses: The Finances of American Arts and Science Graduate Students* (Chicago and London, 1962), pp. 25, 33, 123, 160; B. Berelson, *Graduate Education*, pp. 133–34, 154.

ing from 61 for anthropology, 59 for medicine, and 48 for law — a pattern typical of the more exclusive professions — to 33 for education, 32 for business, 28 for sociology, and 22 for agriculture.[3]

Do historians conform to this general configuration of economic, social, and educational characteristics of those employed in higher education? It is hard to answer with complete confidence, because information about individual disciplines is not nearly as detailed. What we know about history, moreover, is even less than about some of the other fields, especially in the natural sciences. But the available data suggests that history does not diverge significantly from the pattern for higher education as a whole. The report of the National Opinion Research Center, for example, showed a difference of only 3 per cent or less between the 306 graduate students in history and the entire sample of 2,842 graduate students with regard to the fathers' education, the fathers' occupational status, the mothers' education, and the proportion meeting half or more of their undergraduate expenses by their own earnings. Only in the percentage of those for whom no undergraduate expenses were met by the parents was there a greater disparity: 38 for the history graduate students and 30 for the group as a whole. The same similarity between historians and other scholars appears in the Carnegie Commission's survey of professors and the supplementary inquiry by Ladd and Lipset. Whereas the proportion of college-educated fathers was 39 for the entire group, for historians it was 44 per cent, not a highly significant difference.

The most extensive information, however, dealing not only with the social background of those entering academic life at a given time but with changes occurring over the course of a generation, may be found in a study of more than 10,000 Ph.D.'s who received their degree in the years 1935-60, a study by Lindsey R. Harmon prepared under the auspices of the National Academy of Sciences. The samples contain a disproportionately large number of natural scientists, but they also include several disciplines in the social sciences and humanities. The work is so illuminating because, by providing data at five-year intervals for six successive cohorts of recipients of the doctorate, it makes possible an analysis of the shifts which have taken place in the social base of the historical profession and of higher education in general.

3. B. Berelson, *Graduate Education*, p. 133; D. Perkins and J. L. Snell, *Education of Historians*, pp. 46, 229; E. C. Ladd, Jr., and S. M. Lipset, *Divided Academy*, pp. 342-43.

Although for statistical purposes the author combines history and geography into a single category, his figures may be taken to apply, with perhaps some minor deviations, to history alone. Table 3.1 shows that the occupational status of the fathers of the Ph.D. recipients as a whole remained pretty much the same between 1935 and 1960, the percentage of professionals and managers being 48 at the beginning and 46 at the end. For the fathers of historians, on the other hand, the data reveals a slow, irregular decline, from 55 per cent in 1935 to 50 per cent in 1960. It would appear then that before the Second World War history graduate students came from families of modest circumstances, but somewhat above the average for all graduate students. The great influx into higher education after the war had the effect of broadening the social base of doctorate recipients, more so in the case of history than most other disciplines, so that the pattern for historians came to coincide more closely with the overall pattern.

Table 3.2, showing the educational level of the fathers of graduate students, supports the conclusion indicated by the data on their occupational status. It reveals that before the Second World War a substantially higher proportion of the fathers of historians had obtained a college degree than the fathers of graduate students in general, but thereafter the difference diminished. The percentage of the former who had finished college dropped slightly from 19 in 1935 to 18 in 1960, while the percentage for the latter rose slightly from 13 to 14. The figures show a more significant narrowing in the category of fathers who had received advanced training beyond the bachelor's degree. Whereas in 1935 the percentage for the fathers of historians was 22 and for all the fathers 14, by 1960 it had diminished to 14 for the former while remaining at 14 for the latter, evidence of the growing accessibility or "democratization" of the historical profession.

Finally, there is the data given in table 3.3 concerning the level of education attained by the mothers of doctorate recipients. It demonstrates, to begin with, the extent to which admission to higher education was sexually weighted. There was little difference between the parents in the proportion of those who had received only elementary schooling, while a substantially and consistently higher percentage of the mothers than the fathers had finished high school — 26 to 14 in 1935, 24 to 15 in 1945, and 27 to 11 in 1955. But the balance shifts markedly in favor of the fathers in the category of those who had finished college — 13 per cent to 9 in 1935, 13 to 11 in 1945, and 15 to 10 in 1955 — and even more markedly in the category of those who had gone beyond the bachelor's degree — 14 per cent to 2 in 1935, 14

TABLE 3.1 Occupation of Fathers of Graduate Students, 1935–60

Cohort	Group	Number	Unskilled Worker	Semi-skilled Worker	Skilled Worker	White-Collar Worker	Farmer	Manager	Professional	Unknown
						CATEGORY (percentage)				
1935	Total	1355	1	4	12	13	21	19	29	2
	History	59	2	3	8	15	15	14	41	2
1940	Total	1610	2	4	13	13	19	19	29	1
	History	58	2	2	10	7	17	12	48	2
1945	Total	1289	2	5	14	15	16	18	29	1
	History	81	4	9	15	12	11	15	35	0
1950	Total	1627	2	5	14	18	16	16	28	1
	History	77	3	3	12	14	13	29	27	0
1955	Total	1912	3	6	16	16	13	19	26	1
	History	74	0	5	23	18	9	18	26	1
1960	Total	2224	4	6	14	17	12	18	28	1
	History	100	4	6	15	17	7	20	30	1

SOURCE: Lindsey R. Harmon, Profiles of Ph.D's in the Sciences: Summary Report on Follow-Up of Doctorate Cohorts, 1935–1960 (Washington, D.C., 1965), pp. 107–9.

TABLE 3.2 Education of Fathers of Graduate Students, 1935–60

Cohort	Group	Number	HIGHEST LEVEL ATTAINED (percentage)						
			Grade School or Less	Some High School	High School Graduate	Some College	College Graduate	Advanced Study	Unknown
1935	Total	1355	34	8	14	10	13	14	7
	History	59	32	5	7	14	19	22	2
1940	Total	1610	35	8	16	11	12	14	4
	History	58	24	10	7	17	26	14	2
1945	Total	1289	35	9	15	11	13	14	3
	History	81	31	11	14	12	19	11	2
1950	Total	1627	33	10	15	11	14	14	3
	History	77	36	8	18	12	14	12	0
1955	Total	1912	34	10	17	11	15	11	2
	History	74	49	7	11	11	18	4	1
1960	Total	2224	30	11	17	12	14	14	2
	History	100	30	11	12	14	18	14	1

SOURCE: Lindsey R. Harmon, Profiles of Ph.D's in the Sciences: Summary Report on Follow-Up of Doctorate Cohorts, 1935–1960 (Washington, D.C., 1965), pp. 101–3.

TABLE 3.3 Education of Mothers of Graduate Students, 1935-60

Cohort	Group	Number	HIGHEST LEVEL ATTAINED (percentage)						
			Grade School or Less	Some High School	High School Graduate	Some College	College Graduate	Advanced Study	Unknown
1935	Total	1355	31	8	26	17	9	2	7
	History	59	32	7	19	19	12	7	5
1940	Total	1610	32	9	26	18	10	1	4
	History	58	28	7	21	26	14	3	2
1945	Total	1289	31	10	24	16	11	2	4
	History	81	27	14	30	16	10	0	4
1950	Total	1627	30	9	27	17	11	3	3
	History	77	30	12	26	16	13	3	1
1955	Total	1912	30	11	27	17	10	3	2
	History	74	35	9	27	12	14	1	1
1960	Total	2224	26	12	27	17	11	4	3
	History	100	23	13	23	20	13	5	3

Source: Lindsey R. Harmon, *Profiles of Ph.D's in the Sciences: Summary Report on Follow-Up of Doctorate Cohorts, 1935–1960* (Washington, D.C., 1965), pp. 104–6.

to 2 in 1945, and 11 to 3 in 1955. The data, furthermore, reinforces the view that academics in general and historians in particular come typically from a middle-class, indeed, from a lower middle-class background.[4]

Not only do academics as a rule improve their position in society when they become teachers in institutions of higher learning, but they perceive that they are improving it. Their upward mobility, in other words, is the result of a conscious decision or process. In his study, Davis asked the participating graduate students: "In your opinion, how would the *general social standing* of your father's type of job compare with that of a professor in a small liberal arts college?" He chose this level of academic employment as a reference point because it occupies a median position in the social world into which they expected to move. A substantial majority, 61 per cent, said that their father's job was lower, 20 per cent that it was the same, and only 19 per cent that it was higher. It would appear that those who enter higher education realize that they are rising above their social origins, and that realization motivates in part their readiness to endure the hardships of graduate training. This in no way denies the genuineness of their interest in the discipline. Academics generally display a natural propensity for learning, an aptitude for dealing with abstract as opposed to practical problems. Intellectuality is their most obvious common characteristic. But it is also apparent that what attracts them to higher education as a source of employment is not only its intellectual but also its social rewards.[5]

For many graduate students an appointment to the faculty of a college or university offers still another advantage. It frees them from the need to engage in the rough-and-tumble of the economic marketplace. They often feel a distaste, sometimes aggravated by a feeling of inadequacy, for the competitiveness and moneygrubbing which appear to them to pervade life in the office, salesroom, or factory. This cloister mentality is less pronounced in the natural sciences, where the requirements for success in the academic community are not very different from those outside. The university scientist is frequently forced by the nature of his work to deal with corporate interests, industrial needs, and market conditions. The way of life of a prominent chemist or physicist thus resembles in important respects that of a

4. D. Perkins and J. L. Snell, *Education of Historians*, pp. 46, 229; E. C. Ladd, Jr. and S. M. Lipset, *Divided Academy*, pp. 342–43; Lindsey R. Harmon, *Profiles of Ph.D's in the Sciences: Summary Report on Follow-Up of Doctorate Cohorts, 1935–1960* (Washington, D.C., 1965), pp. 101–9.

5. J. A. Davis, *Stipends and Spouses*, p. 26.

business executive or bank officer. But in the social sciences and especially the humanities the boundaries of the campus separate two widely differing behavior patterns and value systems. Those on the inside tend to look on outsiders as materialistic, grasping, unrefined, and lowbrow. They are perceived as Babbitts, uncultured and insensitive, concerned only with sports and local gossip. While academics readily concede that there is more money to be made in industry, finance, government, or even labor, they feel that the life-style in a college or university is more stimulating, more responsive to esthetic and intellectual needs. In short, the milieu of higher education attracts many graduate students almost as much as the opportunity it provides for the pursuit of knowledge.

The wall separating the campus from the surrounding community is not without its intellectual advantages. It enables scholars to view their society with greater detachment than would otherwise be possible. They become more perceptive critics of its dominant attitudes; they can see more clearly through the veil of rhetoric and piety which obscures established institutions. But their isolation can also lead to a complacent narcissism. It encourages disdain for the values of the social order which sustains higher education. Academics tend to see themselves as a small company of the righteous defying the hosts of Philistinism.

The graduate students who regard higher education as an oasis of culture in a materialistic desert frequently also long for a sense of community which only the campus can satisfy. They like associating with the people, professors as well as students, whom they meet at the university. As undergraduates they were often active in school affairs. They joined literary clubs, they took part in scholarly activities, they socialized with friendly faculty members, they enjoyed the feeling of togetherness which comes from closeness to a group of men and women sharing intellectual or cultural interests. Many of them, well-known on campus, were afraid of losing their identity in the impersonal world which faced them upon graduation. They sought therefore to retain a sense of community by remaining in higher education. Some stayed on to do their graduate work in the same institution from which they received their bachelor's degree. Others went elsewhere, but their hope was to return to alma mater, where they had so many happy memories, or at least to find employment at a school with a similar atmosphere and outlook.

This emotional attachment to academic life is most characteristic of those who attended a small liberal arts college or one of the Ivy League schools, where a close relationship between students and teachers is emphasized. But it can also be discovered among graduates of the big, impersonal state institutions and urban universities. At almost any school in the country there are a few professors, sometimes quite a few, who attended it as undergraduates, who were trained in its graduate program, if it has one, who after a few years received an appointment there, or moved directly from graduate student to member of its faculty. For them higher education makes possible a lifelong pursuit of learning in an environment sheltered against the cold winds blowing outside. It means the enjoyment of emotional and psychological satisfactions which only the self-contained academic community can provide.

Closely related to the search for togetherness is a craving for the experience of teaching. Many graduate students are drawn to higher education by this craving even more than by the challenge of scholarship, the stimulation of academic life, or the feeling of community on campus. What appeals to them is the prospect of standing before a roomful of undergraduates, expounding the fine points of the discipline or expressing their views on man, society, and the world. The reason for their interest in pedagogy is more complex than they generally realize. There is, of course, an obvious and altogether valid explanation. The instruction of young minds is an important pursuit. But that is not all. There is also a subtle satisfaction in lecturing to a group of students who seem to hang on every word, writing it down dutifully in their notebooks. For most academics there is something agreeable in standing before an audience, even a captive audience, in being the center of attention, in displaying knowledge and wisdom. The feeling is similar to that which an actor or opera singer experiences when the curtain goes up on a full house. A few years ago a well-known scholar, distinguished in the field of American social history, confided that he felt fortunate to be in a profession which actually paid him for doing something he would be willing to do for nothing. Not all academics are prepared to go so far, but they would probably agree that they find the experience of the classroom stimulating and gratifying.

For those who are attracted to higher education primarily by a desire to teach, formal instruction is only part of their pedagogical activity. They are also the ones most likely to maintain contact with students through extracurricular activities and social gatherings. They usually act as advisers to clubs, societies, programs, and projects. They often eat lunch with undergraduates in the school cafeteria, they have coffee or beer with them in the afternoon, they invite them home for food and conversation, they address them by their first name, and in some cases are addressed by their first name as well. They gradually acquire a reputation of being "regular guys," faculty members with whom you can talk freely, let your hair down. At first, while young instructors or assistant professors, they reinforce their identification with the students by sounding, dressing, looking, and sometimes behaving like them. As the passage of time makes this life-style increasingly incongruous, they adopt a more avuncular manner, becoming reconciled to the generation gap, but insisting that it can be bridged by goodwill, understanding, and sympathy. Finally, they become campus characters enjoying esteem and affection, remembered by generations of undergraduates, celebrated in school anecdotes, part of the golden tradition of alma mater. They help embellish and enrich the texture of life in institutions of learning.

Not only are the graduate students who enter higher education thus impelled by a variety of motives, but they are expected to perform a multiplicity of roles. The several functions of the academic are not mutually exclusive, to be sure. The same man or woman can be an active scholar and stimulating teacher, a campus politician and social lion, a departmental administrator and amateur therapist. But no one can play all these parts simultaneously or with equal effectiveness. Graduate students have greater interest and aptitude for some than for others. Many recognize this while still studying for the doctorate; others find the role for which they are best suited after they get their degree. But eventually they all discover that the requirements for success in one of the functions a professor is supposed to perform are different from and sometimes incompatible with the requirements for success in another. Yet regardless of where their interests and talents lie, they are in theory expected to pursue the same activities and receive the same rewards. The result is that serious tensions are generated in academic life by the tug-of-war between those who emphasize scholarly achievement as the measure of merit — the publication of a book, the completion of an experiment, the organization of a conference — and those who serve higher education by enhancing the quality of life on campus — the teachers, socializers, counselors, and administrators. Behind the outward appearance of a tranquil profession lie conflicts arising out of the disparity of functions and objectives of institutionalized learning.

These problems face all graduate students preparing for employment in higher education. Sometimes they are not aware of their existence, however, until they finish the doctorate and become members of a college faculty. A generation ago universities tended to encourage the view that all members of the academic community, professors and students alike, formed a close-knit intellectual fellowship high above the world of moneygrubbing and careerism in which less fortunate people live. Most graduate students today are more skeptical. They discover the facts of life early in their training. If anything, they tend to exaggerate the competitiveness of higher education, the pettiness and pedantry. They suffer from too few rather than too many illusions. In any case, the spurious otherworldliness which many schools used to affect has ceased to be fashionable.

The greater realism of graduate students regarding academic life has not deterred them from seeking to become part of it. On the contrary, there has been a vast increase since the Second World War of those studying for advanced degrees. But according to table 3.4, the growth in history, while considerable, has been relatively smaller than in higher education as a whole. This proportionate decline conforms to the overall pattern for the social sciences, although in the newer social-science disciplines, those other than economics and history, there was actually an increase. The decline in the humanities was still more precipitous. Even most of the natural sciences, despite the economic boom of the postwar years, showed a substantial drop. The big gainers were engineering, "applied biology," that is, agriculture and home economics, psychology, education, and such "miscellaneous" fields as journalism, library science, and social work.

The relative decline of interest in history reflects partly the growth in the number of subjects offered by higher education and partly the erosion of the central position which historical learning once occupied in the college curriculum. The process of displacement is apparent in many of the disciplines which used to constitute the core offerings in institutions of learning. Foreign languages fell from 5.8 per cent of all doctorates in 1926–30 to 2.5 in 1956–57; "earth science," a collective designation for fields like geography and geology, went from 4.0 to 1.7 per cent; and philosophy dropped from 5.4 to 1.0.

This shift in student interest is obviously connected with the increasing diversity of scholarly disciplines, but it also mirrors a changing view of the relationship between the knowledge required for a liberal education and the training needed for a comfortable livelihood. There was a time when fields like history, philosophy, classics, and modern languages were regarded as the heart of the curriculum precisely because they were far removed from the practical concerns of the marketplace. They represented a form of con-

TABLE 3.4 Ph.D.'s Awarded by Discipline, 1926–57

	PERCENTAGE			
	1926–30	1936–40	1946–50	1956–57
Social Sciences	21.5	19.3	17.2	18.8
History	5.7	5.3	4.2	3.6
Economics	6.6	4.8	3.8	2.7
Psychology	4.6	4.1	4.1	6.3
Miscellaneous	4.6	5.1	5.1	6.2
Humanities	17.1	17.9	15.3	10.3
English	5.5	6.2	4.1	4.0
Fine Arts	0.4	0.8	3.5	2.8
Languages	5.8	6.8	3.1	2.5
Philosophy	5.4	4.1	4.6	1.0
Natural Sciences	45.9	49.7	43.9	38.5
Chemistry	16.8	17.2	15.1	11.4
Physical Science	8.8	8.7	8.5	5.4
Engineering	1.7	2.1	5.6	6.8
Earth Science	4.0	2.8	2.6	1.7
Biological Science	14.6	18.9	11.7	12.6
Miscellaneous	0	0	0.4	0.6
Other	15.5	13.1	23.6	32.4
Agriculture	1.5	2.2	4.8	3.8
Business	0	0	0.7	1.1
Education	13.4	9.9	14.2	17.5
Health Fields	0	0.5	1.0	1.7
Miscellaneous	0.6	0.5	2.9	8.3
Total	100.0	100.0	100.0	100.0

SOURCE: Charles V. Kidd, *American Universities and Federal Research* (Cambridge, Mass., 1959), p. 238.

spicuous consumption; they helped separate the college graduate from the common run of humanity. Their very impracticality made them valuable and attractive. But that attitude has changed. The gradual democratization of the social base of higher education has blurred the distinction between utilitarian skill and humanistic learning. Formerly, a student planning to enter his father's business or take over the family farm would often study Latin and Greek, literature and philosophy, mathematics and history. To-day he is more likely to choose courses directly related to his occupational goals. This explains why the percentage of doctorates in business and commerce rose from 0 in the 1920s to 1.1 in the 1950s, higher than in philosophy, or why the percentage in agriculture rose from 1.5 to 3.3, nearly equaling history. These are relatively minor shifts, considering the entire scope of institutionalized learning, but they suggest the changes which higher education has experienced as a result of rapid growth.[6]

Once a student decides to devote himself to one of the older disciplines like history, he must, before even beginning his formal training, make a decision likely to have a highly important effect on his future career. In seeking admission to a graduate school he faces a crucial choice. Although the number of institutions offering advanced degrees has increased considerably since the Second World War, the number of first-rate departments has not increased accordingly. The same dozen or so which were regarded as leaders in history fifty years ago still enjoy that reputation today. They no longer produce the same high proportion of all Ph.D.'s, but they continue to a large extent to monopolize the better jobs. While changing somewhat from one survey to the next, the list of elite institutions remains remarkably constant, a reflection perhaps of tradition or inertia as much as of unvarying excellence. In the East the names of Harvard, Yale, Princeton, Columbia, and Cornell appear regularly, joined sometimes by Johns Hopkins. In the Middle West the departments generally regarded as the strongest have been Chicago, Michigan, and Wisconsin. Of the Southern universities only North Carolina is frequently included in the list. On the West Coast the outstanding institutions are Berkeley and Stanford. This does not mean that other departments may not be as good or even better than some of those included among the leaders. Reputation lags behind accomplishment, on the way up as well as down. Although getting into the charmed circle may be difficult, getting out is not easy either. Tradition in higher education is so tenacious that a school can live on it for decades.

Yet however inaccurate or unfair the rankings, a prospective graduate student would do well to keep it in mind in planning for admission to a university. The history departments high on the list will be able to do more for him when he earns his degree. They will be the first to learn of good job openings; their recommendations will carry greater weight. They have broader contacts, closer connections, better credentials. While an outstand-

6. Charles V. Kidd, *American Universities and Federal Research* (Cambridge, Mass., 1959), p. 238.

ing scholar will rise to the top regardless of where he got his doctorate, it will be easier for him if he got it from one of the prestigious institutions. As for the average, competent but undistinguished historian, the university at which he studied will make a big difference. With a Ph.D. from a small and obscure school in the provinces, he can only expect a job in an even smaller and more obscure one. But with a Ph.D. from Harvard or Yale, his opportunities broaden; almost all the better liberal arts colleges and universities have several faculty members from such top-rated institutions.

This difference has been ascribed to something called, not altogether accurately, the "old boy network." It is true that scholars, regardless of age, sex, or status, use what influence they have to promote the interests of their students. But the advantage enjoyed by the leading universities is not primarily a result of their greater influence. It reflects rather the fact that these universities are more likely to have strong candidates. Whether it is the prestigious institutions which make their students good or the good students who make their institutions prestigious is an open question. But it is clear that a college looking for a promising young scholar is most likely to find him or her in one of the first-rate graduate schools.

Once a student decides on the university at which to pursue advanced study, he begins his training in accordance with methods and procedures established more than a hundred years ago. He is expected to spend two or three years taking courses designed to provide him with broad mastery of the field. The instruction may be offered entirely in seminar form, that is, in small groups of graduate students meeting under the direction of a senior professor, or in a combination of seminars and lecture courses in which advanced undergraduates participate as well. In either case, the emphasis rests on the mastery of factual knowledge and historical literature rather than critical scholarly analysis.

During this time the graduate student is also required or at least urged to pass proficiency examinations in two foreign languages, formerly French and German, but now usually any two. This requirement is a legacy from the days when a holder of the Ph.D. was supposed to be a cosmopolitan man of learning, able to converse with a scholar from Europe in his own language and to read the important literary and historical works of other countries in the original. Whether many American historians ever lived up to this ideal is doubtful, and certainly very few of them do today. Students specializing in the history of a foreign country often gain fluency in its language through constant use. But for those who have little practical use for a foreign language, for students in American history, for example, the ritual linguistic requirement still enforced by most graduate schools is an obstacle to be overcome with a minimum of time and effort. They generally manage to acquire just enough knowledge to pass the examinations, which are almost never very rigorous, and then they soon forget what little they knew. The value of this minimal ceremonial accomplishment appears questionable, and the profession might do well to abandon a tradition which has so little relevance to the actual practice of the historian's craft.

At some point during this phase of his training, the graduate student will also probably receive the master's degree. It is another of those academic legacies from the days when scholarship was more flexible and diversified. It was then possible, though not common, to find employment in higher education without the doctorate. While the M.A. was always less prestigious than the Ph.D., the recipient was expected to demonstrate scholarly promise and achievement. Indeed, in some cases his career proved more distinguished than that of a holder of the doctorate. But today the master's degree is little more than a decorative title. It is generally awarded about two years after entry into graduate school. It requires as a rule the completion of a thesis of a hundred or so typed pages, in theory a demonstration of talent for original research, in reality little more than a dress rehearsal for the doctoral dissertation. Some departments grant the M.A. on the strength of just course work and a good seminar paper, others require even less, and a few have dropped the degree altogether. As a result of the vast increase in the number of Ph.D.'s, the M.A. is no longer regarded as a sufficient qualification for employment, even by the weaker schools. Its function has therefore become almost entirely psychological and ceremonial. Only for those who leave graduate school without the doctorate in order to become secondary school teachers does it provide a modest increment in salary. Otherwise, it serves as a spur to the students who go on for the Ph.D. and as a consolation prize to those who do not.

The period of formal graduate instruction culminates in an exhaustive examination — known variously as comprehensives, generals, prelims, or orals — by which the candidate is expected to demonstrate that he has mastered a substantial body of historical knowledge and is ready to proceed to the next phase of his training, scholarly research. This examination comes in most cases after two or three years of residence, although many graduate students postpone it as long as possible, finding the prospect unsettling and frightening. While it is usually given in written form, extending over one or two days, in some departments the examination is oral, lasting about two hours. The experience is nerve-racking to almost all candidates, but in fact few fail, and those who do are frequently given a chance to take the examination again. This is not always the case, however. Some universities, even a few well-known ones, admit large numbers of students with undistinguished records, allowing them to study and pay their fees for a few years, and then flunking them out en masse through very rigorous comprehensive examinations. Fortunately, the practice is uncommon. In the great majority of cases, the student who is able to endure the grind and tedium can expect to pass the qualifying examination. Indeed, what is tested in general is not brilliance or even aptitude, but tenacity and assiduity, what the Germans call *Sitzfleisch.*

Having completed the first part of his training by demonstrating familiarity with a body of historical knowledge, the graduate student is ready to begin work on his dissertation. This is designed to show his grasp of method and technique, his professional skill and judgment, and his creative qualities as a historian. It means finding a topic on which he can do original research — a difficult, time-consuming task — and examining a considerable volume of primary material in order to make a serious contribution to scholarship. But the process tends to foster technical skill at the expense of intellectual excitement; it inhibits spontaneity and imagination. The student is taught to be cautious, sober, factual, and balanced, to avoid taking sides or expressing preferences. Hence the doctoral dissertation is typically bland, in spirit as well as style. The circumstances under which it is composed discourage strong convictions or controversial conclusions. They foster a tendency toward the safe, humdrum, and indisputable.

Despite that, the dissertation can play a very important part not only in the training but in the subsequent career of the historian. He will probably never again enjoy the luxury of two or three years of uninterrupted reading and writing. Indeed, since the dissertation is often the only piece of original research he is able to do, many people in the profession live on this academic investment for the rest of their life. After getting their degree, they try to publish an article or two based on the work they did for it. They may even seek to induce some university press to publish the entire dissertation in revised form, though only a small proportion, perhaps less than 10 per cent, will actually succeed. Not only that, their future scholarly writing will frequently be derived from the research which they first began during their years in graduate school. In short, the dissertation is the most important aspect of the training which the professional historian receives.

But it is also psychologically and emotionally the most trying. The bulk of what is taught in graduate school requires primarily diligence and determination. It is in large part a test of endurance, helping to identify those who do well in formal instruction and are adept at getting good grades. Their strong point is mastering the required material and summarizing it on examinations clearly and accurately. The dissertation, however, is another story; it demands talent of a different sort. The student has to make nagging choices and decisions, he must find the right balance between detail and generalization, he must sense what to include and — much more difficult — what to omit. Hardest of all, he must be able to face the prospect of having his work, on which he has lavished so much time and effort, analyzed, dissected, criticized, and perhaps rejected. That takes toughness. Those who are thin-skinned often postpone completion of the dissertation for years by constantly finding more papers, records, pamphlets, newspapers, and periodicals to look at. A powerful instinct, almost maternal in nature, seeks to protect the offspring of their scholarship by delaying its exposure to the world. That is why success in graduate work frequently depends on temperament more than ability. The students who cope most effectively with the pressures of professional training are by and large those who are organized, systematic, placid, and perhaps a little insensitive or even dull. Too much brilliance can be a hindrance, because it is often accompanied by emotional instability and intellectual restlessness which chafe under rigid degree requirements.

While working on the doctoral dissertation, the graduate student is also likely to encounter another decisive influence which will affect his entire professional career: his major professor. Advanced training in history, especially in its latter stages, is conducted in accordance with an apprentice system under which an established scholar supervises and directs the work of a beginner. The assignment of a student to his major professor may take place as soon as he enters the university, or it may be postponed until he decides in which field of history to specialize. But whenever it occurs, it marks the beginning of a relationship which goes far beyond that of master and pupil. To be sure, the official function of the major professor is to guide the training, especially the writing of the dissertation, of the students working under him. He helps them find a topic, he suggests where they might look for sources, he helps shape the direction the research is taking, he reads the chapters as they are being written, making corrections and recommending changes, and at the end he presides at the defense of the dissertation, when the candidate is expected to refute criticisms directed at him by members of the doctoral committee. The supervision by the major professor over his graduate students is the most costly aspect of the entire system of graduate training. No other form of classroom or individual instruction is so generously uneconomical, perhaps even prodigal, in the expenditure of academic resources.

The relationship between professor and student, however, while beginning in graduate school, does not as a rule end there. It often continues to be of central importance in the careers of both. The student now becomes a disciple of the professor, so that the status of the latter affects the prospects of the former. A well-known, widely respected historian can be expected to do more for his students than one with little reputation or influence. Since his recommendations carry greater weight, his protégés gain a significant advantage in the competition for better jobs and higher salaries. That is an important reason why the stars of the profession attract more candidates to their seminars than their run-of-the-mill colleagues. They may be no better as teachers; indeed, some of them are notoriously bad. But their names provide graduate students with contacts and opportunities which would otherwise remain inaccessible to them.

The entire process suggests that it is not the distinguished schools and professors who turn out good graduate students, but good graduate students who help maintain the reputation of the distinguished schools and professors. The training provided by a university, however sound, cannot transform a hard working, uninspired plodder into an imaginative, perceptive scholar. The qualities which the new Ph.D. or, for that matter, the established historian displays are to a large extent those which he possessed before beginning his professional training. Graduate work can polish or sharpen the student's natural talent; it cannot provide a substitute for native ability. It can help the young historian by making him more sensitive to significant issues and unexplored problems, or it can hinder by misdirecting him into blind alleys and petty drudgeries. In either case, it contributes only a small part to his being the kind of scholar he becomes, and that contribution can sometimes be made more effectively in a backwater university with few students than in one which is eminent but overcrowded. In other words, it is not the superior performance of a pedagogical function but the conferral of professional status and occupational advantage which often distinguishes a first-rate from a second-rate graduate school.

This means that for the student the relationship with his major professor is crucially important not only while working for the doctorate, but for the rest of his career. There are letters of recommendation for grants, fellowships, appointments, and promotions. There are nominations to prestigious or influential positions in the profession. There are personal contacts with people and institutions of importance in the academic world. In all these respects the major professor can be of enormous help. But his support exacts a price. The student comes to be identified with his professor's interests and biases; he inherits his quarrels and vendettas; his own work is influenced and sometimes overshadowed by that of his mentor. The latter in turn tends to regard his graduate students as extensions of himself. Their successes become his successes; their achievements confirm his own. Many prominent historians feel subconsciously that their reputation depends at least in part on that of their students. They therefore become protective and uncritical, bestowing on them praise they do not deserve and pushing them for jobs for which they are not qualified. Like overfond parents, they exaggerate the talents of their protégés, rejecting indignantly any suggestion that their judgment is not entirely objective.

The relationship between master and pupil, moreover, can easily cross the boundary of professional concerns and become almost painfully personal. There are cases where the major professor turns into a father, therapist, confessor, and marriage counselor, while the graduate student becomes a son, confidant, secretary, and factotum. Such an association is in the long run unhealthy for both. The apprentice system of graduate training cannot be easily altered, but it might be better if the relationship between professor and student, while remaining cordial, became more impersonal, businesslike, and detached.

If nothing else, a clearer definition of their respective roles would reduce the pressures and ambiguities which prolong the period of study for the Ph.D. On paper it should take no longer to get a doctorate in history than to earn a degree in law, medicine, business, theology, or any other profession. The course work preparing a student for the comprehensive examination can ordinarily be completed in two to three years, while the dissertation, according to some graduate-school estimates, should take about another two years. But such calculations are unrealistic. There are very few students who actually manage to get a doctorate that quickly. A study of doctorate recipients published by the National Academy of Sciences shows that in 1964–66 the total time between the baccalaureate and the doctoral degree in all disciplines was 8.2 years, although the registered time, that is, the period when the student was officially enrolled and working on his graduate program, was considerably less, 5.4 years. In no discipline was the average time elapsing between the bachelor's and the doctor's degree as little as five years, the figure frequently given as the norm for earning the Ph.D.

There were significant variations, however, among the major categories of disciplines covered in the study. The shortest period for completing the doctorate — 6.3 years total time and 5.1 registered time — was recorded by the physical sciences including mathematics, physics, astronomy, chemistry, geology, and engineering. Then came the biological sciences — agriculture, "health sciences," biochemistry, physiology, anatomy, botany, zoology, and biology — with 7.3 years total time and 5.3 registered time. For the social sciences, that is, psychology, anthropology, sociology, economics, and political science, the average number of years from baccalaureate to doctorate was 8.0 total time and 5.3 registered time. The longest term of study for the Ph.D. was in the arts and humanities — history, English, modern languages, classics, philosophy, speech, fine arts, and music — with 9.5 years total time and 5.7 registered time. Within this category history, requiring 8.9 total years and 5.7 registered years, was not as time-consuming as most other disciplines. Only in the classics and philosophy was there a shorter period of study. But compared to the social sciences, history was near the bottom of the list, with only sociology requiring a greater total and registered time for completion of the doctorate.[7]

What accounts in part at least for the long years of study for the Ph.D. is the absence of a fixed timetable for meeting the requirements. Although graduate students in history may know enough to pass the comprehensive examination in the second or third year of residence, their sense of insecurity frequently leads them to delay taking it until the fourth or even fifth year. Still more important is the length of time needed to finish the dissertation. Uneasiness about possible gaps in the research, uncertainty concerning the major professor's expectations, fear of criticism by the examining committee, all contribute to a prolongation of graduate training. As a result, the student is often forced to interrupt his stay at the university, sometimes in the middle, more commonly toward the end, so he can find employment to support himself. But this further delays the completion of the

7. National Academy of Sciences, Publication 1489, *Doctorate Recipients from United States Universities, 1958–1966* (Washington, D.C. 1967), pp. 66–68.

degree, because now he can work on his dissertation only in the evenings and on weekends, when his energies have been reduced by the demands of the job. Thus the lack of a rigid schedule for satisfying the Ph.D. requirements extends the term of study to nearly a decade, longer than in any other profession. How to deal with this problem may be hard to decide, but that it makes earning the doctorate even more of an emotional ordeal is obvious.

Since the period of training is so prolonged, financial support for graduate students becomes of central importance. Yet in the competition for fellowship funds history lags behind most other disciplines, even in the humanities and social sciences. Harmon's survey shows that in the social sciences, comprising history, sociology, economics, and political science, graduate students of history were consistently below average in the proportion receiving support from university or government sources. In 1935 the percentage for history was 24.4, while for the social sciences as a whole it was 32.0; in 1940 the figures were 31.1 and 34.2 per cent respectively; in 1945 they were 33.8 and 37.2. In 1950, when the effects of massive federal support for veterans in higher education were first felt, the percentage in history rose to 50.9, almost equaling the combined social sciences with 51.8. But by 1955 the proportions had dropped and diverged once again to 40.6 and 47.9 per cent, and by 1960 to 40.3 and 43.2. Indeed, in four of the six periods covered by the survey — 1935, 1940, 1945, and 1955 — history was in last place in the social-science category with respect to the percentage of graduate students receiving support. It rose to second place in 1950, but by 1960 it was next to last, ahead of political science by only 0.1 per cent. The pattern suggests that those studying to become historians, though facing a longer period of training than in most fields, are among the least successful in obtaining support from private or public sources.

This impression is reinforced by other studies, some of them more recent. The report of the National Opinion Research Center in 1958–59, for instance, revealed that the percentage of graduate students holding one or more stipends was highest in botany with 89, chemistry with 79, and physics with 78; it was lowest in economics and political science with 45 each, and in history with 34. Even English with 53 and philosophy with 47 were far ahead of history.

A similar pattern of student support emerges from a survey of universities offering the Ph.D. in the behavioral and social sciences conducted under the joint auspices of the National Academy of Sciences and the Social Sci-

TABLE 3.5 Financial Aid for Entering Graduate Students, 1967

| | PERCENTAGE | | |
	Admitted, Offered Financial Aid	Entered, Received Financial Aid	Mean Stipends
Psychology	52	70	$3,007
Geography	45	63	2,928
Sociology	37	60	2,905
Anthropology	33	46	3,080
Economics	32	52	2,990
Linguistics	30	45	3,376
Political Science	28	43	2,877
History	26	43	2,647
Mean	35	53	2,910

SOURCE: *Sociology*, eds. Neil J. Smelser and James A. Davis (Englewood Cliffs, N.J., 1969), p. 140.

ence Research Council. It shows that among the applicants for admission to graduate school in 1967, the percentage of those accepted who were offered financial aid was highest in psychology and lowest in history. The distribution of the proportion of students actually entering graduate school who received financial aid was quite similar. The percentage was once again highest in psychology and lowest in history. Thus for an entire generation, from the middle 1930s to the late 1960s, history was consistently near the bottom of all disciplines in the proportion of its graduate students receiving support. Although there is little statistical information on the period since then, the situation does not appear to have changed significantly.

Not only do relatively fewer graduate students in history receive financial aid, but they receive less of it. To put it another way, those preparing to become historians are less likely to get the lucrative grants and fellowships than those studying in other fields. The report of the National Opinion Research Center makes this clear. As of the late 1950s, the largest proportion of graduate students receiving support who held a stipend of $2,000 or more for the academic year was in the natural sciences. This is not surprising, since research funds from private and government sources are most plentiful in fields whose findings have a direct application in industry, medicine, or national defense. The highest percentages were in chemistry with 63, physics with 60, and botany with 53. Next came, somewhat unexpectedly, philosophy with 45, followed by economics with 44. At the bottom of the list were political science with 30, English and sociology with 29 apiece, and, again in last place, history with 27.

A survey undertaken at the request of the National Academy of Sciences and the Social Science Research Council confirms this pattern by a different method of measurement. Calculating the financial aid received by newly entering graduate students in the behavioral and social sciences in the fall of 1967, it found that the mean stipend was $2,910. The highest amounts averaging $3,376 were awarded in linguistics, followed by anthropology with $3,080 and psychology with $3,007. The disciplines in the middle range were economics with $2,990, geography with $2,928, and sociology with $2,905. The lowest amounts went to political science with an average of $2,877 and, as usual, to history with $2,647. The evidence that history has been less effective in obtaining support than the social sciences or even most of the humanities is thus overwhelming. That fields like physics, chemistry, and biology should do better in the scramble for academic funding is not surprising, given their ties to the world of business and government. But that psychology, sociology, and anthropology or, even more puzzling, philosophy, literature, and the classics were able to acquire a proportionately larger share of the resources for graduate study remains a riddle.[8]

Why has history been so persistently unsuccessful in the competition for financial support? Why is it that only 12 per cent of the historians in the National Opinion Research Center sample of graduate students were able to support themselves by some kind of assistantship, as opposed to 20 per cent of the social scientists, 22 per cent of the humanists, and over 33 per cent of the natural scientists? Why is it that, taking into account all fellowships and assistantships involving research or teaching, only a third of the historians managed to finance their education by these means, in contrast to nearly half of the humanists and social scientists and three fourths of the natural scientists? Why is it that, counting partial as well as full support, only 52 per cent of the historians held some sort of stipend, as against 62 per cent of the humanists, 65 per cent of the social scientists, and 80 per cent of the natural scientists? And why were the stipends which historians received substantially lower? Why were they the only group whose fellow-

8. L. R. Harmon, *Profiles of Ph.D's*, pp. 92–94; D. Perkins and J. L. Snell, *Education of Historians*, p. 50; *History as Social Science*, ed. David S. Landes and Charles Tilly (Englewood Cliffs, N.J., 1971), p. 85; *Sociology*, ed. Neil J. Smelser and James A. Davis (Englewood Cliffs, N.J., 1969), p. 140.

ships in the majority of cases did not cover more than tuition? Why were they forced to take outside jobs more frequently? And why were the outside jobs they took less remunerative, only about 30 per cent of them paying over $4,500 a year for full-time employment during the late 1950s, as opposed to 50 per cent in the biological sciences, slightly more than 50 per cent in the social sciences, and 70 per cent in the physical sciences?

The answer appears to lie in the ambivalent nature of historical learning, in its marginal position on the border between the social sciences and the humanities. Reluctant to embrace the techniques and objectives of the former, yet unable to accept the values and assumptions of the latter, history enjoys the advantages of neither. It falls between two stools. The social sciences have succeeded in gaining prestige and relative affluence by applying the methodology of the natural sciences to the problems facing the individual and the community in everyday life. They may not be able to deliver on everything they promise, but those who control academic purse strings, though increasingly dubious, are not ready to write them off. Their prosperity is likely to continue, at least for a while. The humanities, pursuing a different strategy, have managed to capitalize on their otherworldliness. To many philanthropists, foundation executives, and government officials they seem an island of idealism, a citadel of learning for the sake of learning, in a world grown increasingly materialistic. Their very impracticality makes them suitable for the conspicuous consumption of culture, like poetry, opera, or abstract art.

But history is both too practical and not practical enough. It cannot offer any solution to the problems besetting contemporary society: unemployment, inflation, crime, injustice, emotional conflict, or mental anxiety. It cannot match the esotericism, the reconditeness of scholarly research on Macrobius or the Cambridge Platonists. It cannot tell us where we are going and how we should get there. It cannot pretend to make us better or even wiser human beings. All it can do is bear witness to the past, and the reward for that is meager.

The relative impoverishment of history has not gone unnoticed. Yet while many writers have touched on it, the only systematic attempt to deal with the problem appears in the study of *History as Social Science* which a group of historians headed by David S. Landes and Charles Tilly published during the early 1970s. They began their analysis with a stark proposition: "By comparison with the other behavioral and social sciences, history is a poor relation." It manages to get its share of university funds on the basis of its instructional responsibilities — the criteria for allocation usually include the number of students taught — but "it receives only a pittance from outside sources, which are channeled overwhelmingly, first, to the natural sciences, then to the more 'scientific' and equipment-using of the behavioral and social sciences."

This assertion was followed by detailed statistical data underscoring the privations from which history suffers. The mean annual operating cost per full-time faculty member in departments with a Ph.D. program in anthropology, economics, history, political science, psychology, and sociology was $18,750 in 1967, but whereas psychology, the most favored of the social sciences, spent $24,020, history, the "poor relation," spent only $15,230. The average large department of psychology was using equipment worth $448,120; even in less experimental disciplines like sociology and economics the average large department had a capital stock of $31,050 and $13,820 respectively. History had to rely on a modest supply of typewriters, copiers, and occasional adding machines valued at $2,350. The space per faculty member in the combined group of social sciences averaged 565 square feet, but while the figure for psychology was 1,263, history was again at the bottom of the list with 227. Not only that, in the social sciences other than history a good deal of work was done in institutes and centers which were independent of university departments; that is, they had their own plants, budgets, and offices. Such institutes and centers accounted for 35 per cent of research expenditures in those fields. Since most of them were interdisciplinary in nature, they made it a point to provide room for some historians on their staff. But these constituted a small privileged group which had at its disposal no more than a fraction of the total outlays and facilities for scholarly work.

What was to be done? Landes and Tilly wasted little time railing against fate. They were not concerned with the abstract question of justice in the distribution of scholarly rewards. Their approach was pragmatic and their advice expedient. History must learn to ride the wave of the future, not resist it. Committed to a close partnership with the social sciences, they urged historians to adopt the methods and purposes of their more prosperous sister disciplines. Not only would this revitalize the study of the past, but it would make accessible to the historical profession financial resources which had remained beyond its reach. Indeed, there were already signs that historians had begun to grasp that discretion was the better part of valor. "As new fields of inquiry flourish within history, the division of opinion is changing and the genteel poverty of historical researchers may change as well. An increasing number of historians are working in fields that bring them into interdisciplinary research centers and other forms of contact with more favored disciplines. Since they are better financed and better equipped than their fellows, they inevitably produce a kind of demonstration effect among them."

Still, Landes and Tilly warned, the conclusion of a close alliance between history and the social sciences continued to face serious obstacles. The forces of tradition, of scholarly inertia, remained strong and obstinate. They had been forced to retreat, but they might counterattack at any time. *History as Social Science* described the danger of a scholarly reaction with shrewdness and a touch of irony: "One should not, however, underestimate the significance of an anti-technological backlash among those historians whose interests or temperaments make it difficult or less necessary for them to use the newer techniques or facilities or whose subject areas within the discipline are less favored in this regard. They are tempted to turn privation into an intellectual ideal and to oppose the advantages of others as a source of corruption." Yet in the long run progress would prevail against academic standpattism. There was room for hope; the future was bright. "Social-scientific research will make history richer, more exciting, more valuable, more relevant (that much overused word!) to contemporary concerns and problems."⁹

Here was the voice of triumphant academic entrepreneurship during the postwar boom years. Yet even while Landes and Tilly were describing the shape of things to come, the material circumstances of higher education began to change. The period of prosperity was almost over. Since then history has moved increasingly in the direction of the social sciences, borrowing their concepts, methods, and goals, without measurable effect on that "genteel poverty" in which it has had to live for more than a generation. A few historians have succeeded in getting their full share of the cakes and ale of the quasi-scientific disciplines. A few more have gained substantially increased support, even if not on the same generous scale as psychologists, economists, and sociologists. But most, including those working in fields which are social-scientific in character, have had to content themselves with crumbs and leftovers. History as social science has not done much better financially than history as one of the humanities.

9. *History as Social Science*, ed. D. S. Landes and C. Tilly, p. 142. Cf. ibid., pp. 24–25, 32, 88–89.

The trouble is partly that historians, even those committed to the social-science approach, are not always accepted as bona fide social scientists. They continue to be regarded with vague suspicion and a touch of condescension. They are not as uncompromisingly "scientific" in language and method as the scholars they hope to emulate. After all, their roots were for a long time in the humanities; perhaps they still are. A faint odor of opportunism clings to them, moreover. They are sometimes perceived as latecomers, freeloaders, fair-weather friends. Their conversion is praised and encouraged, but they find it hard to gain the full confidence of those disciplines whose orthodoxy goes back to their beginning. To make matters worse, the massive movement of historians toward a social-science methodology came at a time when the period of academic affluence was drawing to an end. A new stringency began to be felt, even by the natural and the social sciences. The mood of recession, the feeling of scarcity, made historians seeking a partnership with economics or sociology appear not only as converts, but as mouths to be fed, as competitors for shrinking resources. For all these reasons, the growing influence of social scientists on the work of historians has not diminished the disparity in the financial support available to them. History remains near the bottom of the scale of academic affluence.

For graduate students in history this means that they continue to find themselves at a disadvantage. They receive fewer fellowships, their stipends are lower, the outside jobs they get are less remunerative, their dependence on private assets such as savings or investments is greater, and they are forced to borrow more heavily than students in the natural and the social sciences. Limited opportunities for those studying history, moreover, lead to limited aspirations. Expecting to get less support, they ask for less support, according to findings published in *History as Social Science.* Yet in fact the proportion of rejected applications is about the same in all fields. In other words, graduate students in history receive fewer stipends partly because, anticipating that they will not get as much, they do not ask for as much. Landes and Tilly call this being "realistically inured to deprivation," but it may well be that they are needlessly modest in their expectations and excessively gloomy about their prospects. In any case, the continuing disparity in the allotment of academic resources, with its psychological wear and tear, produces a mood of discouragement among those studying for the Ph.D. in history. A survey cited by *History as Social Science* shows that historians and humanists are the most worried and least optimistic about their present financial circumstances and future professional opportunities.

Their anxiety derives not only from their experiences while in graduate school, but from their lower earnings once they get their degree. According to Harmon, the average first postdoctoral salary during the period 1935–60 was highest in the professions and the natural sciences followed by the social sciences. The lowest salaries went to holders of the doctorate in history, geography, the arts, humanities, languages, and literature. The figures themselves are not very illuminating, because they represent only the mean of the first postdoctoral annual earnings, measured at five-year intervals, of six cohorts of Ph.D.'s totaling about 10,000 respondents. But they make possible a ranking by earned income of those with doctorates in more than twenty disciplines immediately after completion of their training. Apart from holders of the doctor's degree in the professions — medicine, education, engineering, pharmacology, and miscellaneous professional occupations — the highest first postdoctoral salaries went to economics ($4,720), the most remunerative of the social sciences, which was ahead of even such established natural sciences as chemistry ($4,670), biochemistry ($4,595), and microbiology ($4,595). Then came genetics ($4,470) and physics ($4,410). Political science ($4,390) was in the middle range of salaries along with physiology ($4,375) and the agricultural sciences ($4,370). The position of mathematics ($4,325) and psychology ($4,300), though surprisingly low, was still above a number of important natural and social sciences: geology ($4,625), sociology ($4,190), botany ($4,030), and zoology ($3,850). The lowest earnings were in history and geography ($3,845), the arts and humanities ($3,745), and languages and literature ($3,630). The pattern of financial rewards in the job market thus resembles closely the pattern in graduate school.[10]

It is easier to explain the disparity in salaries, however, than the disparity in fellowships and assistantships. The reason lies in the nature of the employment of those with a Ph.D. in disciplines for which the chief demand comes from higher education, as opposed to those who also receive job offers from business, agriculture, medicine, or government. The statistical data makes this quite clear.

A detailed report in 1967 sponsored by the National Science Foundation revealed that of the close to 44,000 doctorate recipients during the preceding three years whose postdoctoral work activity was known, 11 per cent held fellowships, 27 per cent were engaged in research, 45 per cent were

10. Ibid., pp. 88–89; L. R. Harmon, *Profiles of Ph.D's*, p. 66.

TABLE 3.6 Postdoctoral Employment by Discipline, 1964–66

	PERCENTAGE					
	Fellowship	Research	Teaching	Admin-istration	Professional Service	Miscel-laneous
History	2	3	88	3	1	3
Social Sciences	7	22	48	4	14	5
Humanities	2	3	89	3	1	2
Biological Sciences	27	39	26	2	1	5
Physical Sciences	16	48	28	1	0	7
All Fields	11	27	45	8	4	5

SOURCE: National Academy of Sciences, Publication 1489, *Doctorate Recipients from United States Universities, 1958–1966* (Washington, D.C., 1967), pp. 86–88.

in teaching, 8 per cent were in administration, 4 per cent performed professional service, and 5 per cent were in miscellaneous occupations. There was a significant difference, however, in the distribution of these activities among the major categories of disciplines. The percentage of those holding fellowships or engaged in research was highest in the physical sciences and the biological sciences. In the social sciences the proportion of those in the nonteaching categories declined significantly. But the sharpest deviation from the general pattern of employment for new Ph.D.'s was in the humanities. No more than 2 per cent held fellowships and no more than 3 per cent were engaged in research, while an overwhelming 89 per cent were in teaching. The rest were scattered here and there. Doctorate recipients in history conformed closely to the overall distribution of pursuits in the humanities.

Even among the Ph.D.'s who were employed in higher education there were significant differences in the proportion of those in teaching as opposed to those in research. While 61 per cent of all recent doctorate recipients were employed by colleges or universities, only 45 per cent were actually providing classroom instruction. In other words, about a fourth of those who held positions in higher education were engaged in activities other than teaching. But there were wide disparities among the various fields of learning. In the physical sciences and engineering 48 per cent of the doctorate recipients were in higher education, but only 28 per cent were teaching. In the social sciences, on the other hand, there was a substantially different distribution of pedagogical and nonpedagogical functions: 64 per cent of the doctorate recipients were employed by colleges or universities, and 48 per cent were in teaching. The highest proportion of classroom instruction among faculty activities, however, was in the arts and humanities, where 89 per cent of recent Ph.D.'s were in higher education and 89 per cent in teaching. The pattern for history coincided almost exactly with that for the arts and humanities as a whole: 86 per cent of the doctorate recipients were in higher education and 88 per cent in teaching, with the 2 per cent employed in elementary or secondary schools accounting for the difference.

Here lies the key to the much lower initial salaries paid to holders of the Ph.D. in history. Their heavy dependence on teaching makes them less competitive in the job market. The statistics published by Harmon prove that of all the activities in which scientists and scholars engage, the least remunerative is classroom instruction (see table 3.7). For the group of doctorate recipients who had gotten their degrees in 1960, the highest mean salary went to those who spent at least half of their time in administration. Close behind were those who divided their time evenly between administration and research. The salary for those who divided their time evenly between administration and teaching was considerably less. Then came those engaged mostly in research, followed by those devoting themselves half to research and half to teaching. In last place were those who spent half of their time or more in teaching. The figures show that in the world of learning the most lucrative initial employment lies in administration and the least lucrative in teaching. But since administration provides jobs for only a small fraction of all Ph.D.'s — 126 out of more than 2,000 in the cohort of 1960 — research becomes the most effective means by which young doc-

TABLE 3.7 Mean Salary by Occupational Group and Cohort, 1965

	1935	1940	1945	1950	1955	1960
Administration	$18,694	$17,733	$16,403	$15,852	$14,427	$12,380
Administration and Research	18,737	18,198	14,544	16,304	15,354	12,196
Administration and Teaching	12,735	14,963	12,419	12,589	11,460	11,454
Research	13,909	14,757	14,299	13,501	11,712	9,508
Research and Teaching	11,374	13,421	13,861	12,221	11,290	9,205
Teaching	11,233	11,075	10,200	10,895	9,993	8,546

SOURCE: Lindsey R. Harmon, *Profiles of Ph.D's in the Sciences: Summary Report on Follow-Up of Doctorate Cohorts, 1935–1960* (Washington, D.C., 1965), pp. 118–23.

torate recipients can obtain the higher financial rewards of a scholarly occupation.

This pattern of remuneration, moreover, remains pretty much constant throughout the career of the typical Ph.D. His salary increases with age and experience, but its relative position on the scale of earnings continues to depend on the function he performs. Those who got their degrees in 1950 were making substantially more money than those who got theirs in 1960, but the distribution of incomes was in most respects quite similar. The highest mean salary, $16,304, went to those who divided their time equally between administration and research, while those who spent half of their time or more in administration were not very far behind. Then in decreasing order came those devoting themselves mostly to research, those who divided their time evenly between administration and teaching, and those who divided their time evenly between research and teaching. The lowest salary by a wide margin was paid to those who spent most of their time teaching.

Even the doctorate recipients who had gotten their degrees in 1935, thirty years before, the senior scholars in the field, now approaching their sixties, conformed to the same pattern as the recent Ph.D.'s. For this cohort the highest mean salary, $18,737, went to those who spent half of their time in administration and half in research. Very close behind, the difference being in fact negligible, were those mostly or entirely in administration. Then came a sharp drop for those devoting most of their time to research, and another drop for those dividing their time equally between administration and teaching. The mean salary for those who were half in research and half in teaching was even lower. In last place, in this group as in every other, were those who spent their time primarily in teaching.[11]

Since for historians classroom instruction is by far the most common source of livelihood, they find themselves restricted to the form of scholarly activity which is least remunerative. Physicists and chemists or, to a somewhat lesser extent, economists and psychologists can find employment outside higher education, where earnings are substantially greater. Here they engage primarily in research, which is a function of scholarship financially more rewarding than teaching. In other words, they have options open to them which are not available to historians. This means, moreover, that even when they accept a position in a college or university, they are able to ob-

11. National Academy of Sciences, *Doctorate Recipients*, pp. 82–84, 86–88; L. R. Harmon, *Profiles of Ph.D's*, pp. 118–23.

tain better terms: a higher salary, greater research support, more equipment and space, and easier access to technical and clerical assistance. Their bargaining advantage lies in the implicit threat that they may otherwise decide to take a nonacademic job. The historian's only choice is to exchange his present academic position for another, and in a time of recession in higher education, that is not a trump card.

Those who argue that history can improve its situation by joining forces with the social sciences overlook the fact that the latter can offer services for which the community is prepared to pay a handsome price. They profess to be able to tell how the economy will look a year from now, how to deal with poverty and crime, how to win the next presidential election, how to restrain the ambitions of the Soviet Union, or how to achieve greater peace of mind. But history cannot attempt to perform any of these services without becoming a mere handmaid of the disciplines with which it is being urged to form a partnership. There thus appears to be no clear way for historians to rise much above the bottom of the scale of earned incomes in the academic world.

To graduate students in history this means that they are not likely to achieve parity with those in the natural and the social sciences. The favorable position of a prominent biologist or sociologist helps improve the position of those studying under his direction. He has greater access to the resources of the government, the foundations, and the business community. He is able to squeeze more support out of the dean or chancellor by a combination of sweet talk and pressure. The grants he receives provide employment for his students; the contacts he has in Washington or New York help them obtain fellowships and assistantships. The financial advantages enjoyed by the natural and the social scientists have a ripple effect which benefits those they are training. The humanists cannot compete in this respect. Since the academic world is to all intents and purposes their only source of employment, they are forced to fall back on the moral function which they claim to perform, on their alleged ability to shape character and conduct. But historians cannot pretend even to that. Without the predictive capacity of the scientific disciplines or the ethical and esthetic content of the humanistic ones, their claim on the resources of higher education is not very strong. Hence the low level of support for those studying in the field. The limited opportunities open to them during and after their period of training are attributable to the competitive disadvantage of their discipline in relation to other disciplines within institutionalized learning.

Yet there is a danger of exaggerating the hardships young historians face. Their privation is after all relative; the financial assistance they receive appears inadequate only by contrast with what is available in other areas of scholarship. Virtually all graduate students in history who have talent, and some who do not, can count on modest support during their residence at the university, not as much as in the natural or social sciences, but enough to enable them to complete their studies. It is doubtful whether the historical profession has lost a single first-rate scholar because of a shortage of fellowships and assistantships.

There is, to be sure, dissatisfaction among those seeking the doctorate concerning the nature of their training and the situation of their discipline. The anticipation and excitement which most of them feel as they begin their studies is soon replaced by a creeping lethargy. They often succumb to a sense of disgruntlement which causes the less gifted or committed to drop out, while those who remain become increasingly blasé about the education they are receiving. According to Berelson, only 20 per cent of the recipients of a Ph.D. in history in 1957 reported two years later that they regarded the present state of the discipline as "very satisfactory." These young scholars, though just starting out on their career, had already become to some extent critical of the profession.

Since they had as yet had little experience beyond the doctorate, however, their reservations must in large part reflect what they had gone through in graduate school. It may indeed seem reasonable to ascribe their lack of enthusiasm to the financial strains they had faced. Such an explanation is disproved, however, by a comparison with recent doctorate recipients in disciplines which are treated more generously than history. For there appears to be little correlation between the degree of satisfaction with a field of learning and the amount of financial support which it receives. To be sure, the most favorable attitude toward the discipline was to be found among the natural sciences, in some of which — mathematics, for instance, with 61 per cent or physics with 58 per cent — most recent doctorate recipients described the current situation in their profession as "very satisfactory." The degree of approval in several other scientific fields, while less enthusiastic, was still substantial: biology with 46 per cent, chemistry with 42, and botany with 38. But why should there have been so much discontent in zoology, where only 33 per cent of the new Ph.D.'s were fully satisfied with their discipline, or in geology with 30 per cent, or in engineering with 29 per cent? In these fields disgruntlement among the younger people was almost as widespread as in history.

The situation in the social sciences is even more perplexing. Here are disciplines which not only seem to have few doubts about their importance, but which are accustomed to receiving generous financial support. Yet the degree of satisfaction among recent doctorate recipients as measured by those with a very favorable opinion of the current state of their field was surprisingly low: 28 per cent in psychology, 21 per cent in economics, 13 per cent in sociology, and 13 per cent in political science. The average for all the social sciences was 23 per cent, the same as in modern languages and only slightly ahead of English with 21 or the humanities as a whole with 22 per cent. Why? Even in the professional fields, which are clearly career-oriented and promise rich rewards, present conditions received strong approval from only a small minority of new Ph.D.'s: 29 per cent in agriculture, 25 per cent in education, and 21 per cent in business.[12]

The doubts which trouble so many young scholars, not only in history but in most other disciplines, cannot be the result of the financial pinch they feel while working for the doctorate. They reflect rather to a considerable extent personal experiences encountered during graduate study, regardless of the area of specialization. It would have been useful if Berelson had provided a breakdown by individual fields of why most new Ph.D.'s regard the state of their profession with less than unqualified approval. But the complaints of those studying for the doctorate in history, and in other disciplines as well, are quite familiar. There are too many lecture courses; they are narrowly centered on a particular country or period; the subjects being taught are not sufficiently important; the professors teaching them are not very interesting; the seminars are too specialized and compartmentalized; there should be more interdisciplinary or comparative offerings; there should be less emphasis on rote memory and more on insight and originality; faculty members are indifferent or inaccessible; patronage and favoritism are rife; the criteria for distributing financial support are vague or unfair. These are some of the more common grievances of graduate students.

There are also complaints of another sort, pertaining not to the quality of the instruction but the relationship between students and faculty. The gulf separating them is too wide. There is not enough intellectual or social contact. They do not constitute a community of scholars but two distinct groups or classes — masters and pupils, the strong and the weak. Why couldn't they mingle and socialize more? Why couldn't graduate students be given a voice in the formulation of departmental policies? Why shouldn't

12. B. Berelson, *Graduate Education*, p. 212.

they help decide what the requirements for the degree ought to be? Why not eliminate or at least curtail the grading system, which is the principal weapon used by professors to maintain their power over students? For that matter, why not give students voting rights on departmental committees dealing with appointments, promotions, and salaries? Why shouldn't their evaluations play a part in the distribution of financial and academic rewards among the faculty? Questions of this sort suggest dissatisfaction not only with the level of support or the content of instruction, but with the subordinate position which students occupy within the system of authority in higher education. They feel themselves defenseless against the whims and caprices of the professors, and while there is little they can do to remedy their weakness, the experience arouses a feeling of resentment among them. This is usually expressed in private conversation or informal discussion, but sometimes it leads to organized demands for a greater role by graduate students in issues affecting their future.

In all fairness, the profession has not remained indifferent to this problem. Especially after the wave of unrest in higher education during the 1960s, history departments engaged in a lengthy process of self-scrutiny and self-criticism. Graduate students and even undergraduates were frequently invited to take part in the discussion of needed reforms. There is hardly a doctoral program which has not been significantly altered in the course of the last twenty-five years. There have been changes, first of all, in the form and content of instruction. Team teaching, involving members of one or several departments, has been greatly expanded. Fewer lecture courses with a narrowly national or periodic focus are being offered. A major shift has taken place from political, diplomatic, and military to cultural, economic, social, and social-science history. The rigor of graduate work has been gradually relaxed. The old requirement of two foreign languages, for example, can now be met in some schools by competence in one language and advanced work in the philosophy or methodology of history. A few departments have dropped it entirely. The comprehensive examination has been made less grueling, psychologically as well as physically, by curtailing its length and scope. The dissertation, though still the centerpiece of graduate training, appears less formidable or intimidating, less of an ordeal, than a generation ago. It has even become common for students to have a voice, though as a rule only advisory, in the educational policies governing them. These are significant innovations in a system of higher learning which had remained virtually unchanged for close to a century.

The reform of subject matter has been accompanied by an effort to improve relations between professors and students. Sometimes this takes the form of workshops, colloquia, and discussion groups where they mingle and exchange opinions concerning professional interests. Sometimes brown-bag lunches, wine and cheese parties, and informal department dinners help foster a sense of togetherness. Members of the faculty are encouraged to invite students to their home; the students often reciprocate. In a few of the less sophisticated places there are folksy attempts to stimulate the spirit of camaraderie: picnics, wienie roasts, beer busts, and baseball games between faculty and students. All these forms of socializing have a common purpose. They seek to narrow the gap between masters and pupils, the old and the young, the haves and the have-nots. They seek to allay discontent among students by demonstrating that professors are human after all, that they are approachable and even likable, and that all historians are one big family.

Yet whether these efforts have reduced to any substantial degree the dissatisfactions which many graduate students feel remains doubtful. There is far less overt rebelliousness among them than in the 1960s. Times and circumstances have changed. But beneath the surface much of the old malaise remains. It can be heard or sensed in what they say and do, in their wishes, complaints, resentments, and fears. This does not mean that the attempt to improve the quality of life in graduate school should be abandoned. It has had and will continue to have beneficial results. But its effect is limited, because the sources of the discontent among students are existential and thus beyond its reach. They lie in the nature of the training they receive, of the life they lead. Grown men and women, in their twenties and thirties, many of them married, some with children, people who could by now have been securely established in a job or business, are forced into an existence which in many respects resembles that of high-school adolescents. They have to grub and drudge for grades; they have to face an endless succession of courses, papers, and examinations; they have to ingratiate themselves with the professors who supervise their work; they have to seek favor with the deans, chairmen, faculty members, and administrative secretaries who decide the race for fellowships and assistantships. And then there is the constant nagging knowledge that the protection of an influential patron is of vital importance in the competition for a good academic appointment. These are demeaning conditions of life for gifted and sensitive young people. They are bound to arouse dissatisfaction.

Worse still, nothing much can be done to change the character of graduate education. The apprentice system, despite its abuses and weaknesses, appears to be not only the best but the only way to train scholars in history. And this means that the subordinate position of graduate students, with the disgruntlement which it breeds, is probably unalterable. We can try to mitigate it by improving the content of course offerings and the quality of personal relations. But such attempts are only a palliative. No amount of sympathy or goodwill can bridge the gulf between professors and students created by differences in age, status, and income. There can be understanding and respect between them, perhaps even affection, but the tensions arising out of opposite interests and separate life-styles seem ineradicable. The pressures and dissatisfactions of graduate training are to a large extent beyond remedy.

What advice should one give then to the young student of history? The best would be to complete the work for the doctorate quickly, to get it out of the way as soon as possible. Nothing can make studying for the Ph.D. a consistently challenging or exciting experience. Those who seek to become professional historians should be urged to fulfill the requirements for the degree without delay. They should strive to overcome the psychological barriers to taking the comprehensive examination and completing the dissertation. Postponement will only intensify their doubts and fears. Above all, they should be warned against making a career out of graduate training. For many students, the financial and emotional strains of working for the doctorate are compensated by the feeling of belonging which they acquire in the university. They live in a residence hall with other students, they eat with them in the school cafeteria, they go to Saturday night parties together, they form friendships, they exchange confidences and complaints, they discuss solutions to the ills of the world, they feel sheltered against the wintry winds blowing outside. But this sort of coziness exacts a price. It is an escape from reality, an imitation of life. The graduate student's existence is in many respects constricted and artificial. It should be treated as an important but passing stage in the education of a historian. A dedicated young scholar will be impatient to complete his term of apprenticeship and to assume the full responsibilities of a master craftsman.

CHAPTER IV

History as a Way of Life

A young scholar who receives an appointment as faculty member at an American college or university becomes part of a community with a character and spirit uniquely its own. Like many major corporate institutions in our society—business, labor, the church, or the armed forces—higher education rests on a complex of values, attitudes, and beliefs which help distinguish it from other groups and interests. While the only criteria for employment at an institution of learning are in theory talent for research and effectiveness in teaching, the new Ph.D. is in practice also expected to display other qualities demonstrating his suitability for academic life. Those who look him over will ask themselves questions which must by their nature remain unspoken. How well will he get along with his colleagues? How congenial will the administration find him? Will his personal lifestyle blend with the general atmosphere of the school? Will he be able to share its loyalties and aspirations? In short, will he fit in? These are matters too delicate to discuss openly during a job interview, but they are always in the back of the mind of those who make appointments. The importance of compatibility and adaptability is as great on the college campus as in the executive suite, on the assembly line, or at an army post.

Fitting in, however, comes in a variety of styles in higher education, depending on the nature and status of the institution. In the Ivy League and in many of the old liberal arts colleges it involves poise, manner, language, and refinement, a certain *je ne sais quoi*. Here the ideal candidate should look, sound, and behave in a particular way. He should come from a particular background, have a particular schooling, display a particular style. He should, to put it briefly, conform to a special concept of what a professor ought to be.

That concept is not shared by all schools, however. The big state universities, most of them in the Midwest and South, perform a different social function and have a different academic ideal. They tend to look with suspicion on the manner and inflection cultivated in the exclusive institutions in the East. They favor a style of behavior which appears to them less affected, more spontaneous. They too emphasize the importance of research as well as teaching, but the aristocratic elegance which can be an asset at Yale or Princeton makes them a little uneasy. They find it precious; it runs counter to their populist sympathies. Those who are seeking a job at one of these universities should keep that in mind.

Finally, there is the largest category of all, the hundreds of run-of-the-mill colleges — some public, most of them private, generally with a small enrollment, usually situated in the hinterland, without the elite status of the Ivy League or the democratic ethos of the state universities — which instruct the great majority of students pursuing a higher education. They lack the resources to become centers of scholarly research; their sole function is teaching. Hence what they look for in their faculty is different from what the leading private and public institutions seek. The candidate for a job in such a school would do well to display qualities appropriate to its modest circumstances. He should appear amiable and jovial, perhaps a little bit of a backslapper, lively in conversation, someone who will be popular in the local community, especially among the influential business people, someone who will get along with the administration, and who will not make the other members of the department feel uncomfortable by too much sophistication.

The material rewards offered by these various institutions differ as widely as their academic aspirations. The most desirable terms of employment — the highest salaries, lightest teaching loads, and best fringe benefits — are found in the elite private universities. Even in a period of financial stringency, their endowments are large enough to enable them to stay ahead of the big state universities, although the gap is slowly narrowing. The public institutions are subject to the scrutiny of a suspicious legislature which looks askance at academic amenities, but their advantage is that they can count on support from general taxation. Since they are thus in a better position to withstand the effects of inflation or recession, they have by now succeeded in surpassing the weaker of the elite private universities. The leading liberal arts colleges are not far behind the well-known state institutions, but then comes a steady decline from the second-class universities and mediocre colleges to the denominational schools, commuter campuses, and community or junior colleges.

The first appointment which a Ph.D. receives is of great importance for his subsequent career. If he gets a job at one of the top schools, he has a fair chance of remaining there or at least moving to a comparable institution. He has thus taken a major step to academic success. But the recipient of the doctorate who is hired by a small, obscure, impecunious school will find great difficulty in trying to get out. He will have a heavy teaching load, little time for research, not much support for scholarship, and no recognition for publishing. The odds will be against him.

How then are the crucial decisions regarding academic jobs made? Why does one graduate student manage to get a position in a prestigious university providing him with an avenue to advancement, while another is banished to a remote provincial school which proves a dead end? The answer is complex, but it involves more than native ability or professional training. In their book on the sociology of the natural sciences, Jonathan and Stephen Cole describe the tacit principle of selection which characterizes most scholarly disciplines:

> In graduate school, certain students are labelled as being "bright" and "promising." They usually become the students of the most powerful and eminent professors. As graduate students, they are given access to greater resources and often have the opportunity to publish papers with their mentors. Perhaps even more important, they pick up self-confidence and the belief that they have what it takes. The "knighted" students of the most eminent professors are also most likely to receive first-job appointments to prestigious academic departments or research laboratories. At these research centers they again have resource advantages and find it easier to publish.[1]

This does not imply, of course, that the graduate students labelled as "bright" and "promising" are in fact dull and untalented. But the question is, Why are some graduate students "knighted," when others who are equally gifted fail to receive attention and recognition? The answer seems to be that the graduate students most successful in getting the good jobs are those who not only have talent, but who have been prudent in selecting a distinguished university for their training, who have become sensitive to the tacit social conventions of higher education, who have learned to make a favorable impression on their academic superiors, and who appear in general to be poised, congenial, stylish, and knowledgeable. Other graduate students who are

---

1. Jonathan R. Cole and Stephen Cole, *Social Stratification in Science* (Chicago and London, 1973), p. 237.

just as gifted may be left behind in the race because they attended a second-rate university, because they do not look or sound very elegant, because they seem awkward in dealing with people, in short, because they lack the style which leading schools want their faculty members to display.

This explanation is supported by the findings of the sociologists Theodore Caplow and Reece McGee, who a generation ago published an illuminating study of the academic labor market. They discovered that in the appointment process of ten major universities, what a candidate for a job had written was not considered of central importance, so that as a rule it was not examined with great care. "The reason why publications, all protestations to the contrary, are not really *read* [is that] men are hired for their repute, and not for what that repute is purportedly based upon. Men are hired, to put it baldly, on the basis of how good they will look to others." Those making the appointments assumed that the grueling training required for the Ph.D. guaranteed a satisfactory quality of teaching and research. "There is very little point in trying to determine how good the man *really* is, or even how good the department opinion of him may be. What is important is what others in the discipline think of him, since that is, in large part, how good he *is*." Caplow and McGee concluded that "prestige . . . is not a direct measure of productivity but a composite of subjective opinion."

The people in higher education whom they interviewed readily acknowledged the arbitrary nature of the selection process. "They don't have to submit credentials," said one respondent regarding senior appointments. "We all know of them. What others think of them is the most important criterion." Another respondent was revealing in his emphasis on prestige, actual or potential, as a major factor. "The biggest thing is that other people think well of him. It's like choosing a wife; you want one that other people will admire too. It's hard to tell exactly how good they are; the opinions of others are presumably related to promise as a scholar. We're also influenced by apparent brightness and possibilities of stimulation for us — and they're supposed to be able to teach, I guess."

But what is even more important than prestige, according to the interviews conducted by Caplow and McGee, is compatibility, the knack of fitting in. The scholarly reputation of a new member of the faculty is of great interest only in the better schools; to many people in the small colleges it is more of a threat than an asset. But all institutions of learning want colleagues with whom they can feel comfortable. This was a frequent concern of the over four hundred faculty members who were questioned in the survey. "We are only interested in people whom the members of the department would be quite competent to assess," said one respondent. Another was very explicit in emphasizing a congenial personality and compatible lifestyle. "[An applicant for a job] had to have a good background in the subject, Ph.D., some experience, research-oriented, bright, hard-working. Good social person, nice person, happily married. Those last two are important." He then went on: "You let some shit in, or someone with marital problems, Christ knows what'll happen. We have trouble enough with the things that happen normally without a paranoid around or someone's wife trying to lay everybody. We hire men to keep; we think personality is tremendously important." The tacit nonacademic or nonintellectual factors in the hiring process — personality, behavior, appearance, and manner — can thus be of greater importance than the explicit criteria of scholarship and teaching.

On the basis of the evidence they gathered, Caplow and McGee suggested that an academic's career was pretty much determined by the time he reached the age of forty. For by then the opinions which others had of him became so crystallized and diffused that the possibility of changing them was slight. "Disciplinary prestige is a feature of a social system, not a scientific measurement. It is correlated with professional achievement but not identical with it." A scholar might, for instance, publish what would under other circumstances be a brilliant contribution. "But if he is too old, or too young, or located in the minor league, it will not be recognized as brilliant and will not bring him the professional advancement which he could claim if he were of the proper age and located at the proper university." There are people in every field of learning to whom this has happened. "Disciplinary prestige, then, has a social and institutional locus," so that the unwritten rules and silent conventions of the academic marketplace will often play a more important role than the official standards or requirements.[2]

These rules and conventions serve to exclude those whose scholarly achievements might qualify them for a desirable position, but whose personal characteristics conflict with the accepted norms of style or conduct in higher education. Before the Second World War they often debarred from academic life people whose ethnic or racial background was different from that of the white, Anglo-Saxon, Protestant ascendancy: Jews, Catho-

2. Theodore Caplow and Reece J. McGee, *The Academic Marketplace* (New York, 1958), pp. 127-29, 158, 160.

lics, Hispanics, Asians, and blacks. The obstacles were usually disguised as inadequacies in scholarship, background, experience, promise, or empathy, but the function they performed was obvious. A tacit bigotry served to protect the traditional social and ethnic composition of the academic community against outsiders, especially Jews, who were attracted to higher education in disproportionate numbers.

The pattern of discrimination used to maintain the genteel tradition in learning began to unravel, however, after the Second World War. The great influx of students and the rapid growth of faculties initiated a democratization of academic life, altering its character in important respects. The social background of the people employed in higher education has become more plebeian, and there has been a substantial increase in the proportion of Jews, Catholics, Hispanic-Americans, Afro-Americans, Orientals, and, more recently, women. A survey conducted by the National Opinion Research Center shows that as early as 1958–59 the religious affiliation of graduate students in history was only 36 per cent Protestant, as against 33 per cent Catholic and 6 per cent Jewish, with another 20 per cent professing no religion. In sociology the percentages were 32, 21, 15, and 28; in anthropology 28, 2, 5, and 62; in political science, 35, 23, 10, and 28; and in physics 32, 22, 9, and 29. A substantial proportion, moreover — 30 per cent in history, 54 in sociology, 65 in anthropology, 41 in political science, and 46 in physics — reported that they attended religious services rarely or never. The high percentage of respondents who had no denominational affiliation — the largest group in the case of anthropology — reinforces the impression that Protestantism has ceased to be a criterion of social acceptability in the world of learning. In general, the religious, ethnic, and social barriers which used to restrict access to higher education have shrunk or disappeared. By now the descendants of the *Mayflower* or the Sons of the American Revolution are outnumbered on many campuses by members of the B'nai B'rith or the Knights of Columbus.[3]

Yet in a fossilized form, the old, genteel WASP tradition lives on. The ethos of academic life still reflects the manner of the New England Brahmin or the Southern gentleman — sedate, dignified, poised, and slightly aloof. Today those who earn their livelihood in colleges and universities may come from a broader social and ethnic background, but they are still expected

---

3. W. O. Hagstrom, "Prolegomena to the Sociology of History and the Sociology of Sociology," mimeographed (Madison, Wis., 1966), p. 2.

in many places to adapt in speech and appearance to the old patrician style. They gradually become absorbed and assimilated. The spontaneity and robustness, the zest and exuberance of recent immigrant strains in American life grow pale in the rarefied atmosphere of the world of learning. The donnish refinement cultivated in the better schools is reminiscent of academic life at the turn of the century, with its courtly manner and aristocratic studiousness. If the founders of the American Historical Association could visit a contemporary campus, they might be puzzled by the swarthy complexions among the professors, they might wonder at the strange-sounding Celtic, Latin, or Semitic names. But the flavor, the atmosphere of college life would not be unfamiliar to them.

The young Ph.D. entering this milieu soon discovers that he has not only found a source of livelihood, but become part of a community governed by its own laws and conventions. To a greater degree than in most other professions, academics are expected to adopt a distinctive lifestyle in performing their scholarly and pedagogical functions. One of its chief characteristics is the close tie between professional duty and private life. The professor does not cease to be a professor when he leaves the office to go home. His occupational responsibilities are inseparable from his social obligations and cultural pursuits. The fact that most colleges and universities are situated in small towns, which cannot provide the anonymity of a big city, reinforces the communal nature of faculty activities, the overlap of individual and collective interests, the intermingling of personal and corporate experiences. The way of life in higher education can best be compared to that of people in certain other close-knit occupational communities: business executives, career diplomats, professional soldiers, and members of the clergy.

Like them, the academic can move from one location to another, from one position to another, confident that wherever he goes, he will find people who share his interests, values, loyalties, and beliefs. Indeed, in his quest for advancement, he should be prepared to change jobs frequently, for to become too attached to an institution of learning — unless it is so prestigious that any move would be a demotion — invites the risk of being labeled a stick-in-the-mud, without drive or ambition. Many of the big names in higher education change employers three or four times, sometimes more often, as they move up the ladder of status and affluence. But after each move they find a social and cultural milieu similar to the one they left. Perhaps that is why personal relations on campus tend to be cordial but a little detached, a little superficial. Not only are colleagues in the department also competitors for salary and prestige, but there is the knowledge that the association may end at any time as the result of a job offer from another school. The departing faculty member will then have to make new friends, while old ones will be remembered in Christmas cards and at professional meetings. The way of life in higher education does not encourage close ties. The dominant mood is one of general amiability.

Yet while personal relations among the faculty are as a rule bland, they are of great importance. Through them an academic helps establish his position in the social hierarchy around which life on the campus is organized. He displays his compatibility and adaptability, he demonstrates his talents and accomplishments, he forms alliances, joins factions, in short, he defines his role or identity in relation to others. The process by which this is achieved is subtle. It has little to do with effectiveness in the classroom or talent for research. It operates rather through informal interaction, through department meetings, committee assignments, casual conversations in the lounge, small pleasantries in the hallway, lunches, cocktail parties, and dinner invitations. Thereby faculty members size each other up, form opinions, probe, feel, judge, or simply reinforce their sense of solidarity.

In some schools members of a department can be seen at noon marching en masse across the street for lunch at the cafeteria. No one is forced to take part in this collective ritual; anyone can stay away as often as he likes. And yet there is an unmistakable feeling that a member who regularly fails to join his colleagues is indicating that he does not really belong, that he does not consider himself part of the group. His absence suggests that togetherness is not important to him.

Similarly, senior colleagues will sometimes take a newcomer aside to urge him to join the faculty club, so that he can lunch there and perhaps drop in for an occasional dinner. It is a smart thing to do, he is told. "You get to meet people from other departments, and they get to meet you. That may prove useful some day."

The most common means of establishing or maintaining a position within the social hierarchy of the campus community, however, is through cocktail or dinner parties. "Entertaining" is a very important aspect of academic life. The purpose of the invitations which members of the faculty regularly exchange is not only to express personal affection but to affirm group solidarity. Thereby they demonstrate their institutional commitment and collective identity. Good food and stimulating drink help generate an expansive atmosphere in which teachers and administrators, veterans and recruits, professors and students mingle and interact.

The mood at such gatherings is relaxed but sedate; the heavy drinking often encountered at parties in affluent suburbs or on army posts is uncommon in academic circles. The tone of the conversation is as a rule chatty rather than sophisticated or profound. It is not very different from what might be heard at parties attended by bankers, businessmen, or other professionals. People talk about the weather, amusing personal incidents, local news, public affairs, or the day's headlines. Rarely will anything pertaining to research or scholarship come up; that would be talking shop. At larger affairs there is often a spontaneous separation of the sexes. The men congregate in groups to gossip about what has been happening in the office or in the profession, while the women, except for the few who are themselves members of the faculty, are likely to discuss personal hobbies, family affairs, community news, and cultural events. The atmosphere — cheerful, cozy, and a little bland — resembles that of most gatherings of middle-class Americans.

Social life in higher education performs still another function beyond the reaffirmation of collective identity. It helps establish a network of ties and obligations with influential people in the college community, a network which can be of considerable advantage. It leads to contacts with the wielders of power on the campus: deans, directors, chairmen, and prominent faculty members. It can mean a nomination to an important committee or an appointment to some administrative post. Those who have achieved a position of authority seek to fortify it by informal interaction with others in such a position, while those who are still seeking to achieve it hope to improve their chances. The personal ties established through social activity, moreover, do not necessarily stop at the boundaries of the campus. They may extend to important people in other institutions of learning. They may enhance a scholar's reputation in the profession. They may lead to invitations to conferences, lectures, symposia, colloquia, and junkets, the signs of "visibility" in higher education. But they require social skills of a high order: amiability, friendliness, and the talent and willingness to entertain.

That is why the right spouse can be a great professional asset in academic life. Someone who is hospitable and an engaging conversationalist is able to do a great deal to further a scholar's career. Thus a married couple often functions as a team, especially in the smaller schools. Indeed, until quite recently it was not unusual for letters of recommendation to dwell on the candidate's wife as well as the candidate himself. The two were frequently described as a "delightful pair" who would add greatly to the social life on campus. While the usual adjectives to describe him were "gifted," "promising," "bright," or the unambiguous euphemism "clean-cut," she was generally portrayed as "delightful," "attractive," "vivacious," and "likable." This tone has now largely disappeared from academic recommendations. The rise of the feminist movement has made people aware that such forms of endorsement are condescending and demeaning to both spouses. But while the tone of academic personal relations has changed, the substance remains to a considerable extent the same. For the average member of the faculty it is still difficult to maintain a clear separation between professional and social life.

Even the cultural and leisure activities in which he engages are more directly affected by his employment than is the case in most occupations. The academic is expected, though this is rarely expressed in so many words, to support local musical, artistic, and literary enterprises. Especially in small towns, there is a tacit assumption that he and his wife will help raise the cultural standards of the community. They may join the school choir or symphony orchestra; they may help organize an exhibition of painting or sculpture by local talent; they may take part in amateur theatricals. In doing so, they will probably meet other faculty and administration couples, some of them quite influential, so that their interest in culture will not go unnoticed. Conversely, it will not do for a professor to be seen too often in local bars and lounges, in nightclubs and places of raffish entertainment. A weakness for low forms of amusement, even if indulged only after working hours, will seem out of place in a serious scholar.

For most faculty members a total commitment to the academic way of life, with its intermingling of private and professional experiences, is not a heavy burden. They generally find it easy to conform to its prescriptions, which coincide with their own inclinations anyway. For faculty wives, however, the campus milieu can create serious personal conflicts; in some cases it may become repressive or destructive. The men are after all doing what they have chosen to do, and if at times they resent the subordination of personal preferences to occupational requirements, they can at least reap the rewards of their conformity. For the women the situation has generally been different. Educated and gifted, in many cases more gifted than their spouses, they have been forced to sacrifice their scholarly or professional ambitions to domesticity. Husband and wife may both start out as promising students of history or literature or mathematics, but after a few years their destinies begin to diverge. Keeping house and raising children make her fall farther and farther behind him. By the time she is ready to return to study or research, it is already too late. She is forced to remain outside or at the fringes of the academic world in which he has carved out a career. There is something poignant about this gradual erosion of hope and aspiration.

To be sure, many faculty wives have been reasonably content with their situation. They have found satisfying outlets for their talents in private hobbies and community activities. For those who have not found the role of helpmate and hostess stimulating enough there are ample opportunities for employment in business or industry. Others have sought a position within the academic bureaucracy, traditionally becoming secretaries, advisers, librarians, or editorial assistants. A few may even obtain teaching appointments — though almost invariably at a rank below that of their husbands — as lecturers, readers, instructors, or visiting assistant professors.

No one dwells on the disparity in the academic status of the two spouses. The subject is awkward. But the fact remains that with rare exceptions the position which faculty wives manage to attain remains inferior to the one their husbands have reached. The situation is beginning to change with the steady influx of women into higher education and a new concept of the roles appropriate to the respective spouses. But this has merely shifted the strains and pressures of married life on the campus. Today there are cases of faculty husbands staying at home, getting a part-time administrative job, or seeking academic employment in another community. The burden of frustration is perhaps being distributed more fairly, but its effect can be just as destructive.

While the pressures of academic life may not be greater than in other pursuits, the means of relieving them are significantly different. Alcohol, drugs, and sex — the common forms of escape in such occupations as music, art, entertainment, advertising, business, and the armed forces — are not unknown on the campus. But the favorite opiates of higher education are causes and politics. They provide an intellectually stimulating diversion from the routine of the classroom and the laboratory. Academics are prominently represented in various movements to improve government and society. They are invariably among those alerting the nation to the dangers threatening peace, freedom, justice, and the environment. Participation with other people of good will in some worthy reform provides them with a sense of transcendent purpose. It helps absorb their surplus energies. There are tactics to be discussed, petitions to be drafted, meetings to be organized, and letters to the *New York Times* to be written. Professors as well as students feel themselves part of something bigger and more exciting than the humdrum of college life.

Then there is the lure of local and national politics, almost always liberal, almost always Democratic. At one time only people in the humanities and the social sciences responded to it in large numbers. Today the natural sciences and even the school of business administration have succumbed as well. There may still be some Republicans left in higher education — especially in the small local or denominational colleges — but they are generally found in the remote reaches of the school of engineering, the college of agriculture, and the R.O.T.C. Among the more fashionable and influential disciplines anyone more conservative than a moderate Democrat would be a rarity. In the typical college town members of the faculty or their spouses often run for the board of education, the city council, or even the mayor's office. They sometimes play an important role in the politics of state government, promoting candidates and organizing campaigns. They may occasionally get into the legislature. But the greatest achievement of the academic amateur politician is to be a delegate to the party's national convention, where exhilaration and hoopla reinforce the sense of making history. In one or another of these forms, politics is the favorite recreation of many people in the world of learning.

Clearly, the main features of history — indeed, of higher education — as a way of life are not very different from those of many other businesses or professions. Why should they be? The problems which arise when large numbers of people with competing talents, ambitions, and purposes work side by side in an institutionalized enterprise are everywhere the same. What is disappointing to some, however, is that men and women employed in higher education, ostensibly committed to the aspirations of the mind and spirit, often behave like those engaged in the self-seeking pursuit of profit. There is the same calculating competitiveness, and sometimes the same pettiness, meanness, and intrigue. Only the rewards are much smaller. In the business world success can frequently be measured in thousands or even millions of dollars, but in academic life people will squabble over a modest raise in salary, over a bit of recognition, a scrap of prestige. To those who are just entering higher education this can be a disillusioning discovery. Most of us would like to believe that the truth shall make us free, free from the trivial concerns and interests of everyday existence. Alas, educational institutions are sometimes incapable of rising above those narrow, selfish concerns which dominate so many other human enterprises.

This picture of academic life may be too gloomy. There may be greater generosity of spirit, a broader vision, a loftier outlook. Yet the same complaints from educators about the provincialism of the academic milieu, about the small-mindedness of a profession consecrated to scholarship, are heard over and over again. There must be some substance to them. During the 1960s William Arrowsmith, chairman of the classics department at the University of Texas, groaned at "the wretched pedantry, the meanness of motive, the petty rancors of rivalry, the stultifying professionalism, [faults] as familiar as the air we breathe. We ourselves endured it and now, intolerably, we impose it on [our graduate students]. It is an old story, best avoided."

An even more bitter complaint appeared at about the same time in an open letter which William G. Carleton, professor of political science at the University of Florida, addressed to a young friend who had just received his doctorate. Colleges and universities, he began, cannot be graded like commodities. "Even the oldest and most distinguished have their mediocrities, their time-servers, their wire-pullers, their beneficiaries of family pull and nepotism, their internal jealousies and conspiracies, their weaker departments, their departments rent with nasty feuds." Although in general he liked the "professional humanists," it was clear to him that "there are among them a disproportionate number of pedants, dogmatists, precious dilettantes, poseurs, and snobs, and a lot of mossy gentility and arid traditionalism."

There are also such "professional rackets," he went on, as writing textbooks in order to capitalize on a captive student market, awarding fellowships and grants to favorites and hangers-on, speculating in real estate, administering rental properties, running cattle or dairy farms, and conducting private consulting businesses. But that was not the worst:

> The most pervasive academic corruptions . . . are of a less tangible and more tragic kind: the gradual oozing away of youthful enthusiasm and idealism, the bureaucratization and impersonalization of procedures, the everlasting angling for place and promotion, the search for a soft and secure life without practical or intellectual competition, the over-emphasis on specialization, mi-

nutiae, and trivia, and the refusal to look to the larger consequences of one's work, its place in the larger whole. There are the pressures to conformity and gentility, the exaggerated concern for what administrators, colleagues, and even the public will think, the fear to teach and write honestly and creatively and the animosity toward those who do, the timid hesitation to be a genuine and spontaneous human being even in one's personal life. Many will say, "But these are the corruptions of life itself, particularly in our kind of industrial society." And I reply: "We yield the good life more often than we need to, and if individuality, spontaneity, and creativity cannot be encouraged in the colleges and universities, are not these institutions abdicating some of their chief reasons for being?"

The situation was not entirely bleak. Higher education had its rewards, especially for those who found it exciting to instruct young minds. "After all these years," Carleton confessed, "I am still charged with a positive thrill when I enter the classroom, and at the end of the period, I often say to myself, 'And to think I get paid for doing this!' With all its drawbacks, college teaching probably still has fewer irritations, anxieties, pressures, and corrupting influences than the other ways by which men make a living. In providing leisure and opportunities for creative activity, a modern university is superior to a Renaissance patron." But there was also the seamy side. The open letter included a grim word of warning to the young Ph.D.: "If you are a successful and popular teacher and a productive scholar, you are likely to arouse the jealousy, malice, and conspiratorial instincts of your less gifted and less energetic colleagues. Remember, Rip, with all its relative advantages and gracious amenities, you are entering what has now become one of the bitchiest professions in the world, and don't let your guard down."

Things had not always been that way, Carleton maintained. They had once been much better. "What a change has come over the academic world since I entered it over thirty-five years ago!" he sighed. "How quiet, unworldly, and innocent it was then, how modest the material surroundings and rewards, how few the opportunities for glamorous careers. College professors were a kindlier, more unpretentious, more humane, more earthy, less 'sophisticated' breed. The home-spun personalities typified by David Starr Jordan, John Dewey, Charles A. Beard, and John R. Commons were in every educational institution. A college campus was certainly no Eden, as illustrated by the fate that befell Beard, but even so, there were fewer pitfalls." That was academic life as it should be, still in a state of primal innocence, before the fall.

Yet during the 1930s, the period to which Carleton looked back with nostalgia, the campus environment had not been essentially different. Many people in higher education were complaining then about the same petty preoccupations, the same meanness, narrowness, and pomposity, which embittered academic critics a generation later. A letter addressed to the editor of the journal of the American Association of University Professors in 1938, for example—the writer of which asked to remain anonymous—sounded as disillusioned with college life as Carleton did in 1961:

> We on the faculty envy each other. The professor does not want any other teacher to have higher standards than he has, to know more than he does, or to be promoted before he is. If the head of the department, or his jackal, is unproductive, it is dangerous to publish an article; if your senior gives no grade lower than B, and you give two D's, your job is in jeopardy—you are an inefficient teacher; and if your standards are so low and your ignorance so great that your promotion seems inevitable, you may be sure that some less fortunate colleague is waiting for an opportunity to impugn your morals. Sloth and envy are the sins which dominate the academic scene, not bigotry. A little bigotry would be welcome evidence that someone cared for matters extraneous to his own right to unearned academic distinctions. It would be evidence that someone, besides a few classroom drudges, was concerned about the students.
>
> I do not believe that we are more unscrupulous, lazy, and envious than other men. If there were no laws against short weights and poisoned food, grocers would doubtless be as corrupt as we are. But there is no restraint placed upon us or upon our employers, and consequently we do not have a freedom, far more important than the freedom to teach unproven theories—we are not free to work for higher standards.

Is this much different from what Carleton was saying twenty-three years later? Was life on the campus during the 1930s "quiet, unworldly, and innocent"? Were professors "kindlier, more unpretentious, more humane, more earthy"? Petty intrigues and minor corruptions have apparently characterized higher education from its beginning as an organized and bureaucratized institution.[4]

People in the world of learning, however, generally accept the "everlast-

4. William Arrowsmith, "The Shame of the Graduate Schools: A Plea for a New American Scholar," *Harper's Magazine* (March 1966): 55; William G. Carleton, "Letter to a New PhD," *Teachers College Record* 63 (1961–62): 199, 203–7; *Bulletin of the American Association of University Professors* 24 (1938): 381.

ing angling for place and promotion" as a hard reality; they regard "jealousy, malice, and conspiratorial instincts" as an inescapable part of the struggle for advancement. In their survey of political scientists, Albert Somit and Joseph Tanenhaus summarized the replies they received from 431 members of the discipline regarding the most important attributes contributing to career success, defined as "the ability to get outside offers." In first place was "volume of publication," with a score of 2.67 out of a possible 3.00, followed by "school at which doctorate was taken," with 2.58. Close behind in third place, with a score of 2.47, was "having the right connections," and in ninth place, with a score of 1.82, was another manifestation of those "conspiratorial instincts" of which Carleton had spoken: "self-promotion" or "brass." These rankings reflect the perceptions of scholars in political science, but Somit and Tanenhaus felt that the situation in other fields was essentially similar. "When one considers," they wrote, "the current proliferation of writing on the organization man, the 'operator,' and the way to succeed without really trying, it does seem unlikely that [political scientists] shall emerge as atypical."

The information obtained by Ladd and Lipset from more than 60,000 professors in nearly 30 disciplines reveals that political scientists are indeed not atypical. Almost half of the respondents agreed that the "highest paid professors get there by being 'operators' rather than by scholarly, scientific contributions." The average for all the fields was 48 per cent, and while there were significant variations among them, none was more than 12 per cent above or below the average. The disciplines in which the view that the highest paid professors are "operators" was most pronounced were social psychology with 60 per cent, mechanical engineering with 58, and botany and zoology with 56. The lowest percentages were in law with 37, economics with 39, and mathemathics and clinical psychology with 41 each. History was almost exactly in the middle with 47 per cent, and political science was slightly above average with 50. The belief that "having the right connections" and a talent for "self-promotion" are among the attributes essential for success as well as the feeling that the highest paid professors achieve their position by manipulative skill rather than scholarly accomplishment clearly suggest a widespread dissatisfaction with the system of rewards in higher education. They indicate that many people in academic life agree with Carleton that they are in "one of the bitchiest professions in the world."[5]

5. Albert Somit and Joseph Tanenhaus, *American Political Science: A Profile of a Disci-*

This does not mean that most scholars feel alienated from the values and conventions of institutionalized learning. Their attitudes vary considerably. Some rail at the obvious contradiction between professed ideals and actual practices; others accept it as one of the failings of an imperfect world; still others approve of the way in which success in higher education can be achieved. How they react depends in part on how well they have done under the established system. But the statistical evidence clearly shows that almost half of the people in academic life believe that manipulative talent is more important in getting ahead than occupational skill.

This perception helps account for the attitude of many faculty members toward the administration. Although those who become presidents, chancellors, provosts, and deans generally start out as teachers and scholars, their real talent lies in entrepreneurship. They display skill in dealing with people, they know how to impress superiors, they seem to have mastered the art of management, to have discovered the secret of advancement. They are effective "operators." But the organizational aptitude which helps them forge ahead in income and status makes them suspect in the eyes of their less successful colleagues. The power they exercise over salaries, appointments, promotions, leaves, and grants reinforces the feeling among the faculty that administrators are shifty and arbitrary, reaping the rewards which should rightly go to those who labor in classrooms and laboratories, not in offices.

To be sure, some academics with entrepreneurial aptitude manage to put it to good use without leaving the ranks of the faculty. Even if uninterested in original research, they get ahead by organizing the scholarly activities of others. They plan, coordinate, and foster the growth of knowledge without taking part in it themselves. They perform a function which can best be described as promotional rather than creative.

In a satirical piece published in 1965 in the *Atlantic*, Irving Howe presented a taxonomy of these professional managers, "new types, far more snappy, aggressive, and up-to-date than the traditional scholar or intellectual." There is first the "research magnate," usually a natural scientist, sometimes a social scientist, rarely a humanist. "He spends as much time in Washington as on his campus. Supervising enormous projects and teaching less and less, he does the work of the world, not the work of the mind." It is not clear to his colleagues or even to him whether he is directing those

pline (New York, 1964), pp. 78–79, 85, 141–44; E. C. Ladd, Jr., and S. M. Lipset, *Divided Academy*, pp. 358–59.

projects because of scholarly interest or because of "strong institutional pressures and worldly inducements." What tempts such people is not money but the idea of power. "Professors whose political experience had been limited to jockeying for the chairmanship of a university department now find themselves close to the centers of national authority — it can make heads reel. Worldly power is a lure both strong and insidious, even among those who regard themselves as principled critics of the society."

Then, on a lower level of intellectual distinction and professional status, comes the "academic entrepreneur," who is "the all-around grubber of university life." He is always busy, but his activity is of more modest scope than what the "research magnate" does. "He arranges conferences for colleagues and attends conferences arranged by colleagues. He consults in behalf of the Rand Corporation, also for a local research institution which has federal money to study 'the changing character-structure in urban society'; he organizes 'teams' of researchers, keen to the fact that foundations like to sip broths made by an excess of cooks." The textbook he has published is now in its seventh edition, and undergraduates who know what is good for them will carefully avoid displaying a used copy. "He writes humdrum articles for the learned journals, sometimes 'helped' by his graduate students. He also writes for the New York *Times* magazine, fearlessly advocating a balance between freedom and authority." His greatest talent, however, lies in preparing applications for foundation support. "He is the Max Weber of 'grant expediters.'"

Finally, at the bottom of Howe's hierarchy of professional bureaucrats, there is the "campus org-man," who antedates academic corporatism, although only since its arrival has he really started to flourish. He may not possess as much influence and affluence as the "research magnate" or the "academic entrepreneur," but like them he is constantly rushing about. "Provide a chore, and he will do it. Not much of a researcher, too little known to be an entrepreneur, he makes himself indispensable at home. He serves on twenty-seven committees, 'advises' students endlessly, keeps in close touch with alumni. He is the delight of chairmen, the joy of deans (soon he too may become —). Every institution needs him, and he makes life a little easier for all of us; but as far as learning, writing, or even teaching is concerned, he simply fills a slot."

The attitude of most faculty members toward the bureaucratic apparatus is less lighthearted than Howe's. They regard administrators with a mixture of resentment and scorn leavened with secret envy and a touch of admiration. For even the most bitter critics of academic officialdom have to concede that the function which it performs is essential for the effective operation of higher education. There may be too many manipulators, politicians, courtiers, hangers-on, and yes-men in the dean's office, usually in subordinate positions, but there are also some gifted, dedicated people who keep the system going day after day in the face of unrelenting pressure. An administrator who has to make the hard decisions regarding academic policy is in an unenviable situation. Whatever he does will be damned. He must judge between opposing factions, he must choose among competing requests and projects. He is expected to settle jurisdictional disputes, scholarly brawls, financial squabbles, and personality clashes. He has to negotiate, arbitrate, cajole, placate, and, when all else fails, decree. It is an emotionally exhausting job. Very few of those who sneer at the school bureaucrats could endure the strain. The truth is, though academics are reluctant to admit it, that in institutionalized learning administrative talent is more rare and at least as important as scholarly aptitude.

Even Carleton, who was no Pollyanna, conceded this point in his open letter:

> It is common in academic circles to belittle deans and administrators, to say that they are fixers with public-relations mentalities who went in for administration after they failed as teachers and scholars; but as you know, all of this is gross distortion. There are all kinds of college presidents and all kinds of deans. (Incidentally, have you noticed with what avidity the most acidulous of these critics ensconce themselves in administrative jobs when opportunities arise?) It seems to me that the American system of administrative control has some advantages over the European system of faculty control, where all too often little oligarchies of established professors tyrannize over the younger men and reduce them to disciples and sycophants.

To some scholars it may sound like heresy, but good administrators earn the high salaries they receive by the emotional risks they take and the mental pressures they endure.[6]

In any case, most academics must necessarily find success outside the bureaucratic apparatus. Not only do they lack the resiliency and toughness which the managerial function requires, but there are too few jobs in administration to satisfy the ambitions of more than a handful. The usual

6. Irving Howe, "Beleaguered Professors," *Atlantic* (November 1965): 117–18; W. G. Carleton, "Letter," p. 200.

way to get ahead, therefore, is through research and publication. In the case of historians this means the writing of articles and books which will gain recognition for the author and prestige for his school. Since the status of an institution depends in part on the professional distinction which its faculty members acquire, and since professional distinction depends to a considerable extent on the volume of publication, professors in the leading universities are under constant pressure to write. This pressure is exerted through the system of rewards, creating tension between those who assert the primacy of scholarly productivity and those who believe that pedagogical skill should be the chief criterion of academic merit.

The battle is becoming increasingly one-sided, however. A gifted teacher will display his talents before two or three dozen students, perhaps before two or three hundred, so that by the time he retires there may be a few thousand alumni who remember his performance in the classroom. A well-known scholar, on the other hand, can reach an audience running into tens of thousands or more. The undergraduates who study under an interesting, stimulating instructor, moreover, will soon be scattered in a variety of businesses and professions far from the world of learning. But a piece of research which a faculty member publishes will be read by the experts whose opinion determines the ranking of universities and departments. The scholarly function is therefore bound to be more richly rewarded than the pedagogical function, at least in the large institutions which compete in the race for recognition and status. In the less distinguished schools, teaching is emphasized more than research; indeed, research is sometimes regarded as an unwarranted diversion of a faculty member's time from undergraduate instruction. Yet by and large prestige and remuneration in higher education are determined by scholarly productivity rather than effective pedagogy.

Material rewards, though high on the academic scale of tacit values, are conventionally described as only indirect or incidental results of scholarship. Those seeking to justify the importance attributed to research generally adduce reasons based on its contribution to pure learning rather than to personal advancement. The chief argument is that a scholar has the duty to expand the frontiers of knowledge. The world of the intellect must be more than an object of contemplation or a means of self-improvement. We ought to become directly involved in enriching its content. Those devoting their life to a scholarly discipline should help make it stronger and greater. Theodore Roosevelt emphasized this point in an article entitled "Productive Scholarship," which he published in the *Outlook* in 1912. "What counts in a man or in a nation," he wrote, "is not what the man or nation can do, but what he or it actually does. Scholarship that consists in mere learning, but finds no expression in production, may be of interest or value to the individual, just as ability to shoot well at clay pigeons may be of interest and value to him, but it ranks no higher unless it finds expression in achievement. From the standpoint of the nation, and from the broader standpoint of mankind, scholarship is of worth chiefly when it is productive, when the scholar not merely receives or acquires, but gives." This has been a classic justification of the historian's craft from its beginning.

But more recently, as learning became institutionalized, another kind of argument has emerged in support of scholarly research. The pedagogical function, so the reasoning goes, cannot really be separated from the cognitive function. The professor who teaches from books alone is providing his students with an inadequate education. Though his manner may be engaging and his presentation interesting, what he says is based entirely on secondhand information. Would you want to learn medicine from someone who has never examined a patient or visited a hospital ward? Would you choose to receive training in the law from someone who has never had a client or been in a courtroom? Would you be willing to study engineering with someone who has never built a bridge or dug a tunnel? And if not, why should a student interested in physics receive instruction from a professor who has never worked in a laboratory or conducted an experiment? Why should a student attracted to literature be guided by a professor who has never done any creative or critical writing? And why should a student who hopes to become a historian be taught by a professor who has never looked at historical materials in a library or archive?

Experience shows that this logic, though plausible, is largely specious. There is in fact very little correlation between achievement in scholarship and success in pedagogy. There are some professors who are great researchers and great teachers, there are others who are great researchers and poor teachers or poor researchers and great teachers, and there are still others, unfortunately, who are both poor researchers and poor teachers. The two aptitudes appear to be separate and different. While the eminent scholar who has made a solid contribution to his field may use it in one or two of his lectures, for the rest of the course he has to rely on what he has learned from others. To be sure, he will sometimes devote a disproportionate part of the semester to problems on which he has worked directly, but that distorts the coverage of the subject matter and deprives the students of the breadth they expect from a good course. In short, research and teaching require disparate skills and talents, so that effectiveness in one does not in any way establish a presumption of effectiveness in the other.

This conclusion is supported by a survey conducted in the early 1940s of 101 economists who were asked to list "the ten living Americans whom they considered to have made the most valuable contributions in their . . . field," and who were told in addition to check the names of "persons known to them to be outstanding as teachers or lecturers." The frequency ratings in the two categories showed no correlation. The scholar at the top of the list of distinguished researchers was mentioned in 75 of the questionnaires, but he appeared only 17 times on the list of distinguished teachers. The scholar in second place was cited by 58 respondents for distinction in research, but by no more than 10 for distinction in teaching. The frequency ratings for the other economists included among the most eminent members of the profession were 56 and 9, 52 and 1, 50 and 12, 50 and 10, 47 and 23, 32 and 11, 30 and 6, and 23 and 1. The figures reinforce the common observation of anyone who has gone to college. There are excellent teachers who never get ahead because they fail to publish, and leading scholars who are deadly bores in the classroom. The instructional and investigative functions are simply unrelated.[7]

The ultimate justification of scholarly research, therefore — and in the case of historians that means writing and publishing — has to be that it is the most challenging, exciting, and satisfying of the various activities in which academics engage. Not everyone will agree with this view. Some find teaching, within the classroom and outside, more rewarding; others may prefer the duties of administration to those of instruction or research. But when we teach, important though that is, we are essentially summarizing, interpreting, and reformulating what we learned from others. We can strive for originality only in the form or structure of what we are presenting, not its content. Similarly, in administration we mostly perform routine tasks which are essential for the effective operation of an institutionalized enterprise, but whose results are largely ephemeral. In research, however, we do something which we hope will prove a permanent contribution to knowledge. We come face to face with the past, with the bewildering variety and randomness of historical data. We strive to reduce its disorderliness to a sys-

7. *The Works of Theodore Roosevelt*, ed. Hermann Hagedorn (20 vols., New York, 1926), XII, 85; L. Wilson, *Academic Man*, pp. 188–89.

tem, to impose a pattern on its irregularity, to find a meaning in its seeming haphazardness. Here we can achieve creativity in the same sense in which the poet, painter, or musician achieves it; we approach a kind of immortality. This challenge brings out the best in us, giving us strength to rise above our own limitations. The experience can be euphoric and exalting; it can even make us, at least briefly, better human beings.

Perhaps that is why it is sometimes disappointing to meet the authors of important historical books which have aroused our admiration. They generally turn out to be no different from the rest of us, sometimes worse. They can be as petty, vain, jealous, vindictive, pompous, or pedantic as any classroom tyrant or campus prima donna. We wonder how someone of so little virtue and character could produce such perceptive works of learning. The answer is that the challenge of productive scholarship enables people to see truths in the past which they ignore in everyday life; it enables them to think more nobly and speak more eloquently than they do in their daily routine. There is something magical about scholarly creativity.

The satisfaction which it provides, however, can be gained only at the cost of the greatest mental and emotional strain. No intellectual task is more demanding or exhausting. An awareness that what he writes constitutes his legacy to learning induces the scholar to commit all his energies and talents; he is pushed to the limits of his capacity. The knowledge, moreover, that his work will be seen by thousands of readers, among them the leading authorities in the field, that he will be exposing his vulnerability, his nakedness, so to speak, intensifies the pressure. Academic research is conducted in an atmosphere of constant tension. The effort required in teaching or administration seems almost modest by comparison.

To outsiders the problems of historical writing may not look very difficult, certainly not as difficult as those of fiction writing. After all, the personalities, events, and denouements are already there. All the historian has to do is embellish them with literary finery and present them in organized form. Such was the view of Samuel Johnson, for example. "Great parts were not requisite for a historian, as in that kind of composition all the greatest powers of the human mind are quiescent," Boswell reports him as saying in 1763. "He has facts ready to his hand, so he has no exercise of invention. Imagination is not required in any high degree; only about as much as is used in the lower parts of poetry. Some penetration, accuracy, and colouring will fit a man for such a task, who can give the application which is necessary." Even the eminent French medievalist Louis Halphen wrote in 1946 that the arrangement of the items in an archival collection, provided nothing has disturbed their original sequence or the sequence can be reconstructed, may prove of great help to the historian. "It is then enough to let ourselves be carried along in some fashion by the documents, read one after another as they appear to us, in order to see the chain of facts reconstituted almost automatically."

He should have known better. Documents may help establish the nature of the events with which the historian deals, but that makes his task harder, not easier. For he cannot change his characters or their deeds; he can only make them more understandable or plausible. Therefore he has to consider their motivations, purposes, calculations, thoughts, and emotions. The facts merely provide the plot; he provides the story. That is why it is possible for scholars examining the same historical data to find different themes and meanings, especially in the great decisive events of the past: the statecraft of Augustus or Charles V, the American or the French Revolution, the Civil War or the First World War, the rise of the Soviet Union or the fall of the Third Reich. But by the same token, the attempt to find new significance in a fixed body of factual material imposes on the historian a task even more difficult than that facing the writer of imaginative literature.

For all these reasons most professors of history do little research and publishing. The strain is so great that they prefer to devote their energies to pedagogy or administration. Even those who would like to engage in creative scholarship often find themselves afflicted with writer's block; they cannot face the moment when they will have to sit down with a blank sheet of paper before them waiting to have something written on it. They therefore seek escape through various conscious or subconscious subterfuges. Sometimes they swear that there is nothing they would rather do than write, but classroom instruction and committee work always keep getting in the way. At other times they complain that the complexity of their project is constantly forcing them to examine more data or to read new documents. In fact they are simply nervous, reluctant scholars trying to postpone their rendezvous with the muse.

This helps explain why many of the books dealing with historical research dwell on the psychological obstacles to productive scholarship. "Consider that a likely cause of the distaste for beginning is that writing is for all of us an act of self-exposure," Jacques Barzun and Henry F. Graff point out to their readers. "Writing requires that we create some order in our thoughts and project it outside, where everybody can see it. The instinct of self-protection, of shyness, combines with the sense of our mental confusion to make us postpone the trial of strength." Barbara W. Tuchman is even more emphatic. Writing, in her opinion, "brings a sense of excitement, almost of rapture; a moment on Olympus." It is, in short, "an act of creation." But it is also very hard work. "One has to sit down on that chair and think and transform thought into readable, conservative, interesting sentences that both make sense and make the reader turn the page. It is laborious, slow, often painful, sometimes agony." There is therefore a strong temptation to delay the ordeal of creativity by prolonging the period of preparation. "Research is endlessly seductive," she warns; it can become a form of subtle self-deception.[8]

Such admonitions are frequently ignored. Despite horror stories current in academic circles about the unrelenting pressure to do research, despite the stern precept to young faculty members to "publish or perish," people in higher education do relatively little scholarly writing. They do more in the large and prestigious schools than in the small and obscure ones, more since the Second World War than before. But intellectual productivity on the campus is on the whole surprisingly modest.

A survey in 1929–31 of 1,257 college teachers in 35 institutions of learning affiliated with the Methodist Episcopal Church showed that no more than 32 per cent of them had made a contribution to published literature during the preceding five-year period; the average number of contributions per faculty member, moreover, was only 1.3. An inquiry sponsored by the American Historical Association concluded in 1927 on the basis of about 260 replies that fewer than 25 per cent of the Ph.D.'s in the field were "consistent producers." Yet the figure did not seem disappointing to those who prepared the report. "It is possible that the percentage given for history is not unreasonably low in comparison with other subjects," one of them wrote. The situation among mathematicians was not significantly different. In his study of the 1,188 people in the United States who had received the doctorate in mathematics between 1862 and 1933, R. G. D. Richardson found that 46 per cent wrote no published papers after graduation, 19 per cent wrote only 1 paper, 8 per cent 2 papers, 11 per cent 3 to 5 papers, 6 per

---

8. *Boswell's London Journal, 1762–1763*, ed. Frederick A. Pottle (New York, London, and Toronto, 1950), p. 293; Louis Halphen, *Introduction à l'histoire* (Paris, 1946), p. 50; Jacques Barzun and Henry F. Graff, *The Modern Researcher* (New York, 1957), p. 351; Barbara W. Tuchman, *Practicing History* (New York, 1981), p. 21.

cent 6 to 10 papers, 6 per cent 11 to 20 papers, 2 per cent 21 to 30 papers, and 2 per cent wrote more than 30 papers.

Though exact comparisons are hard to make, the relative volume of scholarly publication appears to have increased during the postwar period. It has nevertheless remained quite low, considering the emphasis in higher education on research and writing. According to Berelson, the percentage of Ph.D. recipients in history in 1947–48 who published one or more titles in the course of the following decade was 34, and the average number of publications per recipient was 0.5. The figures for English were 61 and 2.2, and for philosophy 63 and 2.8. In the natural sciences both the percentage of publishing Ph.D.'s and the average number of publications per Ph.D. were substantially greater, but not by as much as might be expected in view of the greater expenditure of time, effort, and money on research in those disciplines: 89 and 6.1 in chemistry, 86 and 5.7 in biology, 77 and 4.9 in physics, and 68 and 4.0 in mathematics. The figures for psychology, the only one of the social sciences included in the survey, were 77 and 5.4. Bear in mind, moreover, that the apparent disparity in productivity between the humanities, among them history, and the natural sciences exists in part because in the former disciplines books are the most important means of disseminating scholarship, while in the latter articles are the rule. Remember also that team research, very common among the natural and social scientists, is rare among the humanists. All in all, it appears that a heavy emphasis on scholarly productivity is found only in the more distinguished institutions, and even there the warning to "publish or perish" is not always rigidly enforced.[9]

The amount of research would be even smaller without the system of material and psychological rewards used to encourage it. The most obvious inducement is the prospect of a bigger salary and swifter promotion. This is not always the case, to be sure. The low-ranked schools generally attach little importance to scholarly productivity. Indeed, a study of all the 802 academic appointments and promotions at Indiana University between 1885 and 1937 found that "there has been no close relation between promotion and publication." Quite the opposite. "On the average, the person

9. Floyd W. Reeves et al., *The Liberal Arts College* (Chicago, 1932), p. 323; Marcus W. Jernegan, "Productivity of Doctors of Philosophy of History," *American Historical Review* 33 (1927–28): 2; R. G. D. Richardson, "The Ph.D. Degree and Mathematical Research," *American Mathematical Monthly* 43 (1936): 199, 201, 209–10; B. Berelson, *Graduate Education*, pp. 54–55.

who has reported on a piece of research or formulated some creative or interpretive writing and has either published or had it accepted for publication has not been promoted as rapidly as the person who confined his activities to classroom teaching and social affairs." But that would no longer be true at Indiana University or at any other large school with a claim to distinction. Today the deans and chairmen in leading institutions carefully scrutinize the research activities of their faculty members. Not only that, voluminous publication leads to professional recognition, which in turn means greater influence and income. Thus the more than four hundred political scientists surveyed by Somit and Tanenhaus ranked the amount of scholarly writing first among the attributes important in getting outside offers, which is the quickest way to rise on the scale of academic remuneration.

Scholarly productivity, furthermore, can provide a form of gratification which is of even greater importance to most academics than money; it can provide prestige. Writing about "the social structure and chances of success," the sociologist Karl Mannheim observed that "there is something in the nature of cultural achievements in our society that ensures that their primary reward is unstable subjective success — i.e., fame — and that other supplementary guarantees of objective success associated with it are regarded as merely accessory." As far as the "professional intelligentsia" is concerned, "work is primarily motivated by the *desire for recognition.*"

This contention is supported by Talcott Parsons and Gerald M. Platt, who argue in their book on the university system that growing competition for the best products of the graduate schools has sometimes made professional getting ahead easier, "but in another context the pressures of the 'rat race' have increased." There has been a demand for greater academic achievement through research as well as for greater professional responsibility through the attainment of office in scholarly associations and the acceptance of membership in study councils of governmental funding agencies. "The successful homo academicus is not being encouraged to rest on his oars; he is a member of a heavily burdened occupational group." They cite a study of the Harvard faculty of arts and sciences, which found that associate professors who had gained tenure felt more anxious about their professional performance than assistant professors who had not. Their anxiety focused not only on research but also on "faculty citizenship." Such feelings remain constant throughout the academic's career, so that as he advances in the competition for money and status, salary raises cease to be important primarily as an enhancement of purchasing power and became increasingly a measure of personal merit.

There is ample evidence that productive scholarship is closely related to the fulfillment of psychological as well as material needs. Using the information provided in 1955 by close to 2,500 social scientists, including historians, Paul F. Lazarsfeld and Wagner Thielens, Jr., constructed an index of productivity — based on the doctoral dissertation, published articles, papers read at professional meetings, and scholarly books — which turned out to have a high correlation with the achievement of prestigious positions. Thus, 79 per cent of those with a score of 4, the highest on the scale, had held office in professional organizations, and 51 per cent had served as consultants to nongovernmental agencies. Of those with a score of 3, 57 per cent had held office in professional organizations, and 43 per cent had served as consultants to nongovernmental agencies. The percentages for those with a score of 2 were 40 and 21; for those with a score of 1 they were 33 and 23; and for those with a score of 0 they were 23 and 11. In short, the amount of scholarly publication determines in large measure the extent to which the demand for personal recognition can be satisfied.[10]

That the various forms of pressure used to increase the amount of research have resulted in a larger output is clear. But have they expanded the quantity of scholarship at the expense of quality? Have they diluted its value and importance in order to inflate its size and scope? There are those who claim that encouraging talented but lazy academics to spend more time in the library or laboratory is bound to have a beneficial effect. J. H. Hexter, for example, rejects the view that "history produced under conditions of labor rather like those of the more satanic early nineteenth-century textile mills will be worthless." Can people with little taste for historical work really do anything worthwhile? he asks. The answer, according to him, is an emphatic yes. "The notion may not make happy those generous souls who, confusing their wishes with actuality, believe that competence waits on dedication. It does not. There are lovable, enthusiastic, and inept oafs in our profession, and there are deplorable, nonchalant, and skillful idlers. When the latter are routed out of their sacks and driven to labor in the

10. A. B. Hollingshead, "Climbing the Academic Ladder," *American Sociological Review* 5 (1940): 390; A. Somit and J. Tanenhaus, *American Political Science*, p. 79; Karl Mannheim, *Essays on the Sociology of Knowledge* (London, 1952), pp. 242, 272; T. Parsons and G. M. Platt, *American University*, pp. 161–62; P. F. Lazarsfeld and W. Thielens, Jr., *Academic Mind*, p. 9.

vineyard they always beat the former hands down in the judgment of their peers."

Many people in higher education find this argument unconvincing, however. In their opinion, the pressure to publish may occasionally transform an academic sluggard into a productive scholar, but more often it mechanizes and routinizes learning, depriving it of spontaneity and boldness. As he embarks on his career, the young Ph.D. who has to decide what path to follow to achieve success is tempted to lay claim to some small, obscure subject which he can monopolize without the danger of serious competition. He will choose to specialize in myths and superstitions in seventeenth-century Languedoc or in labor relations in the woolen trade in England under the Restoration. Secure in this little fiefdom, he will publish vigorously, read by only a handful of experts, but spared the risks to which the scholar working on a broad subject is exposed. In time he may expand a little, from seventeenth-century Languedoc to seventeenth-century Gascony or from Restoration England to England under William and Mary and perhaps Queen Anne. He will thus begin to replicate himself, so to speak, doing the same work in a different form over and over again. The entire process suggests that a good part of the increased scholarly productivity resulting from material and psychological pressure can best be described not as a lasting contribution to knowledge but as a quest for raises, promotions, and outside offers. The system of rewards tends to subordinate the higher purposes of learning to the practical calculations of getting ahead.

It is illuminating that the political scientists in Somit and Tanenhaus's survey ranked "volume of publication" first among the factors in career success, giving it a score of 2.67, while "quality of publication" was in fifth place with 2.22. Even more significant were the results of another survey, conducted in 1969 under the sponsorship of the Carnegie Commission on Higher Education, of about 58,000 faculty members from more than 300 four-year colleges and universities. They revealed a widespread dissatisfaction with the insistence in the large institutions on scholarly productivity. A majority of the respondents, 57 per cent, felt that "big contract research has become more a source of money and prestige for researchers than an effective way of advancing knowledge." The percentage of those who believed that undergraduate education would be improved if there were less emphasis on "specialized training" and more on "broad liberal education," code words for rejecting research, was also about 57. Nearly half, 48 per cent, agreed that "many of the highest paid university professors get where they are by being 'operators.'" The concentration of research funds in the major universities is "corruptive" of the schools getting them, in the opinion of 36 per cent, including 35 per cent of the respondents from the large institutions, which are most successful in obtaining grants. Finally, about 25 per cent of all faculty members in the survey and about 33 per cent of those thirty-five and younger thought that their fields were too research-oriented.[11]

Criticism of the importance attached to scholarly productivity takes a variety of forms. There is first the argument that it forces the scholar to become preoccupied with procedure and detail, blinding him to the broader significance of what he is doing. "We are getting absorbed in method," Harold J. Laski warned in the late 1920s, "to the exclusion of an anxiety about the results our methods attain." The effect could be seen in the growing number of vast treatises "in which the text is drowned in a terrifying apparatus of notes and bibliographies and excursuses and appendices." The reader got the sense that neither he nor the author had seen the wood for the trees. There was also "the passion for the *inédit*," however insignificant, and the yearning to publish something somewhere at any cost. "We have got to remember that one takes a journey for the sake of the destination" was Laski's injunction.

A generation later Eric Ashby, another critic of higher education on both sides of the Atlantic, wrote with even greater concern about the effect of scholarly research on the nature of learning:

> The young man who is inspired to devote his career to the real purpose of a university, which is teaching at the frontiers of knowledge, finds himself obliged to enter a different career: The rat-race to publish. And to publish what? It must be "original": minuscule analyses of kitchen accounts in a medieval convent; the structure of beetles' wings — some beetle whose wings have not been studied before; the domestic life of an obscure Victorian poet; the respiration cycle of duckweeds. All, no doubt, interesting, all, in a way, at the frontiers of knowledge, even though it is crawling along the frontier with a hand-lens; all original, in the sense that no one has done them before; but all (with some few exceptions) so secondary to the prime purpose of a university.

This was essentially an elaboration of the view of the majority of the respondents in the Carnegie Commission's survey who had felt that "big con-

11. J. H. Hexter, *Doing History* (Bloomington, Ind., and London, 1971), pp. 94–95; A. Somit and J. Tanenhaus, *Political Science,* p. 79; Seymour M. Lipset and Everett C. Ladd, Jr., "The Divided Professoriate," *Change* (May–June 1971): 58.

tract research" did not constitute "an effective way of advancing knowledge."

In the opinion of William Arrowsmith, the worst thing about coerced productivity is not what it does to scholarship but what it does to scholars. By forcing them to publish against their will, it warps their character, cripples their personality. It encourages pedantry and ostentation. Look at the actual argument or contribution in a piece of published research, he urged. It may take up no more than a fraction of the total space. The rest is a parade of learning, indications of familiarity with the history of the problem or citations to show expertise, whose chief purpose is to establish the scholarly credentials of the author. "Half of every journal is filled with these unlovely exercises exacted by the code; the other half of the issue is announcements, lists of membership, and obituaries." No wonder that an alarmingly high proportion of what is written in most fields is "simply rubbish or trivia," that an alarming percentage of the books published by the university presses "have no business being published," and that an alarming number of scholarly projects receiving grants, fellowships, stipends, and other forms of support are simply "not worth supporting."

How does all this pretense and dissimulation, this "blaze of malice," affect the people who are forced to engage in it? "There is no more sickening spectacle in the modern university," according to Arrowsmith, "than that of the men whose very natures have been violated in order to suit the requirements of a system whose reasonableness and value have never yet been ascertained." Since very few people are fitted by nature or bent to become scholars, learning suffers, for those forced to play the part of scholars necessarily reflect little credit on the part they play. "It is these reluctant scholars whose efforts, born of constraint and willful persistent hope, lack vigor. And it is their efforts which fill the learned journals, deaden the air at learned conventions, and fill the seasonal lists at the university presses."

The most systematic criticism of the emphasis on publication, however, comes from those who maintain that it detracts from the main purpose of an institution of learning: classroom instruction. Sometimes their argument asserts that research and teaching make conflicting demands on the energies of a faculty member, so that what he devotes to one must of necessity be obtained at the expense of the other. At other times their logic is more flexible, conceding that research is important, but so is teaching; the rewards for each should therefore be comparable. The defenders of this position like to remind us that pedagogy has historically been the chief function of higher education, and that those who engage in it have no greater duty than to mold the character and sharpen the intellect of students. They quote Woodrow Wilson's definition of what learning should provide. "The educated man," he had declared in 1909 while still president of Princeton, "is to be discovered by his point of view, by the temper of his mind, by his attitude towards life and his fair way of thinking. He can see, he can discriminate, he can combine ideas and perceive whither they lead; he has insight and comprehension. His mind is a practised instrument of appreciation. He is more apt to contribute light than heat to a discussion, and will oftener than another show the power of uniting the elements of a difficult subject in a whole view; he has the knowledge of the world which no one can have who knows only his own generation or only his own task." What greater responsibility can any institution have than to educate such a man?

This view appeals primarily to academics in the smaller schools, where classes are large, teaching loads heavy, and salaries low. They look with envy and resentment at their more fortunate colleagues who hold positions in the elite institutions and enjoy more favorable working conditions. Yet even among faculty members in the leading universities there are a few who speak of the need for greater recognition of good teaching. They are motivated variously by the hope of improving the quality of instruction, by a feeling of professional solidarity, by the wish to reduce systemic inequalities, or by a guilty conscience.

Sometimes they make a very persuasive case. In the opinion of Dexter Perkins, who wrote voluminously on the diplomatic history of the United States, the academic historian could not fulfill his educational responsibility by publication alone. Successful pedagogy was also of great importance. To be sure, "good college teaching is possible only when the teacher is well trained in the methods of research. It is possible only when the teacher constantly seeks to enrich his knowledge of his subject." Classroom instruction can degenerate into deadly routine without the spirit of scholarship. But the reverse is also true. "Exclusive, or even exaggerated, attention to research for those who are also teachers presents dangers of its own. It makes for indifference to the work of the classroom. It can, and sometimes does, destroy that friendly and stimulating relationship between teacher and student which is at the heart of education. It may reduce history to a mere display of technique rather than illumine it as a great humanistic discipline. It often restricts the researcher to communication with specialists in his own field, to the neglect of the immense values to be derived from history by undergraduates and laymen."

The key to avoiding this danger is the importance which school administrators attach to effective teaching. "Do they think chiefly of publication, and of publication on a quantitative basis? Do they assess publication in terms of the significance of what is published, or without regard to this criterion? Is a badly written article on a minute subject given the minor importance it deserves, or does it count just about as much as the published development of a new theme with insight and skill?" Perkins made a plea for greater recognition of the distinguished teacher, even if his scholarly output is small. "There are men who go on learning all their lives but who never get down to putting their knowledge on paper. There are scholars — I use the word advisedly — whose range of interests is so broad that they cannot bring themselves to the kind of investigation that is so much esteemed in the academic world. There are scholars — again I use the word advisedly — who diffuse wisdom in their classes, wisdom that is the fruit of reflection and experience, but who have a meager output in terms of highly specialized scholarship." He had become convinced on the basis of his long teaching career that "we think too little of the values of history in terms of the classroom, too little of the men who make the classroom a place of joy, as distinguished from the productive scholars who care little for communication in any form." The words were music to the ears of countless academics — overworked, underpaid, unappreciated, and disgruntled — in backwater colleges and universities throughout the country.[12]

There is no evidence, however, that all the talk about the value of good teaching has done anything to redress the balance between research and pedagogy. On the contrary, scholarly publication is becoming progressively more important than classroom performance, at least in the elite institutions. The political scientists surveyed by Somit and Tanenhaus ranked "teaching ability" last among the ten attributes contributing to career success, giving it a score of only 1.29, whereas blind "luck or chance" was in seventh place with 2.06. There are important reasons, moreover, why a reversal of this trend appears unlikely. With the shift of emphasis in higher education from cultivation and style to proficiency and achievement, Wilson's "educated man" began to seem an anachronism. The qualities which

12. H. J. Laski, "Foundations, Universities, and Research," pp. 300–301; Eric Ashby, "Universities Today and Tomorrow," *Listener* 65 (1961): 959; W. Arrowsmith, "Shame of the Graduate Schools," pp. 54–55; *Papers of Wilson*, ed. A. S. Link, XIX, 282–83; D. Perkins and J. L. Snell, *Education of Historians*, pp. 4, 11.

he embodied became irrelevant as a result of the democratization of organized knowledge. Once the prestige of an institution of learning came to depend less on the social distinction of its students and more on the scholarly distinction of its faculty, the importance of teaching was bound to diminish. Today status in the profession has far outstripped performance in the classroom as the chief criterion of merit.

This problem is compounded by the difficulty of evaluating good teaching. Scholarship can at least be measured, counted, and weighed. To assess it in this way often means sacrificing quality for quantity, a complaint frequently heard in academic circles. But at least there is something palpable, something concrete, which can be used as a yardstick. The appraisal of good teaching, however, is almost entirely subjective and intuitive. What is being analyzed is so subtle, so elusive, that depending on the predisposition of those making the judgment, the same performance in the classroom can be described as either good or bad. That is why the promotion of a faculty member who is neither a productive scholar nor an effective administrator is often justified on the ground that "so-and-so is a good teacher." The proposition, though undemonstrable, is also incontrovertible.

This is a point which academics and administrators are reluctant to concede. They argue not only that there is such a thing as good teaching — which is no doubt true — but that it is possible to describe what it is with reasonable accuracy. Still, their attempts to identify the ingredients of effective pedagogy rarely go beyond high-flown oratory. Thus a generation ago Harry J. Carman, dean at Columbia University, demanded such lofty qualities in college teachers that no one could possibly attain them:

> Our liberal arts colleges want teachers who are persons of attractive personality, insight, sensitiveness, and perspective — persons who have a happy disposition and a sense of humor and who have an urge to be guides, philosophers, and friends of students — persons whom students seek out and index in their mind as grand persons and wonderful teachers. We need teachers who have moral strength, a sense of beauty and spirit, the seeing eye, the watchful soul, the inquiring mind. We want teachers who are free of conventional prejudices and fears, and who are articulate and skilled in conversation. Above all, we want them to have a quenchless desire to instruct and inspire youth and to derive great satisfaction from assisting students to see the relationship between learning and life.

A group of educators studying the recruitment and selection of college faculties came up with another list of the essential qualities of the successful teacher. It was more specific than Carman's without being more useful as a measure of classroom performance: "1. Emotional control and maturity; 2. A 'B' average intellectual ability; 3. A deep interest in students and other people; 4. A vital enthusiasm for the subjects taught; 5. Imagination, inventiveness, and curiosity; 6. A strong drive and persistence." This list could form the basis for a systematic and objective evaluation of teaching, their report maintained. "If agreement can be reached on these suggestions, it should be possible to devise tests which would provide, at least, partial answers. Without such agreement and subsequent certification, any approach to aptitude tests for teachers would be illusory."

Educators in a practical field like engineering were as effusive and imprecise in their description of good teaching as those in the liberal arts. Thomas K. Sherwood, dean of engineering at M.I.T., ranked "intellectual capacity" as "the first essential quality in a teacher of engineering, or of any other branch of higher education." Then came a requirement that "the teacher be deeply interested in students," followed by a requirement that he have "wide interests outside his professional field." In fourth place was "a group of personal traits such as enthusiasm, integrity, fairness, and sympathy"; in fifth place was "mechanical competence in the sense of being articulate and tending to business"; and finally there was "knowledge of the field he is teaching."

H. P. Hammond, dean of engineering at Pennsylvania State College, spoke of three chief classes of characteristics by which a college administrator could recognize promising young instructors: "a liking for students and the ability to get along with them and to command their respect; the desire, and the knack, of getting students to do things and to discover things for themselves; and the ambition, backed by inherent capacity, to get ahead through development of knowledge, ability, and interest." All of this, of course, had to be based on "good character, health, and mental capacity."

But Andrey A. Potter, dean of engineering at Purdue, almost outdid Carman: "Unbounded and contagious enthusiasm has always been a principal characteristic of the great teacher, which he radiates in the sparkle of his eye, the vibrance of his voice, his animation, and his vigor. Intellectual curiosity, good habits of study and of reading are essential qualifications." Not only that, "his general education, his professional attainments, and his culture must command the respect of his students, academic colleagues, and the public." Most important, however, "a teacher must live up to high ethical standards. He must not condone dishonesty, deceit, trickery, or the evasion of the laws of the land on the part of his students or colleagues. He must have the ability to inspire and instill in his students sound character, worthy ambitions, an insight into right living, an understanding of the meaning of liberty, and an appreciation of human sanctity."

The flood of words rolled on without providing any practical help in the determination or evaluation of good teaching. Perhaps there is no way of measuring the immeasurable, but then why the orotundity? As early as 1937 an article on the assessment of teaching ability complained that "during the last three decades nearly 500 studies have been made in an attempt to secure a more adequate knowledge of the factors that condition success in teaching," yet "the problem is still largely unsolved." The article concluded that "the current investigations have in general made but slight contribution to the study of the measurement of teaching success, and have not suggested new technics for the study of the problem." Indeed, "increasing evidence seems to indicate the futility of studying isolated teacher traits."

The situation has not changed since then; we are no closer to the measurement or prediction of teaching ability. Yet since the academic value system insists that good teaching is important and must be rewarded, higher education is forced to devise some measure of effective classroom performance. Thus, for lack of any other norm, it tends to equate good teaching with popular teaching, just as it tends to equate fruitful scholarship with voluminous scholarship. And since under a curriculum which has become largely elective classroom enrollment is the most direct measure of popularity, numbers provide the chief criterion of merit in pedagogy as well as learning.[13]

The acceptance of class size as a yardstick of teaching effectiveness, however, increases the psychological burden on the world of learning. Every campus has a few faculty members who have a reputation among the undergraduates as spellbinders. Their classes are always full, because the student grapevine has it that a college education is not complete unless you have taken at least one course with Professor Smith. The less popular colleagues

13. A. Somit and J. Tanenhaus, *Political Science*, p. 79; Harry J. Carman, "The Preparation of Liberal Arts Teachers," in *The Preparation of College Teachers: Report of a Conference Held at Chicago, Illinois, December 8–10, 1949, Sponsored by the American Council on Education and the U. S. Office of Education*, ed. Theodore C. Blegen and Russell M. Cooper (Washington, D.C., 1950), p. 18; Lloyd S. Woodburne, "Recruitment and Selection: Report of Work Group I," in ibid., p. 62; Andrey A. Potter, "What Kind of Teachers Do the Colleges Need?" in ibid., p. 27; Thomas K. Sherwood, "Teacher Qualifications and Development," *Journal of Engineering Education* 39 (1948–49): 414–15; H. P. Hammond, "How to Recognize and Reward Good Instructors," ibid., p. 504; T. L. Torgerson, "The Measurement and Prediction of Teaching Ability," *Review of Educational Research* 7 (1937): 242, 245.

of this star pedagogue, jealous and a little spiteful, whisper that his renown has been acquired by the trivialization of his subject and the generosity of his grading. He has low standards, little knowledge, less scholarship, and no depth; he plays to the gallery. Such charges are not always unfounded, for the popularity of a teacher can depend on many things. Sometimes his sincerity, dedication, and enthusiasm captivate the students, but more often mannerisms and idiosyncrasies account for his success. He tells risky stories, he expresses outrageous opinions, he dresses in a flamboyant style, he has an exotic accent, he behaves in an unconventional manner. He shouts, whispers, gesticulates, smiles, growls, struts, and attitudinizes. He has stage presence. There is a bit of ham, a touch of show biz about many spellbinders in academic life. Some of them admit this quite readily. "We do not really teach," George L. Mosse, who is a very exciting lecturer, once confided. "We perform."

But if the performance in a classroom reflects the personality of the teacher, it follows that effective teaching cannot be learned. There are pedagogical techniques which can be improved through training and practice. We can learn to speak more distinctly, write more legibly, express an idea more clearly, or organize a lecture more logically. We cannot thereby become virtuosos in the classroom, however. In pedagogy we generally reach our maximum effectiveness quite early, earlier than in most pursuits, and thereafter even the most intensive investment of time and effort will yield only a marginal return. A professor who is dull and plodding in daily life cannot become transformed into a spellbinder in the lecture hall, no matter how carefully he reviews his notes or prepares his outline. One who has imagination and vivacity, on the other hand, seems able to captivate his students almost without effort. It is not how much he knows or how long he prepares which makes him a popular teacher, but what he is. And since there is little we can do to change what we are, there is little we can do to change how we teach. This reality, which is hard to accept, contributes to the pressures and frustrations of higher education. Except for the would-be scholar, the faculty member forced to do research for which he has no taste, there is nothing more pitiable than the would-be spellbinder struggling in vain to win popularity in the classroom.

The various strains and ambiguities of academic life help aggravate a widespread sense of inferiority among professors in America. They feel that society does not really appreciate them, that it regards what they do as peripheral to the main concerns of national life. The gradual democratization of the social base of faculty recruitment has intensified this lack of self-esteem. There are frequent complaints that scholars in other countries, where higher education is more elitist and academic rank more prestigious, receive greater recognition.

In 1930, for example, Abraham Flexner, who had written a seminal report on the reform of medical education, spoke bitterly about the contrast in the situation of the European and the American academic. "The truth is that, with exceptions, of course, the American professoriate is a proletariat, lacking the amenities and dignities they are entitled to enjoy. Amenities are provided in plenty for the well-to-do students, who have club houses, fraternity houses, and at times luxurious dormitories; not, however, for the teaching staff. Thus a very small part of our unheard-of national wealth, even in the most cultivated and complacent section of the country, is devoted to the uses to which a civilized society would attach, and assuredly some day must attach, the highest importance."

A decade later Marten ten Hoor, dean of the college of arts and sciences at Tulane, expressed the same sense of grievance. "There has gradually been developing in my mind a scholar's passion to inquire into the why and the wherefore of the striking difference between the European and the American attitude toward the college professor," he wrote. "Why is it, I have been asking myself, that in Europe an ordinary mortal, when he sees a professor, tips his hat, whereas in these United States he taps his forehead? Why is it that in Europe the professor is the jewel of the salon while in the United States he is the skeleton at the feast? Why is it that in Europe a professor is a lion who is diligently hunted by the arbiters of society, while in the United States he is as a lone ass braying in the desert?" The answer seemed to be that the American academic "is the symbol of society's perpetually violated but perpetually renewed vows. He is thus at the same time the savior and the scapegoat of the society in which he lives and has his being. And that is why, in a very real sense, society is his most implacable enemy." Ten Hoor concluded that the species *Professor Americanus* "will be in the future exactly what he has been in the past, and what he is in the present; namely, a prophet without authority, a preacher without unction, an orator without sex appeal, a martyr without a crown."

The rapid growth of higher education after the Second World War has done little to allay this feeling of being unappreciated. It may indeed have intensified it by widening the social gap between academic life and the more prestigious business and professional occupations. In the survey conducted by Lazarsfeld and Thielens in 1955 of about 2,500 social scientists and historians, the participants were asked how they thought they would be ranked by leaders of the community—specifically, by a typical businessman, a typical congressman, and a typical trustee of the college where they were employed—in comparison with the manager of a branch bank, an account executive of an advertising agency, and a lawyer. The results showed that most academics felt they would be assigned a position near the bottom of the scale. Their guess was that the average rank of professors on the businessman's list would be 3.3, and on the congressman's list 3.2. Even a trustee of the school where they were faculty members would, in their opinion, rank them no higher than 2.5. The figures suggest the extent to which people in academic life believe that the outside world, especially business and government, has little regard for the achievements of scholarship.[14]

The resentment engendered by this perception may help explain the increasingly critical attitude among academics toward the accepted values and practices of American society. Although institutions of learning have in the past been generally more progressive or reformist than the community at large, they have also accepted and defended its basic beliefs. Indeed, this has been one of their chief claims to support by the community. Professors may have questioned some of the opinions and policies of the established order, but not its underlying principles and assumptions. While an occasional radical or two could always be found on the college campus, the dominant political mood was unmistakably middle-of-the-road.

The period since the Second World War, however, has seen a significant shift to the left in the world of learning. The Carnegie Commission's survey of student and faculty opinion conducted in 1969 showed that 5 per cent of the more than 60,000 participating professors described themselves as left, 41 per cent as liberal, 27 per cent as middle-of-the-road, 25 per cent as moderately conservative, and 3 per cent as strongly conservative (see table 4.1). The proportion of leftists and liberals was greatest among the social sciences and humanities. In medicine, on the other hand, the percentages were only 2 and 40, in mechanical engineering 2 and 23, in agriculture 0.1 and 17, and in civil engineering 0 and 22. History was well above

---

14. Abraham Flexner, *Universities: American, English, German* (New York, London, and Toronto, 1930), p. 208; Marten ten Hoor, "The Species Professor Americanus and Some Natural Enemies," *Association of American Colleges Bulletin* 26 (1940): 404–5, 415; P. L. Lazarsfeld and W. Thielens, Jr., *Academic Mind*, pp. 11–12.

TABLE 4.1 Political Attitudes of Professors by Discipline, 1969

	Left	Liberal	Middle-of-the-Road	Moderately Conservative	Strongly Conservative
History	12	54	21	13	1
Anthropology	15	56	16	13	0
Economics	8	56	21	13	2
Political Science	13	59	17	10	0.1
Psychology	7	59	22	12	0.4
Sociology	17	60	18	5	0.1
English	10	51	21	16	3
Fine Arts	4	46	22	26	3
Philosophy	15	53	21	8	4
Botany and Zoology	2	37	29	31	1
Medicine	2	40	29	27	2
Chemistry	2	37	33	23	5
Mathematics	5	36	30	27	2
Physics	4	49	24	22	2
Civil Engineering	0	22	40	33	5
Electrical Engineering	3	37	31	25	6
Mechanical Engineering	2	23	25	44	6
Agriculture	0.1	17	30	48	5
Business	1	30	29	34	6
Education	3	41	29	26	0.3
Total	5	41	27	25	3

SOURCE: Everett Carll Ladd, Jr. and Seymour Martin Lipset, *The Divided Academy: Professors and Politics* (New York, 1975), pp. 368–69.

average in the proportion of left and liberal faculty members, but nowhere near the top.

A similar distribution was obtained by Everett Carll Ladd, Jr., in his study of antiestablishment attitudes among academics as measured by the signers of eight petitions opposing the war in Vietnam which were published in the Sunday *New York Times* between October 1964 and June 1968. The data was used to establish a "Profession Representation Index," computed by dividing the percentage of all full-time faculty members in a given field into the percentage of all signers of the petitions from that field. Thus an index figure of over 100 meant that the field was represented among signers to a higher degree than among faculty members as a whole. By this calculation, the social sciences had the highest score with 251, then came the humanities with 132, the physical sciences were next with 122, and then the life sciences with 114. The disciplines with substantially below-average scores were fine arts and engineering with 60 apiece, education with 18, business with 10, and agriculture with 6. History's score was 166, ahead of the humanities but far below the social sciences.

To be sure, this radical change of political attitudes in higher education must be seen as part of a general redefinition of national ideals and purposes in America. But the process has been far more drastic among academics than in the population at large. Thus in the 1964 presidential election 78 per cent of the faculty members in the Carnegie Commission's survey supported Johnson, and in the 1968 presidential election 58 per cent supported Humphrey, considerably higher proportions than the electorate as a whole. In history the percentages were 90 and 79, and even these figures were exceeded by some of the social sciences like clinical psychology, anthropology, and political science.

It is clear, moreover, that the trend to the left in academic life does not represent a broadening of the range of political beliefs, but rather a shift in focus from one set of attitudes to another. Only 25 per cent of the participants in the Carnegie Commission's survey described themselves as moderately conservative and 3 per cent as strongly conservative; the proportions in the social sciences and humanities were even smaller. The data suggest that the elitists, bigots, and racists, who were once fairly numerous in higher education, have now been replaced to a large extent by reformers, radicals, and activists. That may be an improvement, but the compass of political beliefs has not thereby expanded but merely shifted. It remains relatively narrow.

How are we to account for these far-reaching ideological changes? Why should a profession whose members are so bent on upward mobility, so fond of the bourgeois amenities, so addicted to an establishment lifestyle be so critical of the establishment's dominant civic and social values? The answer remains unclear; we are too close to the problem to see it distinctly and objectively. But a highly suggestive hypothesis was advanced in 1969 by the historian David M. Potter in a fragment entitled "Historical Aspects of the Rejection of or Disaffiliation from the Prevailing American Society," which was not published until after his death.

The key to an understanding of the change in accepted beliefs and attitudes in America, according to Potter, lies in the replacement of an established patriciate by a new elite. The old order might have survived the failure of prohibition, the trauma of the great depression, and the trend toward a regulated economy, "if the Anglo-Saxon leadership and the leadership of businessmen had retained its remarkable vigor." But the greatest vigor was now to be found elsewhere. In business a class of nonowning managerial bureaucrats, who lacked a proprietary sense of power and responsibility, displaced the old entrepreneurs. In technology a class of engineers, technicians, personnel managers, social scientists, and other "experts" acquired a dominant voice in the conduct of affairs. As research and development became essential for industrial growth, scientifically trained people, who often came from the wrong side of the railroad tracks, started to call the tune. Unexpectedly the "traditional, beloved, sleepy, futile" institutions of learning became dynamic, indispensable suppliers of research personnel and social expertise. "College faculties – as impotent a class as has ever been accorded a status of gentility – suddenly began to feel the stirring of virile power." In short, the pedagogues became intellectuals, "the first sizable cadre of intellectuals that America has ever known," and soon they started to throw their weight around.

The new intellectuals, like the new immigrants – "and a disproportionate number in fact were of immigrant stock" – formed an opposition to the existing order, and for good reasons. While the immigrants had been excluded from the mainstream of society, the academics had been underpaid, patronized, and ignored. Now they were suddenly given the opportunity to pass judgment on the established system, and even to inculcate that judgment in the children of the old entrepreneurial class. American society, like most successful societies, had constructed an elaborate folklore about its virtue and merit. But the academics proceeded to zero in to do a demolition job

on that folklore, "without, perhaps, considering exactly why they were doing it, or indeed what it was that they were doing." The result was a drastic
change in the relationship between higher education and the social order
which had historically supported it, Potter concluded.

This thesis of traditional outsiders continuing to rail at an established
system in which they have now become a new elite is both subtle and ingenious. It may help explain the discrepancy between the private tastes and
ambitions of academics and their public attitudes and pronouncements. It
may also help connect the radicalization of the political outlook in higher
education with the democratization of its social base. But an objective evaluation of all its implications must wait until we can see it from a greater
distance and with greater detachment. More immediate is the danger of a
backlash in the community against the iconoclastic doctrines preached in
the world of learning. Once the self-critical mood in American society passes,
higher education may cease to be regarded as the vanguard of progress and
be criticized instead as a breeding ground of discontent. That has happened
before. And then the academics may discover that it is always risky to attack the political and social system which provides them with a livelihood.

The philosopher Robert Paul Wolff, a "self-proclaimed radical" in politics
as well as education, warned against this danger as early as the 1960s. Institutions of learning are at present sanctuaries for social critics who would
find it very hard to make a living anywhere else, he wrote. "Who but a university these days would hire Herbert Marcuse, Eugene Genovese, or Barrington Moore, Jr.? Where else are anarchists, socialists, and followers of
other unpopular persuasions accorded titles, honors, and the absolute security of academic tenure?" But once the university declares itself to be po-
litically committed, Wolff worried, its faculty will be investigated, its char-
ter revoked, and its tax-exempt status abolished. The president of a school
who protects his dissident faculty members with an appeal to the sanctity
of academic freedom may seem majestic in his defense of principle. Yet that
principle should not be placed in jeopardy lightly. "It is a bitter pill for the
radicals to swallow, but the fact is that they benefit more than any other
segment of the university community from the fiction of institutional neu-
trality." For the time being, therefore, both students and professors would
be well-advised to hide behind the slogans of *Lehrfreiheit* and *Lernfreiheit*,
abandoning the attempt to politicize the campus. "If this advice is too cautious to satisfy their revolutionary longings they may look on the universities as those protected base camps which, Mao Tse-tung tells us, are the

foundation of a successful protracted guerrilla campaign." The disciplined radical should practice discretion as well as valor.[15]

To most academics, however, the danger of an anti-intellectual reaction appears remote. They continue to enjoy both the relative affluence which higher education has gained since the Second World War and the ideological freedom to criticize the existing social order. Indeed, their bleak view of the established system on and off the campus is often combined with a high degree of satisfaction with institutionalized learning as a way of life. This disparity is most apparent in the social sciences and humanities. A comparison, presented in table 4.2, of the findings of Berelson's survey in 1959 of close to 2,000 members of the graduate faculties in 92 universities with the findings of the Carnegie Commission's survey in 1969 and Ladd's and Lipset's supplementary survey in 1972 of over 60,000 professors is highly illuminating. The former tried to determine what proportion of the participants believed that the present state of their discipline was "very satisfactory"; the latter, what proportion was "strongly satisfied" with their career choice. The results revealed a striking disjunction in most fields outside the natural sciences.

Thus in physics and mathematics most respondents considered the state of the discipline very satisfactory and felt strongly satisfied with their career choice, while in chemistry almost half of the respondents approved of the state of the discipline and more than half expressed satisfaction with their easier career. In the social sciences, on the other hand, satisfaction with the discipline diverged much more sharply from satisfaction with the career, especially in political science, economics, and sociology. Among the humanistic disciplines there was comparable data only for English, but this field as well as history conformed to the general pattern for the social sciences.[16]

All of this suggests that most academics continue to find higher education an attractive career, now perhaps more than ever before. They may complain of weaknesses in its structure or operation, and yet it provides them with considerable personal satisfaction. Some faculty members like

15. E. C. Ladd, Jr. and S. M. Lipset, *Divided Academy*, pp. 66–67, 368–69; Everett Carll Ladd, Jr., "Professors and Political Petitions," *Science*, 163 (1969): 1425, 1428–29; *History and American Society: Essays of David M. Potter*, ed. Don E. Fehrenbacher (New York, 1973), pp. 352–53; Robert Paul Wolff, *The Idea of the University* (Boston, 1969), pp. 75–76.

16. B. Berelson, *Graduate Education*, p. 212; E. C. Ladd, Jr., and S. M. Lipset, *Divided Academy*, pp. 352–53.

TABLE 4.2   Attitudes of Academics toward Discipline and Career, 1959–72

	PERCENTAGE	
	Satisfied with the Discipline	Satisfied with Career Choice
Physics	64	59
Mathematics	59	56
Chemistry	48	60
Psychology	40	58
Zoology	29	{57}
Botany	25	
Sociology	21	67
History	19	66
Economics	17	58
English	10	61
Political Science	6	49

SOURCE: Bernard Berelson, *Graduate Education in the United States* (New York, Toronto, and London, 1960), p. 212; Everett Carll Ladd, Jr. and Seymour Martin Lipset, *The Divided Academy: Professors and Politics* (New York, 1975), pp. 352–53.

the atmosphere of the campus, the sense of community, the feeling of togetherness. Others become absorbed in the excitement of academic politics, the endless race for advantage and status. Still others enjoy the experience of teaching and guiding students. But most important, there is greater freedom in higher education than in any other profession to study, think, write, and create. There are pressures and tensions, to be sure, grievances and resentments. Yet there is also the opportunity to explore new concepts, to express original ideas, to seek learning and truth. Such an opportunity is invaluable to men and women with a genuine interest in intellectual pursuits. For those who can meet its challenge, history, despite serious shortcomings, can still provide a satisfying and rewarding way of life.

CHAPTER V

The New History and the Old

The democratization of the social background of historians and the radicalization of their political outlook help explain recent changes in the content and methodology of the discipline. History had traditionally dealt with the deeds and accomplishments of elites, of individuals and groups playing a dominant role in society. The great themes of historiography were typically a king's reign, a minister's statecraft, a general's campaign, or a saint's holiness. Sometimes a secular movement or a collective ideal would provide the subject for a historian's work: the rise of a famous dynasty, the triumph of a true religion, the conquest of a distant continent, or the emergence of a powerful nation. But the purpose of all such history was to justify the established order, to portray its origins and celebrate its achievements.

This does not mean, however, that historians were pliable and uncritical, that they were simply bards or minstrels singing the praises of the powers that be. For many of them history was a stern judge punishing wickedness and rewarding virtue. The lessons it taught could be learned only by studying the errors of the past. Therefore they did not hesitate to point out the weaknesses of their protagonists: rancor, selfishness, rashness, indolence, or vanity. They did not restrict their historiography, moreover, to the *res gestae* of monarchs, warriors, and politicians. They would often deal with public attitudes, economic developments, class relations, and cultural institutions.

Especially after the seventeenth century, historical learning broadened its scope to include society, economy, psychology, and culture. "For what will still be left for the author of a political history," asked the German scholar Johann Christoph Gatterer in 1767, "if he is to say nothing about religious affairs, nothing about the situation, natural condition, and products of countries or about his evaluation of the industriousness, business, and strength of nations, and finally, nothing about their arts and sciences?" Such a meager history, he suggested, would consist only of a chronological list of rulers embellished with descriptions of official ceremonies, accounts of court and love intrigues, and narrations of wars and battles. Forty years later August Ludwig von Schlözer made the same point in a book on statistical theory: "History is no longer merely the biography of kings, the chronologically accurate enumeration of royal successions, wars, and battles, and the account of revolutions and alliances. This was the style of almost all men in bygone days during the Middle Ages, and we Germans still wrote history in this wretched style half a century ago, before the British and French aroused us from our sleep through better examples." Certainly the golden age of historiography which opened after the Napoleonic Wars did not deal exclusively with reigns, campaigns, and treaties. The great masters of the craft — Macaulay, Ranke, Michelet, Parkman, Prescott, Mommsen — were more than chroniclers, genealogists, or storytellers. They had a clear grasp of the diversity and multiformity of collective human experience.[1]

They did, however, accept the view that historical learning should focus on the bearers of authority and wielders of power. Princes, courtiers, generals, governors, and prelates were in their opinion more important than peasants, workers, soldiers, servants, and clerks. Here and there, behind their portrayal of the highborn and the mighty, the broad masses could be seen in dim outline: their labors, aspirations, feelings, and resentments. But it seemed self-evident to most scholars that a Charles V or Louis XIV had had a more profound effect on the course of history than the Spanish villagers or French artisans who had lived under their rule. What historians wrote rested on underlying assumptions regarding the relative significance of the various kinds of data which the past presented for their consideration. They established a hierarchy of values in determining the importance of what had happened, a scale of priorities by which they decided which part of collective experience was worth preserving in historical memory. The criteria they used expressed an implicit judgment concerning the structure of authority in state and society.

1. J. C. Gatterer, "Vom historischen Plan und der darauf sich gründenden Zusammenfügung der Erzählungen," *Allgemeine historische Bibliothek von Mitgliedern des königlichen Instituts der historischen Wissenschaften zu Göttingen*, I (1767), 24–25; August Ludwig von Schlözer, *Theorie der Statistik. Nebst Ideen über das Studium der Politik überhaupt* (Göttingen, 1804), p. 92.

It is in this respect that the new history which emerged after 1945 differed most sharply from the old. It too rested on tacit assumptions regarding the relative importance of the various sorts of information the historian encounters in his research. But these assumptions were not those of the old historiography. Reflecting the changed social position and political outlook of the scholar, the new history was critical of the elites who had monopolized historical learning in the past. It found its heroes among the poor, oppressed, exploited, and ignored. It maintained that Spanish rustics in the sixteenth century or French handicraftsmen in the seventeenth were in fact of greater significance than a Charles V or Louis XIV. Kings and generals were increasingly replaced in the limelight by the rural and urban masses.

There were unmistakable ideological and political implications in this transformation of historical values. "From Rocroi to Crulai," wrote the French scholar Emmanuel Le Roy Ladurie, one of the most eloquent defenders of the new history, "from Waterloo to Colyton — these four place-names could be said to sum up the course taken over the past hundred and fifty years by a certain school of history, from the resounding, action-packed historiography of the nineteenth century, *battle-history*, to the silent, mathematical resurrection of a total past represented today in *historical demography*." Obscure villages like Crulai and Colyton in Normandy and Devon might not be as famous as great battlefields like Rocroi and Waterloo. "Nor have the learned works inspired by these tiny peasant communities appeared in massive editions or provided scenarios for films based on best-sellers." And yet, thanks to these villages and to a few others like them, thanks to their parish registers, and thanks to pathfinding genealogical studies in Geneva and Canada, the important techniques of family reconstitution were first developed and tested. "Without flourish of trumpets, these techniques have shed new light on past societies." This was the voice of the new history.[2]

Its challenge to the values and assumptions of traditional historiography took a variety of forms. There was first of all a rejection of the grand themes of traditional scholarship. Never before had historical learning been so severe in its portrayal of the beliefs and purposes of the established order. The dominant elites, accustomed to the center of the stage, were suddenly elbowed aside by outsiders and aliens, by those whom society had once humiliated and scorned.

Thus in American history the Pilgrim Fathers landing on a wild New

2. Emmanuel Le Roy Ladurie, *The Territory of the Historian* (Chicago, 1979), p. 223.

England shore and the Southern cavaliers fighting and dying for a lost cause ceased to be treated with uncritical admiration. Not even more plebeian protagonists like settlers crossing the Western plains in their covered wagons or small farmers resisting the banks and railroads succeeded in retaining their honored place. Instead, yesterday's antiheroes became the heroes of today: blacks, Indians, Orientals, women, immigrants, city residents, slum dwellers, sweatshop workers, labor organizers, and political radicals.

In European history a similar shift took place. Monarchs, ministers, diplomats, and generals were increasingly left to novels and movies, to the writers of best sellers and potboilers. Their goals were rejected, their ambitions condemned. Serious scholars turned instead to the broad masses, mute since the beginning of history: peasants, laborers, handicraftsmen, strikers, rebels, bandits, poachers, chiliasts, enthusiasts, criminals, and madmen.

There was also a great increase in the number of historians of the Third World, but their attention no longer centered on the explorers, missionaries, conquerors, and governors who had sailed from Europe. They were more interested in the indigenous societies and native cultures, in the great states and thriving civilizations which had been destroyed by the white man's coming, and in the victims of his ruthless expansion: slaves, peons, coolies, and fellahs. The outlook of these scholars was generally anticolonial, critical of the role played by the West, and sympathetic to the struggle against imperialism. Indeed, many of them went native, ideologically speaking, feeling themselves closer in spirit to the radical intelligentsia of the region they were studying than to the policymakers and politicians of their own country.

The new history not only changed the scale of values by which the significance of historical experience was determined. It also discovered fields for scholarly investigation which had been unknown or ignored. It sought to see the past "from below," from the point of view of the humble millions whom historical learning had overlooked. What was life like for the nameless, forgotten masses on whose toil the elites had built their domination? The new historical learning turned from themes of war, diplomacy, and politics to the common, everyday experiences of the lower classes. The British scholar E. J. Hobsbawm maintained in 1971 that the bulk of interesting work in social history in the preceding ten or fifteen years had clustered around the following topics or complexes of questions: "(1) Demography and kinship; (2) Urban studies insofar as these fall within our field; (3) Classes and social groups; (4) The history of 'mentalities' or collective consciousness or of 'culture' in the anthropologists' sense; (5) The transformation of societies (for example, modernization or industrialization); (6) Social movements and phenomena of social protest." Scholarship had previously avoided such subjects, because they were implicitly subversive of established institutions and loyalties. Now it turned to them for precisely the same reason. They became a means of understanding the errors of the past and the possibilities of the future. They became an instrument of social reconstruction.

Other practitioners of the new history were less concerned with the processes of change in society than with manifestations of its changelessness. That is, they began to look for institutions, practices, customs, and attitudes which seemed impervious to time, providing the community with stability and permanence. French historians in particular, expressing their views in the influential periodical *Annales,* urged scholars to reach below the surface of events, to find a substratum of unchangeable reality beneath the ebb and flow of transitory occurrences. They emphasized the *longue durée,* a system of periodization measured not in years and decades but centuries and millennia, where past, present, and future meet and interpenetrate. They made a sharp distinction between "structure" and "conjuncture," between those characteristics of society which remain resistant to change and the fortuitous happenings which may appear crucial while they are occurring, but which can be seen in retrospect as only ripples on a vast ocean. They spoke of the role of "mentality" in history, of collective feelings and attitudes in the community which explain the response of masses of people to common experiences. Above all, they warned against a preoccupation with "event," with the chance occurrence which diverts the attention of the scholar from the underlying forces shaping human destiny. Only a history dealing with those forces deserved to be called history.

The introduction of new values in historical learning led to the adoption of new techniques, for methodology is logically bound to reflect ideology. The old school had employed methods appropriate to its assumptions regarding the importance of patriciates and elites. It examined public and private documentary materials, usually in libraries or archives, which illuminated the activities of the wielders of power. There were memoranda, letters, speeches, memoirs, decrees, newspapers, periodicals, and proceedings. These materials were studied and assessed, compared with one another, and arranged to form a coherent narrative which was objectively true to the historical data, but which also expressed a subjective evaluation of its importance. The emphasis in this kind of scholarship was on clarity, organization, style, and literary skill. In the right hands, such a narrative could become a compelling work of learning read with interest by professionals and amateurs alike. The techniques which the historian was taught stressed the need to remain dispassionate, to weigh carefully the reliability of the evidence, and to judge with impartiality, *sine ira et studio*. He could, of course, never keep himself out of his work entirely; how he interpreted the past was bound to reveal how he regarded the present. But although his view of history expressed his view of society, he had to confine his predispositions within the limits imposed by objective facts emerging from the evidence.

The new school adopted different techniques of scholarship suited to different categories of data. The documentary materials used to analyze the activities of individuals and small groups were inappropriate for the study of large masses. Therefore a new methodology began to take shape which was designed not only to deal with historical information on a broader scale than had been attempted in the past, but also to provide more precise, more "scientific" results than had been attainable by conventional research procedures.

The first of the new techniques to emerge was quantification or "cliometrics," the analysis of large bodies of numerical data, usually with the aid of computers, which could reveal interrelationships overlooked by traditional research. To be sure, the use of statistics in works of history had not been unknown to earlier generations of scholars; quantification was not as revolutionary as some of the quantifiers claimed. There can be no question, however, that the application of statistical techniques to historical evidence became far more common and accepted after 1945.

The second major methodological innovation was "social-science history," the use in historiography of concepts and insights developed by the social sciences, particularly sociology and anthropology. Its rapid spread suggested that many historians were becoming more interested in how classes and communities respond and adapt to change than in how dynasties and aristocracies acquire and exercise power. It reflected the shift of emphasis from policies and diplomacies to processes and institutions.

Finally, out of the intellectual ferment generated by the new school emerged a group of psychohistorians, scholars who maintained that the methods of psychology, psychiatry, and psychoanalysis could be applied to historical data to provide a deeper understanding of the behavior of individuals and groups. Since those methods rested on an insight into the intimate life of patients suffering from nervous or mental disorders, psychohistorians began to look for evidences of the intimate life of past generations, evidences which had been ignored by traditional scholarship, partly out of moral inhibition, but mostly because they were too disparate and ambiguous to be usable under the accepted criteria of historical validity.

Lawrence Stone, a judicious and critical member of the new school, described with gentle irony its effect on the historical discipline after thirty years of innovation and experimentation: "Historians are therefore now dividing into four groups: the old narrative historians, primarily political historians and biographers; the cliometricians who continue to act like statistical junkies; the hard-nosed social historians still busy analyzing impersonal structures; and the historians of *mentalité*, now chasing ideals, values, mindsets, and patterns of intimate personal behavior—the more intimate the better." His tone suggested that the promises of the pioneering period of the new history had not all been fulfilled.

There could be no question, however, that it had brought about a profound change in the way the past was perceived by professional scholarship. Although political, diplomatic, military, and biographical history have not been abandoned, they have come to be regarded as hackneyed and old-fashioned. The French have been especially vehement in denouncing what they call *histoire événementielle*, a history which deals with happenings and contingencies rather than structures and patterns, a history which in their opinion is only chronology and gossip. According to Jacques Le Goff, a director of studies at the Ecole Pratique des Hautes Etudes, "the *Annales* school loathed the trio formed by political history, narrative history, and chronicle or episodic (*événementielle*) history. All this, for them, was mere pseudo-history, history on the cheap, a superficial affair which preferred the shadow to the substance. What had to be put in its place was history in depth—an economic, social, and mental history." He pronounced "the old political history" dead but not yet buried, "a corpse that has to be made to lie down."

Le Roy Ladurie was equally implacable, breathing death and destruction to traditional history. "Present-day historiography, with its preference for the quantifiable, the statistical and the structural, has been obliged to suppress in order to survive," he wrote. "In the last few decades it has virtually condemned to death the narrative history of events and the individual biography. Such genres, not unworthy of attention and sometimes quite justifiable—though perhaps too inclined, in the interests of narrative pace, to leap from massacre to boudoir or from bedchamber to anteroom—still survive today in our cultural supermarkets, thanks to the multiplication effect of the mass media." But now the muse of history had come to disdain those "long sequences of simple and uncomplicated events" of which the historians of the old school were so fond. "As we all know, she has turned towards the study of structures, the persistent patterns of the 'long term,' and the collection of data amenable to serial or quantitative analysis." Anything standing in the way of this revolution would have to be swept away.

The fervent tone of many of the new historians reflected a feeling that they stood on the threshold of a major scholarly breakthrough. But they must be ruthless in destroying conventional methodology in order to achieve a deeper insight into historical experience. There was something exciting and exhilarating about the prospect. Even H. Stuart Hughes, whose field was old-fashioned intellectual history, became caught up in the enthusiasm of imminent discovery. The historian's task, he declared, was not finished when the contents of "the documents" had been established. On the contrary, it just began. "The truly exciting problems of interpretation — whose mere existence the more unsophisticated among us had scarcely suspected — nearly all lay in the future." Those problems could only be solved by a synthesis of art and science in history, and yet many historians were bewildered by the mediating character of their discipline.

In particular, the growing affiliation of history with social science seems more of a threat than an opportunity. In the minds of historians wedded to the tradition of history as a branch of literature, the new emphasis on methodological rigor suggests the abandonment of something infinitely precious. The fear of scientific attachments may be rooted in unfortunate early experience: it may go back to college days, when a young scholar with a strongly literary bent found himself inept in the laboratory. It may reflect an aesthetic distaste for scientists as cultural barbarians with no feelings for language. It may mask a sense of inferiority: after all, scientists have no trouble in understanding what historians write, but the reverse is far from true. In any case, a great many historians seem to feel that if their subject should become too scientific it would forfeit its soul — it would lose the quality of color and adventure that first inspired them to embark on historical studies at all.

Here I strenuously object. I have never argued — and I do not propose to argue now — that history should strive for the exactitude of the more precise sciences. I resist any notion that historians should alter their characteristic vocabulary and mode of presentation, that they should cease to think of their subject as a branch of literature. The dilemma, I believe, is quite false. History can become more scientific — more conscious of its assumptions and its intellectual procedures — without losing its aesthetic quality. Indeed, an explicit recognition of history's place among the sciences may enhance the intellectual excitement it conveys. It may add a new dimension to the old sense of historical adventure.

In the years following Hughes's plea for a new history, his hopes were realized even more fully than he had expected. The discipline became reorganized and transformed; there was a drastic change in the values by which it had traditionally been governed. Yet it is clear that the effects of this historiographical revolution were neither as sweeping nor as beneficial as its advocates had assumed. The old history, which was always more than storytelling and scandalmongering, has survived. It can still be found, not only in novels and films, but in solid works of scholarship which continue to enlarge our understanding. The new history broadened the scope of the discipline, but its usefulness in the solution of methodological problems proved variable and limited. The contrast between traditional and innovative approaches to historical learning no longer seems as stark as a generation ago. Indeed, there appears to be emerging an uneasy coexistence between the two, a grudging mutual toleration, reflecting a more generous appraisal of the old history and a more sober evaluation of the new. The enthusiasm of the early period of experimentation has given way to a mood of somber reassessment.[3]

Consider the rise of cliometrics, the methodological innovation closest to traditional scholarship. There had always been historians whose work had involved the measurement of statistical data on a large scale to determine the direction and intensity of historical development. They could be found most commonly in economic history, which is by its nature dependent on quantification. Herbert Feis's *Europe, the World's Banker,* published in 1930, or Earl J. Hamilton's *American Treasure and the Price Revolution in Spain,* published in 1934 — the former dealing with international finance before the First World War, the latter with the inflationary effect of precious metals from the New World in the sixteenth and seventeenth century — could just as easily have been written fifty years later. But cliometric techniques were employed by scholars in other fields of history as well. Crane Brinton's *The Jacobins,* precociously subtitled *An Essay in the New History,*

3. E. J. Hobsbawm, "From Social History to the History of Society," *Daedalus* 100 (1971): 33; L. Stone, "Revival of Narrative," p. 21; Jacques Le Goff, "Is Politics Still the Backbone of History?" *Daedalus* 100 (1971): 4, 12; E. Le Roy Ladurie, *Territory of the Historian,* p. 111; H. S. Hughes, *History as Art and as Science,* pp. 3–4, 20.

which appeared in 1930, was an attempt to analyze the social foundations of a political ideology; and Marcus Lee Hansen's *The Atlantic Migration,* published in 1940, examined the movement of population from Europe to America prior to the Civil War. In short, there was theoretically nothing new about quantification. As early as 1804 Schlözer had argued that a knowledge of reigns, successions, wars, battles, revolutions, and alliances was not enough to enable the historian to understand a nation's way of life, that is, "whether it was happy or miserable; what was the state of its agriculture, its commerce, and the other forms of livelihood; how it established industry or sank into indolence." Yet all these questions deserved consideration in any scholarly account of a country's development, he maintained. "The historian must deal with them by virtue of the position he holds; he must therefore be a statistician. Or to put it in other words, history is the whole and statistics is a part of it."

What distinguished the cliometric movement after the Second World War was the broader application of its technique and the more rigorous formulation of its method. First of all, areas which had in the past been considered beyond its scope — political, social, cultural, religious, or even biographical history — were now reexamined in the light of statistical analysis. Second, the processes of quantitative evaluation became more exact and complex, so much so that only an expert in cliometrics could fully understand some of them. Their justification was that they could reveal connections and patterns in historical evidence which had remained undiscoverable by other techniques. A different, more exciting way of studying the past seemed to emerge, leading to sounder conclusions, deeper truths, and richer rewards. A generation of young scholars, armed with logarithms, coefficients, indices, and regressions, began to search for bodies of statistical data from which to extract a more precise understanding of collective experience. Some of them were able to make a significant contribution to learning, but others lapsed into an arid abstruseness no more illuminating than the old dryasdust monographic literature based on legal or diplomatic documents. Indeed, in many cases cliometrics ceased to be a useful instrument for solving historical problems; historical problems rather came to be studied because they could be solved with the aid of cliometrics. The means tended sometimes to obscure the ends, technical virtuosity to overshadow common sense, and methodological incantation to substitute for intellectual creativity.

To be sure, many of the practitioners of quantification cautioned against exaggerated expectations. They tried to point out that cliometrics was still an experimental technique, that its effectiveness was not fully known, and that its utility was narrowly limited. In the introduction to a book on quantitative research which they edited, William O. Aydelotte, Allan G. Bogue, and Robert William Fogel described its scope with disarming modesty. "A number of members of the profession," they began, "have come to hope that a variety of different kinds of historical problems, heretofore discussed only in rather general terms, can by . . . means [of quantification] be treated more effectively and brought closer to a solution on the basis of ordered knowledge." Indeed, considerable experimentation by scholars along these lines "has produced results that have already attracted a good deal of attention." Yet there were serious barriers to communication between quantitative and nonquantitative historians. The latter sometimes had unrealistic expectations of what cliometrics could do, that is, what could be claimed for it or "what they think is wrongly claimed for it." Those who were uninitiated in the field "tend to expect a breadth of scope and a degree of certainty from statistical investigations which it is not in the nature of the method to yield." The demand for findings which were indisputable, explanations which were complete, or laws which were universal was "the stuff that dreams are made of and would not be seriously considered for a moment by those who have any considerable experience with this kind of research."

It would even be a mistake, the authors went on, to imagine that the results of quantitative research in the limited areas where it is applicable would be or could be expected to be conclusive or final. This was in part because cliometrics was still a relatively new scholarly technique. But more important, "it is not in the nature of the statistical method, or of any other research method for that matter, to produce definitive answers to major questions." The lack of finality in the results of scholarship was a familiar story, and yet "unrealistic demands in regard to quantitative research are sometimes made by the uninformed, and it is not always appreciated that quantifiers also suffer from disabilities."

It would thus be wrong to think that the use of numbers furnished the historian with a security which other forms of evidence were unable to provide, or that "a set of papers that use figures will, for this reason, be definitive." The accuracy of the calculations could not guarantee the accuracy of the conclusions regarding the substantive questions being investigated. There might be mistakes in measurement. There might be difficulties in establishing a system of classification so clearly defined that there was no question which items or individuals belonged in which categories. There might be inconsistencies in the results obtained from different kinds of data. Most important, "statistical manipulations merely rearrange the evidence; they do not, except on an elementary level, answer questions, and the bearing of the findings upon the larger problems of interpretation in which historians are interested is a matter, not of arithmetic, but of logic and persuasion."

Those who believed that the categories in a large statistical project would be entirely unambiguous, the authors concluded, or that the results would clearly point to a single position, or that there would be no doubt about what the findings meant had simply not had experience with the practical problems of this kind of research. What quantification, like the other methods of scholarship, tried to do was not obtain full knowledge of reality but an increasingly close approximation to it, what might be described in a mathematical metaphor as "the asymptotic approach to truth." Although statistical techniques could not lead to absolute validity, they could bring us closer to findings which were affirmable with a certain degree of confidence.

The various arguments in defense of cliometrics were restated even more modestly, gracefully, and winningly in Aydelotte's collection of essays on quantification in history. Here he conceded once again that statistical methods could be applied only to a limited number of historical questions, and that "employing them when the evidence is inadequate or imprecise may, in effect, amount to nothing more than using the superficial trappings of systematic investigation to cover up loose thinking." Still, quantitative techniques seemed feasible, under special circumstances, for some kinds of scholarly research, that is, where the evidence permitted their use. "There seems reason to believe that a discriminating use of these methods can considerably facilitate the study of certain problems." Who could quarrel with such a diffident formulation? Aydelotte even admitted that some advocates of quantification came close to arguing that its techniques were the only means of arriving at reliable knowledge, so that the scholarly achievements of the prequantitative era could be safely disregarded. "It is absurd, however, to contend that there is any exclusive road to knowledge, that intellectual rigor can be achieved only by the use of figures, or that the value of research depends on the kinds of techniques used rather than on the intelligence with which they are applied."

Indeed, Aydelotte warned, "those who proclaim quantification as a new gospel of salvation, invalidating all earlier work, do the cause more harm than good." There was a danger of concentrating on methods and neglecting the purposes which those methods were designed to serve. In any case, the adoption of a new technique could not guarantee the possession of intelligence. Some young scholars, moreover, having committed themselves to a high standard of exactness, might deliberately avoid important tasks which they felt could not be handled with sufficient precision; they might not even understand those larger issues. "A preoccupation with getting everything just right may make them unable to see beyond the ends of their noses." Yet the main object of quantitative methods in history was simply to carry us a little farther on our way, making possible certain assertions about a subject which could not have been previously advanced with the same confidence. Those methods, though not generally regarded as empirical, might at least have heuristic value. "The arbitrary rejection of techniques for refining the evidence and making our grasp of it more precise not only fails to cure the disease but aggravates it; it works directly against our best hope for a further understanding of our problems." In short, cliometrics could make a contribution, modest but useful, to the historian's insight into the past.[4]

Aydelotte's appeal for methodological acceptance was so ingratiating as to be almost irresistible. It had quiet charm; it sounded eminently fair. But not all quantifiers spoke in the voice of sweet reasonableness. There were hotspurs among them who scorned the diffidence displayed by the moderates. Cliometrics was not only a new scholarly technique, they maintained; it was a superior scholarly technique. The results which it provided were more precise, the conclusions more reliable, the truths more profound. The historians making these claims did not affect false modesty; they did not hesitate to make an invidious distinction between stodgy tradition and exciting innovation. Edward Shorter, for example, in his handbook on the use of the computer in scholarly research, declared jauntily that "this guide should permit the historian whose previous experience has been confined solely to Plain Old History to use modern electronic techniques."

Similarly, Le Roy Ladurie conceded that certain fields of history were still not at the stage where they could be studied cliometrically, but that was because they had not yet reached their full development. Such promising

4. A. L. V. Schlözer, *Theorie der Statistik*, pp. 92–93; William O. Aydelotte, Allan G. Bogue, and Robert William Fogel, "Introduction," in *The Dimensions of Quantitative Research in History*, ed. William O. Aydelotte, Allan G. Bogue, and Robert William Fogel (Princeton, N.J., 1972), pp. 4, 8, 10–11; William O. Aydelotte, *Quantification in History* (Reading, Mass., 1971), pp. 3, 14, 20, 31, 96–97.

disciplines as historical psychology, to give one illustration, remained resolutely qualitative. They were still conceptualizing their approaches, building coherent models, and acquiring the credentials which form an essential preliminary to statistical analysis. But sooner or later, "even in the more esoteric branches of history, it must surely be the case that there will always come a moment when the historian, having worked out a solid conceptual basis, will need to start counting: to record frequencies, significant repetitions, or percentages." Only calculations, however tedious or elementary they might seem, could ultimately validate the data which had been gathered, showing whether it extended beyond the anecdotal to the typical or representative. "To put it in its most extreme form (and it is an extreme so remote and in some cases so beyond the scope of present research as to be perhaps only imaginary), history that is not quantifiable cannot claim to be scientific."

David Herlihy went even farther. To him quantification was an advanced stage in the evolution of historical learning to which all members of the profession would have to adapt as their discipline became more exact and sophisticated. It was a tool of research which the scholar must master in order to meet the responsibilities of his calling. "The historian of the 1980s may not have to be a programmer, but he will have to know how the computer can assist in all phases of his work. Otherwise, he would be derelict in his duties as a scientist and as a historian." The nonquantifiers in the profession happening to read those words must have felt a slight pang of guilt.

Although the cliometric moderates proved more accurate in their assessment of what quantification could achieve, the militants were more exciting. Their vision of a historical science which could produce precise answers to complicated questions about the past was more inspiring than the claim that statistical analysis might under certain circumstances make a contribution to the solution of some research problems. The militants generated a mood of anticipation which attracted large numbers of historians, most of them beginners, to the study of cliometrics. In the course of a generation these youthful converts helped shift the focus of historical learning from literary narrative toward quasi-scientific methodology.

J. Morgan Kousser tried to measure the magnitude of this shift in the period 1961–78 by counting the number of statistical tables for each hundred pages of text in five leading learned periodicals: the *American Historical Review*, the *Journal of American History*, the *Journal of Modern History*, the *Journal of Southern History*, and the *William and Mary Quarterly*. These periodicals, with a combined circulation of approximately 48,500 in 1978, represented roughly the scholarly interests of most professional historians in the United States. Kousser's calculations showed that the average number of tables per hundred pages in all five journals rose from 1 in 1961–64 to 2 in 1965–69, 4 in 1970–73, and 5 in 1974–78. There were significant variations, however, between the two major fields of history covered by the data. In the *Journal of Modern History*, which deals almost exclusively with Europe, there was only a modest rise in the average number of tables, from fewer than 0.5 in 1961–64 to 1 in 1965–69, 2 in 1970–73, and 3 in 1974–78. Similarly, the figures for the *American Historical Review*, which devotes about half of its space to European history, showed a relatively moderate growth in statistical tables, from fewer than 0.5 in 1961–64 to 3 in 1965–69, but then a drop to 2 in 1970–73 and 1974–78. The periodicals devoted primarily to American history, on the other hand, had a much more pronounced tendency toward quantification. The average number of tables in the *Journal of Southern History* went from 2 in 1961–64 and 1965–69 to 4 in 1970–73, and 6 in 1974–78; in the *William and Mary Quarterly* from 2 to 4, 6, and 5; and in the *Journal of American History* from fewer than 0.5 to 2, 6, and 8. The data suggests that while quantitative techniques have spread in all fields, their influence has been significantly greater in American than in European history.[5]

The ready acceptance of cliometrics reflected the excitement generated by the hard-core quantifiers, but its actual achievement was more in keeping with the prediction of the moderates. The new methodology proved invaluable in certain fields of history such as demography, urbanization, and industrialization. In others it played an important though not indispensable part; for example, public opinion, political behavior, and voting patterns. In most fields, however, it has been of little or no value. In a few it has even been counterproductive, diverting energies and resources which might have been more profitably invested in other approaches. Cliometrics has no doubt had a profound effect on the study of history; it has won a secure place among the accepted methodologies of the discipline. Yet while it has been fruitful in some areas of research, in others it has led only to confusion

5. Edward Shorter, *The Historian and the Computer: A Practical Guide* (Englewood Cliffs, N.J., 1971), p. vii; E. Le Roy Ladurie, *Territory of the Historian*, p. 15; David Herlihy, "Quantification in the 1980s: Numerical and Formal Analysis in European History," *Journal of Interdisciplinary History* 12 (1981–82): 135; J. M. Kousser, "Quantitative Social-Scientific History," pp. 437–38.

and disappointment. There may be room for disagreement about its long-range effect, but few scholars will maintain that it has lived up to all the claims made in its early days of youthful exuberance.

The disenchantment with a technique which had initially been greeted with drumbeat and fanfare aroused considerable *Schadenfreude* among members of the old guard, who had maintained all along that quantification promised more than it could deliver. Their fear had been that cliometrics would undermine the humanistic and literary foundations of the discipline. Carl Bridenbaugh expressed this fear as early as 1962 in his presidential address to the American Historical Association. "The finest historians will not be those who succumb to the dehumanizing methods of social sciences," he warned. "Nor will the historian worship at the shrine of that Bitch-goddess, QUANTIFICATION." History offered values and methods radically different from those of cliometrics, because it dealt with the "mutable, rank-scented many." It would fail if it did not show them as individuals. The historians of the future would have to acquire a sense of countless individual men leading their daily lives, acting in time and place, or there would be no comprehension of what they had experienced. "Only then will accounts of men in groups or men in the mass, analyses of forces, of trends, and the whole paraphernalia of graphs and tables make any sense to posterity."

Oscar Handlin's criticism of cliometrics was more subtle. His argument was not that it dehumanized or mechanized historical learning, but that by its methodological pyrotechnics it diverted attention from the fundamental issues in scholarly research. Some studies employing quantification "make modest contributions to the understanding of problems posed by examining conventional sources." Their technique, which involves classifying and counting, helps make the task of scholarship more expeditious, but it demands no shifts in conceptualization. The years in which cliometrics rose to prominence "have increased methodological sophistication but have brought no substantial alteration in point of view." As for the computer, it brought historical statistics, which "had drifted into mechanical and electrical bypaths and gotten entangled with dreams of robotlike intelligence," back to the practical world of ones and twos. It eliminated the need for immense amounts of paper work, but it solved no intellectual problems. "Although its pipe attracted numerous followers, especially those favored with generous foundation grants, it did not transform the practice of history." On the contrary, questions of logic and of conformity to reality became even more urgent in the face of large, total, inflexible systems. Manuals on the use of electronic methods generally told the reader how to do it; they did not explain to him what was being done. "To the extent that the excitement obscured underlying issues, the new hardware impeded understanding." Technique had become more important than purpose.

The cliometricians might have dismissed Bridenbaugh or even Handlin as old fogies resentful of the avant-garde, but could they ignore the views of well-known scholars who had once shared their faith? David S. Landes, long a champion of the new history, had used its insights and techniques in his own work. Yet in his presidential address to the Economic History Association in 1977, he expressed doubt about some of the central assumptions of quantification. "The data of economic history consist in large part of those qualitative, nonquantitative bits that have always been the concern and delight of the conventional historian," he admonished. "The sorting and counting may come later, but someone must find and report the raw material that goes into tables and time series." Even more surprising, he conceded that "many, if not most, of the important questions that we have to deal with do not lend themselves — at least not as yet — to quantitative treatment." There were the technical obstacles to statistical analysis. "Sometimes the numerical data are lacking. There are whole areas of history where we probably will never have the numbers we need. Sometimes we have the numbers, but they do not tell us enough." Yet more significant were the inherent limitations of cliometrics. "Quantitative methods are only a tool; they are not the heart of the matter. The heart of the matter is ends rather than means."

Landes concluded with an exhortation which could have come from the most conservative member of the old guard. "We too have to be concerned not only with the processes of getting and spending, with charts and tables and aggregates and averages, but with people, with employers and workers, merchants, industrialists, and craftsmen, with the knowledge and the ignorance, the reason and the passion that go into economic decisionmaking at all levels." Not even Bridenbaugh would have quarreled with that.

The most moving confession of lost faith, however, came in 1979 from Lawrence Stone, who, though never a blind partisan of quantification, had shared its hopes and adopted its methods. "It is just those projects that have been the most lavishly funded," he now conceded, "the most ambitious in the assembly of vast quantites of data by armies of paid researchers, the most scientifically processed by the very latest in computer technology, the most mathematically sophisticated in presentation, which have so far turned

out to be the most disappointing." He complained that twenty years after
the rise of cliometrics, after the expenditure of millions of dollars, pounds,
and francs, only modest results have been achieved. "There are huge piles
of greenish print-out gathering dust in scholars' offices; there are many tur-
gid and excruciatingly dull tomes full of tables of figures, abstruse algebraic
equations and percentages given to two decimal places." Admittedly, many
valuable new findings and even a few major contributions had been made.
In general, however, the sophistication of the technique had exceeded the
reliability of the data; the usefulness of the results appeared to be in inverse
correlation to the mathematical complexity of the methodology and the gran-
diose scale of the collection of statistics.

"On any cost-benefit analysis the rewards of large-scale computerized history have so far only occasionally justified the input of time and money."
Most of the major problems of historical scholarship seemed as insoluble
as before, perhaps more so. Agreement on the causes of the English, French,
or American revolutions was as remote as ever, despite the enormous effort
to analyze their social and economic origins. Intensive research in demographic history had only increased the historian's bewilderment. "Quantification has told us a lot about the *what* questions of historical demography, but relatively little so far about the *why*." The important issues
concerning slavery in America remained elusive, despite the use of sophisticated techniques on a massive scale. Urban history was cluttered with data,
yet mobility trends were still obscure. No one was sure whether English
society in the seventeenth and eighteenth centuries was more open and mo-
bile than the French, or whether the gentry or the aristocracy was rising
or falling in England before the Civil War. "We are no better off now in
these respects than were James Harrington in the seventeenth century or
Tocqueville in the nineteenth."

What could be learned from this failure of quantification? Stone's response seemed to reveal a sadder and a wiser man:

> It may be that the time has come for the historian to reassert the impor-
> tance of the concrete, the particular, and the circumstantial, as well as the
> general theoretical model and the procedural insight; to be more wary of quan-
> tification for the sake of quantification; to be suspicious of vast cooperative
> projects of staggering cost; to stress the critical importance of a strict scrutiny
> of the reliability of sources; to be passionately determined to combine both
> quantitative and qualitative data and methods as the only reliable way even
> to approach truth about so odd and unpredictable a creature as man; and

to display a becoming modesty about the validity of our discoveries in this most difficult of disciplines.

There was something touching about this farewell to the youthful enthusiasm which had captivated so many historians impatient with the intrinsic limitations of their craft.[6]

In the course of a single generation quantification thus completed the transition from bold experimentation to jaded conventionality. Its evolution provides a lesson in hubris and nemesis, for the early heady exuberance has now dissipated in reconditeness and esotericism. It has become apparent that many important questions in historical scholarship — most of them, indeed — simply do not lend themselves to analysis by statistical techniques. Even where those techniques are applicable, they often provide only partial or incomplete answers. Their results have to be supplemented and checked by the use of more traditional research methods. But most important, cliometricians, like other historians, are at the mercy of their sources. The records which the past has left are inexact and incomplete. The scholars of a later generation, whether quantifiers or nonquantifiers, cannot correct the flaws in the data they examine. No methodology, however sophisticated, is able to compensate for the omissions and distortions in statistical as well as documentary materials. No mathematical formula can rectify the mistakes of a tax collector who did not know how to balance his accounts, a parish priest who was careless in recording births and deaths in his village, or a census taker who got tired of counting and started guessing. While quantification gives the appearance of precision, its specificity is often spurious. It is as fallible, it rests on faith as much as those methods of scholarship which rely on nonquantifiable data. It will remain an important tool of learning, but no more so than other, more conventional techniques of research.

The development of social-science history has followed by and large the same pattern as cliometrics. There was first the phase of bold pioneering and iconoclastic innovation. The complacency of a discipline which had tended to look down on upstart competitors in related fields was suddenly shaken by a group of young historians who argued that the social sciences

6. Carl Bridenbaugh, "The Great Mutation," *American Historical Review* 68 (1962–63): 326–27; O. Handlin, *Truth in History*, pp. 11, 206; David S. Landes, "On Avoiding Babel," *Journal of Economic History* 38 (1978): 6–10; L. Stone, "Revival of Narrative," pp. 12–13; idem, "History and the Social Sciences in the Twentieth Century," in *The Future of History*, ed. Charles F. Delzell (Nashville, 1977), p. 39.

were not the rivals but the allies and teachers of history. Scholars who ignored the methods and findings of the social scientists, they warned, would do so at their peril.

The members of the History Panel of the Behavioral and Social Sciences Survey concluded that "the changing character of historical evidence, the development of new techniques and concepts in related disciplines, the growing body of research by nonhistorians into historical problems — all of these imply that even those historians who are not themselves working in social science have to learn to read it and use it, if only to teach their students." To an increasing extent, they maintained, research vital to historians was taking place outside history. In such areas as collective biographies of the occupants of particular social and occupational statuses, studies of the social origins of elites, histories of political behavior and participation, economic history, demographic history, ethnic history, and local history, much or most of the innovative and exciting work was being done by the social sciences. Insofar as they were cut off or cut themselves off from this growing body of scholarship and the source material on which it rested, historians were the poorer. They had always prided themselves on being the guardians and evaluators of primary historical evidence, while the theorists and generalizers of the other social sciences had been content to rely on processed materials and secondary sources. Historians could not abandon this custodial function now, for without it history would cease to be a critical and scientific discipline. "In short, the history student of today must learn social science statistics, computer techniques, model-building, and ancillary skills. . . . He has to learn these for the same reason that he learns foreign languages — because without them he cannot read the relevent literature and use the relevant sources."

Since such a far-reaching change in the methodology of history implied a drastic revision in the training required for its study, the panel urged that "departments of history should introduce into the curriculum a substantially larger number of courses defined by themes and problems, (war, revolution, power, urbanization, agrarian society, for example), alongside the traditional courses that treat of units of space and time (such as the United States after 1865, Europe since 1815, Renaissance Europe)." To encourage the creation of such courses, institutions of higher learning should support collaborative instruction by faculty members from several disciplines. Moreover, departments of history, like departments in the other social sciences, should recognize the importance of mathematics, statistics, and computer programs, requiring their students to master these skills in addition to the foreign languages which had traditionally been part of their training. This meant that "graduate students should be permitted to do up to half their fields in other disciplines (as against the one outside field typically permitted at present) and should be exempted from those distribution requirements that make it impossible to undertake serious training outside history without sacrificing preparation in the area or areas of principal interest." Only by a sweeping reform of the instruction they received could young scholars be prepared for the challenge of the new history.

Such a reform was clearly overdue, the panel maintained. The other social sciences had already adopted many innovative techniques; they had long since learned to live with equations, numbers, regression analyses, and the unconscious. Historians, on the other hand, or at least many historians, had still not come to terms with "these uncomfortable intruders on a world of art, intuition, and verbal skill." Yet history had always been a borrower from other disciplines, and in that respect social scientific scholarship was simply another example of a process which had been going on for a long time. The flow of knowledge and insight, moreover, had always moved in two directions, so that history had also been a lender. The social sciences would undoubtedly be much poorer without a knowledge of the historical record. In short, only through symbiosis could social scientific and historical learning achieve full development.[7]

This youthful exuberance and pioneering zeal, this sense that history is about to break the methodological chains restraining its growth, have now largely disappeared from the writings of the new historians. They have been replaced by somber reflection. But here and there a faithful follower still speaks of social-scientific history with undiminished enthusiasm. "Where sociology and history flow together, rapids form," says Charles Tilly in the preface to a collection of his essays published in 1981. "Four very different men—Samuel Beer, George Homans, Barrington Moore, Jr., and Pitirim Sorokin—pushed me off to start my navigation of those rapids. Now, nearly 30 years after that launching, let me record my debt to them for pointing me toward adventure."

The adventure for which Tilly feels grateful is the shift in historical learning from deeds and policies to processes and institutions. His own work deals, as he puts it, with "conflict and collective action," with "revolutions,

7. *History as Social Science*, ed. D. S. Landes and C. Tilly, pp. 1-2, 74-75, 91-92, 142-43.

rebellions, collective violence, strikes, demonstrations, [and] food riots," and with "related ways of gathering to act on shared interests and grievances." These concerns are connected by a larger question. "In the West of the last few hundred years, how did the development of capitalism and the concentration of power in national states affect the ways that ordinary people could — and did — act together on their common interests?" he asks. From this question the scholar can move in several directions, toward "the general characteristics of capitalism and national states," for example, or toward "the logic of collective action," or toward "the problems involved in joining the history and sociology of these large subjects." Whatever the direction, the destination is a new kind of history with themes and purposes more relevant than those of conventional historical learning.

Lawrence Stone's approach to social-science history is somewhat different. His essays, he tells us, reflect a shift from social, economic, and political change to a change in values, religious beliefs, customs, and patterns of intimate behavior. "In this shift the essays do not merely reflect changes in my perspective upon the past, but rather a more general shift in the 1960s and 1970s from sociology to anthropology as the dominant source of new ideas in the historical profession in general."

A good illustration is provided by a comparison of his *Crisis of the Aristocracy, 1558–1641,* which was published in 1965, and his *Family, Sex and Marriage in England, 1500–1800,* which appeared in 1977. The former analyzed the position of the nobility in England before the Civil War, relying partly on data obtained by cliometric techniques to describe the peerage in society, the inflation of honors, economic change, the structure of power, estate management, business, officeholding and the court, credit, conspicuous expenditure, marriage and family, education and culture, religion, and the crisis of confidence. The latter opened with "the demographic facts," that is, marriage, birth, and death, and then turned to "the open lineage family" between 1450 and 1630, depicting its structure and values and its affective relationships. Next came a section on "the restricted patriarchal nuclear family" from 1550 to 1700, which examined the decline of kinship, clientage, and community and the reinforcement of patriarchy. This was followed by "the closed domesticated nuclear family" from 1640 to 1800, with chapters on the growth of affective individualism, mating arrangements, the companionate marriage, and parent-child relations. The last section, entitled simply "sex," analyzed upper-class attitudes and behavior, presented a few case histories of gentlemanly sexual behavior, and concluded with plebeian sexual behavior. The difference in subject matter between the two books reflected the shift of emphasis in the new history from a sociological to an anthropological approach.

The application of the techniques of anthropology to historical study could be seen even more clearly in Natalie Zemon Davis's essays on society and culture in France during the early modern period. Here the familiar themes of scholarly research on the golden age of French civilization were replaced by unorthodox studies in what might best be called anthropological history. They focused on the ordinary, everyday experiences of the common people, their folkways, attitudes, beliefs, habits, and activities. "These essays are about peasants and even more about artisans and the *menu peuple* of the cities," the author explained. "The very rich, the powerful, the learned, and the priestly are described primarily in relation to the lives of the 'modest'—as they reacted to them, conflicted with them, or shared their activities and beliefs. The interaction between Society and Culture and the balance between tradition and innovation are thus explored only for certain segments of the social order."

But how was a historian to find sources for the lives of people who were mostly illiterate? How was he to determine not only where the sources were, but what they were? Research of this kind, according to Davis, was not only a matter of scouring libraries for popular playlets, poems, and pamphlets or of sifting criminal and judicial records, welfare rolls, notarial contracts, and militia or financial lists for a mention of the humble and the poor. It was also a matter of recognizing that forms of associational life and collective behavior are not merely items in the history of the Reformation or of political centralization, but are cultural artifacts. "A journeymen's initiation rite, a village festive organization, an informal gathering of women for a lying-in or of men and women for storytelling, or a street disturbance could be 'read' as fruitfully as a diary, a political tract, a sermon, or a body of laws." Similarly, a book or a proverb could not only speak for its author or reader, but provide a clue to relationships among groups of people or among cultural traditions.

The subjects dealt with in Davis's essays illustrated the use which can be made of such unconventional research techniques: the social experiences which helped form Protestant consciousness among male artisans; the relation of religious sensibility to the treatment of poverty; the sources of Protestant allegiance among some groups of urban women; the range of political and social uses for carnivalesque topsy-turvy and festive organization;

the reversal of sex roles in rites and festivities; the underlying order in the violence with which crowds defended their religion; the interaction between literate and oral culture; and proverbial wisdom and popular error in regard to medicine. The conclusions about social structure in early modern Europe emerging out of these essays were described in highly abstruse terms: "I picture a many-dimensional chart in which the axes of measurement represent qualitatively different kinds of power, property, and control, as well as other variables — such as sex and age — that can determine social organization. Different hierarchies may connect in various ways but are not reducible one to the other without some important social transformation." It would thus be a mistake to think only of "persons or families mapped onto a one- or two-dimensional chart according to their property, power, prestige," or some other single category.[8]

To those steeped in the classical tradition of historiography, such language often sounded suspiciously like cant. It made them uncomfortable; sometimes they found it incomprehensible. But their objection to social-scientific methodology was based not only on its unfamiliarity. They also felt that there is a fundamental difference between history, with its emphasis on the individual and unique, and science, with its quest for the regular and repetitive. Their position has been summarized most persuasively by Isaiah Berlin, a philosopher with a keen interest in historical learning. "May it not be that to be unscientific is to defy, for no good logical or empirical reason, established hypotheses and laws," he asked, "while to be unhistorical is the opposite — to ignore or twist one's view of particular events, persons, predicaments, in the name of laws, theories, principles derived from other fields, logical, ethical, metaphysical, scientific, which the nature of the medium renders inapplicable?" This was precisely what was being done by those theorists who were generally characterized as fanatical because their faith in a particular pattern was not restrained by a sense of reality. "The attempt to construct a discipline which would stand to concrete history as pure to applied, is not a vain hope for something beyond human power, but a chimera, born of a profound incapacity to grasp the nature of natural science, or of history, or of both." What separated the two was not ignorance or prejudice, but a fundamental difference in ultimate purpose.

8. Charles Tilly, *As Sociology Meets History* (New York, 1981), pp. xii–xiii; Lawrence Stone, *The Past and the Present* (Boston, London, and Henley, 1981), p. xi; Natalie Zemon Davis, *Society and Culture in Early Modern France* (Stanford, 1975), pp. xv–xvii.

Traditional historians did not always perceive the problem in such stark terms. Some favored peaceful coexistence. C. Vann Woodward argued that détente and cooperation between history and the social sciences were preferable to an endless cold war. Considering the direction in which the two were moving, each drawing closer to the other, there appeared to be ample meeting ground and a promise of closer relations. "I would hope that the social scientists will approach history with questions as well as with answers, with the desire to learn as well as to teach, as allies with common interests and not as imperialists seeking aggrandizement. If they do, then the prospects of mutual commerce, cultural interchange, and peaceful coexistence with [them] would seem propitious." Something about this language suggested a lamb proposing fruitful collaboration to the wolf.

Express or implicit doubts about the applicability of social-science techniques to the study of history were not confined to the old guard. Many scholars who had at first embraced the methodology of the social sciences later came to express reservations about its usefulness in historical research. Often there was impatience with its failure to find some underlying pattern, some grand design in the data which it sought to analyze. "How far has the research of recent years advanced us toward a history of society?" asked Hobsbawm. "Let me put my cards on the table. I cannot point to any single work which exemplifies the history of society to which we ought, I believe, to aspire." There had been important advances recently toward the study of certain types of society, he conceded, particularly those based on slavery in North and South America or on a large body of peasant cultivators, in Europe and Asia, for example. "On the other hand, the attempts to translate a comprehensive social history into popular synthesis strike me so far as either relatively unsuccessful or, with all their great merits, not the least of which is stimulation, as schematic and tentative."

There were other strictures as well. Stone reproached both the social-science and the cliometric historians for failing to make their findings accessible to interested but nonexpert readers. They had written only for a small coterie of devotees and specialists. There was an intelligent nonprofessional public which wanted to learn "what these innovative new questions, methods and data have revealed," but which could not stomach "indigestible statistical tables, dry analytical argument, and jargon-ridden prose." The structural, analytical, and quantitative scholars had therefore been increasingly talking to one another and to no one else. "Their findings have appeared in professional journals, or in monographs so expensive and with such small print runs (under a thousand) that they have been in practice almost entirely bought by libraries." The only way to halt this drift into reconditeness was to return to the style of literary narrative which had traditionally characterized historical learning, Stone suggested.

The social-science methodology, however, suffers from still another weakness, more serious than esotericism. To an even greater extent than quantification, it rests on a flimsy data base. The historical records which the past has left reflect the authoritarian, oligarchic, and hierarchical structure of preindustrial society. Though generally inadequate, they deal far more extensively with dominant than with subordinate classes. They tell us quite a bit about kings and generals, but very little about peasants and artisans. They dwell on public, not private, behavior. The application of even highly sophisticated research techniques to an inexact and incomplete body of evidence cannot correct its distortions and omissions.

The social-science historian is thus like a curator of ancient art who tries to piece together a Roman mosaic out of a handful of scattered fragments. The result may be plausible, but it can never be more than an imaginative reconstruction. The methodology employed leads to conclusions which are frequently ingenious and persuasive; they may even be valid. But can we be sure that they represent an objective reality, not a subjective perception? Do the scattered bits and pieces of information about the life of the lower classes in sixteenth-century France clearly support the contention that a charivari outside the home of some elderly widower who had married a much younger woman was motivated by a wish to placate the dead spouse, show concern for the children of the first marriage, and above all, express resentment at the improper diminution of the pool of nubile young females? Are the diaries of Samuel Pepys, Robert Hooke, William Byrd, Sylas Neville, and James Boswell sufficiently representative to form a solid basis for generalizations about the sexual behavior of English gentlemen during the seventeenth and eighteenth century? Can any German newspaper in the first half of the nineteenth century, even the *Augsburger Allgemeine Zeitung* — sixteen pages in length or less, preoccupied with diplomacy and politics, indifferent to economic and social questions — provide enough reliable data for a percentage distribution of formations which participated in popular disorders, with categories like "simple crowd," "crowd with ideological identity," "artisans," "unskilled or factory workers," "students," and "disorderly military"?

In short, the factual underpinning of the social-science methodology is often too weak for the burden of hypothesis and generalization which it must support. The result is a history not more but less scientific than older forms of historical scholarship. It is even more impressionistic and intuitive, even more dependent on faith and imagination. Every work of historiography becomes at some point a subjective re-creation, requiring, like poetry, a willing suspension of disbelief. But in social-science history that point is reached even sooner than in the more traditional branches of the discipline. The limitations which the nature of historical data imposes on the scholar are intrinsic and insurmountable. No historian can escape them, the social-science historian least of all.[9]

The disparity between evidence and conclusion, between hypothesis and result, is still more apparent in psychohistory, the most controversial of the scholarly innovations characterizing the new history. On the one hand, it is closely related to the most familiar and traditional form of historical learning — biography. But on the other, it seeks to apply to that ancient art the most recent techniques and theories of psychiatry and psychoanalysis.

To an age profoundly influenced by the Freudian insight, nothing has seemed more natural than to utilize it in the exploration of an individual mind or the collective mentality of an earlier generation. Indeed, soon after the First World War, the young Harry Elmer Barnes, a scholarly maverick all his life, wrote — in a psychological rather than historical journal — that history must learn to apply the findings of psychology to the study of important figures in the past. "The modern psychological historian who accepts the Carlylian interpretation of history will need to revise the famous phrase that history is 'collective biography' to read that history is the record of the 'collective sublimation of the neuroses and psychoses' of the great personalities of history," he maintained. "It becomes, therefore, quite evident that we can in no way escape the task of applying the new psychological mechanisms to the study of the leading personalities, at least to those in modern times, where we have some adequate body of evidence to serve as the basis for investigation." We might not be able to go much beyond "the borderland of exploration" in the unconscious of people who are no

9. Isaiah Berlin, "History and Theory: The Concept of Scientific History," *History and Theory: Studies in the Philosophy of History* 1 (1960–61): 31; C. Vann Woodward, "History and the Third Culture," *Journal of Contemporary History* 3, no. 2 (1968): 34–35; E. J. Hobsbawm, "Social History to History of Society," pp. 42–43; L. Stone, "Revival of Narrative," p. 15; Richard Tilly, "Popular Disorders in Nineteenth-Century Germany: A Preliminary Survey," *Journal of Social History* 4 (1970–71): 20.

longer alive, but without knowing at least something about their basic complexes, our understanding of the significance and causation of their thoughts and actions would remain imperfect.

Most historians, unfortunately, did not believe that they should concern themselves with problems of interpretation, Barnes complained, and even those who did were likely to go on for a long time rejecting startling and original innovations like "the psychology of instincts, behaviorism, and above all, the new dynamic psychology of the unconscious." But there was no reason to despair of a discipline which had advanced from a Gregory of Tours in the sixth century to such great masters in the twentieth as Frederick Jackson Turner, James Harvey Robinson, and James Thomson Shotwell. "We can even believe that a century hence a knowledge of that branch of psychology which Freud and his followers have elaborated will be regarded as a tool of the historian which is as indispensable to his success as [a manual on diplomatics] is to the present-day student of historical documents."

It was clear to Barnes that new methods and standards, derived from "modern dynamic psychology," would have to be adopted by interpretive biographical scholarship, if it were to become more than a contribution to descriptive literature. "Vital biography must deal with those intimate features of private life which reveal the deeper complexes in the personality, and cannot content itself with a superficial presentation of certain objective achievements nor accept as valid expressions of doctrine which may be only elaborate forms of disguise or extended secondary rationalizations." Childhood experiences in particular would have to receive close attention, for it was a cardinal fact of analytical psychology that the complexes determining the major outlines of personal behavior were formed and fixed during childhood and adolescence. Through an insight into the psychological wellsprings of human motivation, the historian would gain a deeper understanding of the past, Barnes concluded.

He was right in predicting that most historians would reject for the time being the applicability of psychiatric and psychoanalytic theory to history. But during the period of innovation which opened after the Second World War, the climate became more favorable to the kind of psychohistorical study he advocated. The most important and most surprising convert to the new subdiscipline was William L. Langer, who had gained wide recognition for his writings in the most traditional of fields, diplomatic history. In 1957, already in his sixties, he startled the audience listening to his presidential address before the American Historical Association by dwelling on the im portance for historical learning of recent findings in psychology. He pointed out that during the preceding fifty years the scope of the discipline had been greatly extended. Even such familiar fields as political and military history had become more comprehensive and analytical; they had been reinforced by research in the social, economic, intellectual, scientific, and many other aspects of the past, some of them quite remote from what had once been considered history. There was unlikely to be much further "horizontal expansion," but there was still room for "penetration in depth," so that the "newest history" would no doubt be more intensive and less extensive. Specifically, an urgent need existed to deepen historical understanding through the use of the concepts and findings of modern psychology. "I do not refer to classical or academic psychology which, so far as I can detect, has little bearing on historical problems, but rather to psychoanalysis and its later developments and variations as included in the terms 'dynamic' or 'depth psychology.'"

It was lamentable, Langer declared, that historians had remained indifferent to psychoanalysis, for it appeared to have a great deal to contribute to the solution of historical problems. Many years of clinical work by hundreds of trained analysts had fortified and refined Freud's original theory of human drives, the conflicts to which they lead, and the means by which they are repressed or diverted. Psychoanalysis was no longer regarded as merely a therapy; it had become generally recognized as a theory essential for the study of the human personality. How then could the historian, who must be at least as much concerned with people and their motivation as with impersonal forces and causation, fail to make use of its findings? "Viewed in the light of modern depth psychology, the homespun, common-sense psychological interpretations of past historians, even some of the greatest, seem woefully inadequate, not to say naive. Clearly the time has come for us to reckon with a doctrine that strikes so close to the heart of our own discipline."

The arguments advanced by Langer were repeated during the next few years by a group of scholars, not all of them professional historians, who formed the vanguard of psychohistory. Hans Meyerhoff, whose field was philosophy, maintained that psychoanalysis and history had a great deal in common, first of all, because a historical method formed an integral part of psychoanalytic theory and therapy, and second, because psychoanalysis, though formulated as a strictly psychological theory, could not be divorced from a study of history and society. The similarities in method between the two disciplines made it possible to look at psychoanalysis not as a branch of the general sciences — biological, medical, or psychological — but as a branch of history.

Bruce Mazlish, one of the leading psychohistorical scholars, wondered how history, "the one discipline that deals especially with man's past and seeks explanation of that past largely in terms of men's motives," could so resolutely ignore the one science — or at least attempt at a science — which focused on research into precisely those areas. "Historians study man's collective past; psychoanalysts study his individual past. Surely, one would have thought that a mental bridge could be built to connect the two investigations."

H. Stuart Hughes went a step beyond that. To him the two investigations were more than similar; they were identical. "Psychoanalysis is history — or possibly biography," he told a psychiatric training group at a Boston hospital. The analyst recognized this, although he did not as a rule say so explicitly. His professional and moral goal, moreover, was the same as the historian's, namely, "to liberate man from the burden of the past by helping him to understand that past." The classic problem facing the historian — the explanation of human motives — would find in psychoanalysis a richer fund of understanding than could be provided by any other discipline, and in a form peculiarly congenial to the historian's mind. For its rules of evidence and relevance were highly permissive, and it was constantly alert to the symptomatic significance of the seemingly trivial. "What a less imaginative method might dismiss out of hand, the analyst (or the historian) may well put at the center of his interpretation. In this sense, history in its turn is psychoanalysis: in their study of motive the two show the conviction that everything is both relevant and random, incoherent and ordered, in the all-inclusive context of a human existence." Here was the basic justification for the assumptions of psychohistory.[10]

Not all of those assumptions were entirely new, to be sure. Historians

---

10. Harry Elmer Barnes, "Psychology and History: Some Reasons for Predicting Their More Active Coöperation in the Future," *American Journal of Psychology* 30 (1919): 362, 375-76; idem, "Some Reflections on the Possible Service of Analytical Psychology to History," *Psychoanalytic Review* 8 (1921): 27; William L. Langer, "The Next Assignment," *American Historical Review* 63 (1957-58): 284-87; Hans Meyerhoff, "On Psychoanalysis as History," *Psychoanalysis and the Psychoanalytic Review* 49, no. 2 (1962): 4; Bruce Mazlish, "Introduction," in *Psychoanalysis and History*, ed. Bruce Mazlish (Englewood Cliffs, N.J., 1963), p. 2; H. S. Hughes, *History as Art and as Science*, pp. 47-48.

have always recognized that an insight into human character and motivation — into the way men and women behave and interact, into the way they respond to challenges and problems — was essential for an understanding of the past, especially in the writing of biographical history. That was why so many important biographies have been the work of nonacademic scholars, of historians whose experience had been shaped by the world of affairs — politics, administration, business, or journalism — rather than the college campus. But the kind of psychological discernment which had traditionally been acknowledged to be important in historical scholarship could be acquired through practical action and observation, through life itself. What the historian, like the writer or the artist, needed to obtain it was innate sensitivity rather than formal training.

Saul K. Padover, the biographer of Jefferson, Marx, Joseph II, and Louis XVI, emphasized this point indirectly, asking whether the life of a great historic figure could be written satisfactorily with the same technique and method, and from the same viewpoint, as conventional historiography. "Is it possible to explain a great man — say a Jefferson or a Lincoln or a Jesus — by nothing more than a constant, meticulous, minute reference to documents? Do documents, which are themselves historic accidents, illuminate the internal dynamics of a person? Or does one require other and auxiliary means — such as imagination, psychological insight, psychosocial techniques?" Without such auxiliary means, Padover suggested, the reader could not obtain a clear or vivid picture of the subject of a biographical work.

John A. Garraty, editor of the *Encyclopedia of American Biography*, was more explicit. It seemed to him, he said, that biography and psychology had always been related disciplines. Their early "intuitive interrelationships," moreover, had been recently supplemented by the more conscious and scientific efforts of each to profit from the work of the other. "Psychological knowledge has aided modern biographers in understanding their subjects, and biographies have been used by psychologists interested in the study of genius, heredity, social movements, and many other topics." There was room for further development, however. "Scientific psychological methods ought to be thoroughly investigated by biographers, while psychologists should more often turn to biography as providing a source of psychological data," Garraty proposed.

But this was not nearly enough for the members of the psychohistorical school. They rejected as unscientific the traditional implicit or informal connection between history and psychology. Langer spoke with scorn about the "homespun, common-sense psychological interpretations of past historians," which appeared to him "inadequate" and "naive." The disparagement of historical biography, he maintained, which had once seemed fashionable on the ground that leading personalities were only pawns of major forces beyond human control and understanding, had now been abandoned by an age which had seen its Lenins, Stalins, and Hitlers. "If we are to understand the world-shaking and world-shaping events of either the past or the present, we historians need all the help that other disciplines can provide — not only economics, geography, demography, and so on, but also and especially psychoanalysis." There were some psychoanalytic institutes which already taught survey courses for the nonprofessional, and that was all to the good. "But it would be better yet if, at the major universities, basic courses in psychoanalysis could be offered, designed especially for students in various fields, such as literature, art, and history, where competence in the psychological field is essential or at least desirable." By the same token, analysts wishing to engage in historical studies would do well to enroll in some systematic course in historical method and criticism in order to gain greater familiarity and aptitude in the handling of evidence.

Hughes welcomed all such proposals. A full psychoanalysis would no doubt be too long and costly for most Ph.D. candidates, he conceded; some would even be temperamentally unsuited for it. "In a few cases, however, it might be precisely what was called for, and I trust that foundation funds would be forthcoming to finance such a venture." He hoped that in the future a significant minority of young historians, especially those concerned with the psychological aspects of historical interpretation, would go through personal analysis under the guidance of experienced clinicians. The others might be able to work out a shorter program in consultation with the psychoanalytic institutes which had been established near some of the major universities. "Nothing less, I believe, will be adequate to the needs of historical understanding in the second half of the twentieth century."

Systematic training in psychoanalysis, according to the psychohistorians, would enable the biographer to portray his subject with greater insight and understanding. He would then see more clearly through the various forms of self-vindication by which the mind seeks to obscure its underlying drives and motivations. Without such training, he would always remain at the mercy of the documents, misled by their omissions and distortions. Erik H. Erikson, a psychoanalyst who had turned to historical biography, emphasized the methodological inadequacies of conventional historiography. "We cannot leave history entirely to nonclinical observers and to professional historians," he wrote, "who often all too nobly immerse themselves into the very disguises, rationalizations, and idealizations of the historical process from which it should be their business to separate themselves." A skilled analyst, on the other hand, could not only understand the documentary materials more fully; he could rise above them, filling in their gaps and correcting their mistakes. "A clinician's training permits, and in fact forces, him to recognize major trends even where the facts are not all available; at any point in a treatment he can and must be able to make meaningful predictions as to what will prove to have happened; and he must be able to sift even questionable sources in such a way that a coherent predictive hypothesis emerges." Could the conventional historian get that from his training?

Donald B. Meyer, whose field was American social and intellectual history, wrote in a review of Erikson's life of the young Luther that the book's contribution lay not in discovering new facts but in interpreting old ones more accurately and intelligently. Traditional scholars were asking, as usual, whether the author had turned up any "fresh" data, whether he had gone to untapped sources. But the frequency with which this question was used as a test of professional competence, Meyer maintained, was, "to put the matter bluntly," a measure of the "theoretical bankruptcy" of history. The biography of a man like Luther showed why. "New Luther sources will always be welcome, but there is plenty of room for progress for anyone who knows how to use the basic, available sources. Erikson's book is based, not on fresh data, but upon data refreshened, rescued from suppression, from invention, and from reduction." This was the new methodology's most important function.[11]

The theoretical justifications of psychohistory sounded very persuasive, but its practical achievements have remained disappointingly small. The scholars who accepted its principles and utilized its teachings were for the most part, Langer conceded, "those who have undergone analysis themselves." Having experienced the effectiveness of the psychoanalytic tech-

11. Saul K. Padover, "Architect of Policy," Saturday Review of Literature, October 20, 1951, p. 16; John A. Garraty, "The Interrelations of Psychology and Biography," Psychological Bulletin 51 (1954): 580; W. L. Langer, "The Next Assignment," p. 287; idem, "Foreword," in The Psychoanalytic Interpretation of History, ed. Benjamin B. Wolman (New York and London, 1971), pp. viii–ix; H. S. Hughes, History as Art and as Science, p. 65; Erik H. Erikson, Young Man Luther: A Study in Psychoanalysis and History (New York, 1958), pp. 20, 50; "Review Essays," History and Theory: Studies in the Philosophy of History 1 (1960–61): 292–93.

nique in therapy, they became convinced of its usefulness in historical study as well. Yet in most cases practice refused to conform to theory. A disproportionate share of the psychohistorical scholarly literature was devoted to showing why psychohistory should be or how it could be written, rather than to actually writing it. Reality failed to live up to expectation; methodology outstripped creativity.

Psychohistory did stimulate the study of collective attitudes and beliefs, of what came to be labeled *mentalité:* the life cycle of infancy, childhood, adolescence, and adulthood in Plymouth Colony in the seventeenth century; the concept of insanity under the *ancien régime* during the seventeenth and eighteenth centuries; the view of crime and punishment in France during the eighteenth and nineteenth centuries; or the changing attitude toward death in Western society since the Middle Ages. But more often psychohistory turned to biography, to the use of psychoanalytic insights in the study of an individual personality. Erikson's book on Luther was the best-known and most successful of these psychohistorical portraits, but there were several others depicting prominent figures, both living and dead. Most historians, however, including most new historians, regarded them with skepticism. They seemed scholarly curiosities, methodological sleight of hand, speculative applications of an arcane psychoanalytic theory to a familiar body of data. How could their findings be tested by the usual criteria of historical learning? How could they be checked, weighed, confirmed, or rejected? To escape such questions, psychohistory withdrew into reconditeness even earlier than cliometrics or social-science history. It became largely a scholarly cult, mystical and hieratic, separated by its doctrine and ritual from the great mass of the uninitiated, standing aloof from the mainstream of the historical discipline, its members communicating only with one another.

This isolation, abstruseness, and sacerdotalism have been acknowledged even by those who had at first welcomed the psychohistorical school. Stone, though sympathetic to experimentation, has stated point-blank that "psychohistory is so far largely a disaster area—a desert strewn with the wreckage of elaborate, chromium-plated vehicles which broke down soon after departure." Robert Waelder, professor of psychoanalysis at Jefferson Medical College in Philadelphia, was more restrained. He reiterated the familiar view that "psychoanalysis . . . seems to hold the promise of a deeper understanding of history." But then he conceded: "After three-fourths of a century, the actual results of psychoanalytic study of history are disappointing. There is nowhere a new vista; the actual applications of psychoanalytic viewpoints to history are few and often speculative. Some have been products of the poetic imagination." Robert G. L. Waite, author of a psychohistorical study of Hitler, complained about "well-meaning colleagues [who] proceed to demonstrate in their writings not the complexity of history, but its apparent simplicity." So seductive was psychoanalysis, "at least to the newly converted amateur," that the intricacies of the historical past became reduced to simplistic psychological analysis. "In short, any historian knows how much bad history has been written by those who are long on psychological theory and short on historical evidence."

Even Erikson, the star of the psychohistorical school, declared that he had come to use the term "psychohistory" only with "tacit quotation marks," for "I would not wish to associate myself with all that is done in the name of this term." He had read some analyses of great figures like Jefferson which "treated what these persons said or wrote as if their utterances had been free associations in the course of more or less voluntary confessions and admissions of the kind patients make in the clinical context." This was simply bad methodology. The inner person of a historical figure, "in all its uniqueness and yet also in its conflictedness and failures," had to be seen, for better and for worse, as prototypical for his time and as fulfilling specific needs in the lives of those who followed his direction.

All this raises troubling questions. Why has the application of psychoanalysis to history, which on the face of it seemed so promising, turned out so barren? Why have the psychohistorians, who sought to broaden and deepen historical understanding, shrunk to a small, isolated coterie? The problem appears to lie in a basic difference of methodology between treating the symptoms of a patient who can interact with and respond to a therapist, and examining the actions of a historical figure who can be studied only through incomplete and sometimes misleading documentary materials.

Oscar Handlin, a perceptive critic of the new history, put his finger on the crucial distinction between the psychoanalyst and the psychohistorian. "The fundamental mode of analysis is unavailable to the historian," he pointed out. "The patient is not there to answer questions. The process of diagnosis is difficult enough for the skilled therapist, who can ask and listen after passing through a long apprenticeship and analysis, and who, even so, often yields to the impulse to pontificate." It could not be applied by do-it-yourself practitioners to characters who were not subject to interrogation, and without it the psyche of the subject guarded its secrets inviolably. "Only where evidence exists, can theory complement it." The danger in the wave of psy-

choanalyzing by followers of the psychohistorical school lay in their sub-
stitution of a theoretically grounded formula for evidence. "At the points
at which the data ran out, the historian no longer confessed ignorance or
maintained silence; he reached for a bit of clinical verbiage in a pretense
of knowing." This effort was bound to fail, for aside from the difficulty of
choosing among competing and kaleidoscopically changing theories, borrowings from Erikson, Freud, Jung, or Adler could add no force to what
the analysts themselves had written. "Even when the borrowings did not
degenerate into absurd reductionism, they stifled the imaginations of authors who allowed typology to obscure individual personality traits, and
of readers who might otherwise have found their own way of filling in the
empty spaces in the record."

The methodological differences between psychoanalytic therapy and historical research have been emphasized even by some writers on psychohistory who were sympathetic to its objectives. In his pioneering essay of 1919
on the need for cooperation between psychology and history, Barnes recognized the problem. "It must be remembered," he acknowledged, "that it is
difficult for the most skillful practising psychiatrist to get far enough into
the patient's unconscious to secure enough data to effect a cure without from
fifty to one hundred hours of direct personal questioning, and it is not to
be supposed that the most complete biography, diary, or autobiography
would present anything like that amount of direct personal information."
The tendency of conscious expression, moreover, which constituted the major part of written or spoken records, was toward the "displacement, rationalization, projection, symbolizing or otherwise disguising of the real dynamic motives and impulses in the unconscious." Even the most honest and
reliable individual might and often did assign motives or reasons for his
particular act or policy which were "as far from the real truth as the statements of the most notorious liar of his generation."

The same problem was discussed forty years later in an article by Fritz
Schmidl in the *Psychoanalytic Quarterly* on the relationship of psychoanalysis to history. "Severe difficulties are encountered when psychoanalytic
methods are applied to any other discipline," he warned, "and they are particularly disturbing when applied to history." To look at any phenomenon
psychoanalytically meant to investigate it from the point of view of unconscious motivation; indeed, psychoanalysis was the only method which made
an investigation of the unconscious possible. It was therefore not surprising
that, while the disciplines of psychoanalysis and history had a great deal

in common, the application of psychoanalytic techniques to problems of history had remained casual and frequently unsatisfactory. "The main reason for this is that psychoanalysis requires the cooperation of a living person. The fragments of factual information or of products of the imagination available to the historian are never a substitute for the tremendous wealth of material that is unearthed in an individual psychoanalysis." This was basically "an insurmountable difficulty," although some valuable results could no doubt be achieved if historians became familiar with "certain typical gestalten" known and understood by psychoanalysts.

To summarize, the creative tension between analyst and analysand, established at the cost of considerable time and effort, which often leads to the resolution of psychological conflicts cannot be replicated in the relationship of the historian to his data. Unable to penetrate the veil of rationalizations and plausibilities with which his subject disguises his underlying motivations, the psychohistorian is often forced to fall back on textbook typologies and classroom theories. His findings cannot be tested, as in a clinical analysis, by the patient's state of health. They can be neither confirmed nor refuted, neither proved nor disproved. They have to be accepted on faith. Psychohistory has seemed at times closer in spirit to metaphysical speculation or theological disputation than to empirical scholarship.[12]

Indeed, the new history as a whole can now be seen as less radical or innovative than it had first appeared. Born at a time when the historical profession was becoming socially and culturally democratized, when the traditional functions and justifications of historical learning were eroding, it seemed to offer a way out of the obsolescence with which the discipline was threatened. Nurtured on government grants and supported by philanthropic foundations, it held out the promise of revitalized scholarship relevant to the needs of a changing society. For those who were caught up in the excitement of the new history, it was a time of ferment and rejuvenation, of pioneering and iconoclasticism. But that period is now drawing to a close, and we can see it more clearly than in its intoxicating springtime.

---

12. W. L. Langer, "Foreword," p. ix; L. Stone, "Revival of Narrative," p. 14; Robert Waelder, "Psychoanalysis and History: Application of Psychoanalysis to Historiography," in *Psychoanalytic Interpretation of History*, ed. B. B. Wolman, p. 3; Robert G. L. Waite, "Adolf Hitler's Anti-Semitism: A Study in History and Psychoanalysis," in ibid., p. 192; Erik H. Erikson, *Dimensions of a New Identity: The 1973 Jefferson Lectures in the Humanities* (New York, 1974), pp. 12, 14; O. Handlin, *Truth in History*, pp. 273–74; H. E. Barnes, "Psychology and History," p. 361; Fritz Schmidl, "Psychoanalysis and History," *Psychoanalytic Quarterly* 31 (1962): 535–36, 545.

The scholars who had shared its hopes and achievements still look back with regret to what had once been, warmed by their memories against the chill breezes which are beginning to blow. Thus in the introduction to a collection of his essays published in 1981, Lawrence Stone reflected a little sadly on the waning golden age to which he had made an important contribution:

> I feel myself fortunate to have lived through, and taken some part in, so exciting a transformation of my profession. If, as seems likely, the flow of new recruits into academia is going to be very severely restricted over the next fifteen years for lack of job opportunities, it is probable that intellectual stagnation will set in, since it is from the young that innovation comes. If this happens the past twenty-five years will come to be seen as something of a heroic phase in the evolution of historical understanding, squeezed in between two periods of quiet consolidation of received wisdom.

Other scholars regard those years less nostalgically. But there is at least widespread agreement that the new history has entered a period of retrenchment, introspection, defensiveness, and rigidification. Stone himself has conceded that "warning signals are flying about threats of a new theoretical dogmatism and a new methodological scholasticism." It is therefore not too early to make a tentative appraisal of the results of the great transformation which historical learning has undergone since the Second World War.

Its most enduring achievement has surely been a richer understanding and broader vision in the writing of history. The traditional emphasis on the processes of politics, diplomacy, and warfare in Europe and America has been reduced or supplanted, partly by a growing interest in the Third World, partly by an increasing concern with the way of life of ordinary men and women. A statistical survey by Robert Darnton of doctoral dissertations in history completed between 1958 and 1978 showed a striking shift toward social history, especially in such subdivisions as immigration and ethnicity, labor history, black history, urban history, and women's and family history (see table 5.1). The big losers were the established fields which had once dominated the discipline. The percentage of doctoral dissertations in political history, for instance, which had been five times greater than the percentage in social history in 1958 and three times greater in 1968, fell below social history in 1978. Other traditional areas, such as international relations, intellectual history, and economic history, also suffered heavy losses. As for constitutional history, it disappeared almost entirely, with only 1 doctoral dissertation out of a total of 431 completed during a six-month period in 1978. This distribution of research specialties is not likely to change

TABLE 5.1 History Dissertations by Research Specialty, 1958–78

	PERCENTAGE		
	1958	1968	1978
Social History	6.8	10.4	27.1
Black History	1.0	2.1	4.9
Immigration and Ethnicity	1.5	1.9	2.8
Labor History	0.4	1.9	3.0
Urban History	0.4	0.5	2.8
Women's and Family History	1.0	1.1	3.2
General	2.5	2.9	10.4
Constitutional History	1.5	0.5	0.2
Cultural History	2.5	3.2	5.8
Economic History	7.5	4.8	3.5
Intellectual History	10.5	9.5	8.8
International Relations	10.5	12.7	9.3
Political History	34.3	33.4	23.7
Other	26.4	25.5	21.6

SOURCE: Robert Darnton, "Intellectual and Cultural History," in *The Past before Us: Contemporary Historical Writing in the United States,* ed. Michael Kammen (Ithaca, N.Y., and London, 1980), p. 353.

significantly in the near future. It reflects a long-term shift of scholarship from personalities, events, and conjunctures toward patterns, structures, and institutions or processes, evolutions, and developments. Historical learning will not soon return to the preoccupation with elites and patriciates which had once characterized it.

The enlargement of scholarly vision, however, has been accompanied by a widening gulf between history and literature, between scholarship and culture. The intelligent, educated public, which had once read historical works with interest and understanding, has increasingly turned to amateur popularizers with the narrative skill which professionals no longer consider important. Many of the new historians had initially maintained that their scholarship would make history more relevant to the needs of contemporary society, thereby enhancing its general appeal. The questions they were asking, according to Stone, were those "which preoccupy us all today." Instead of feeding their audience on the "pabulum of popular biographies and textbooks," they were dealing with power, authority, and leadership; the relationship between political institutions and social patterns and values; attitudes toward youth, age, illness, and death; sex, marriage, contraception, and abortion; work, leisure, and consumption; religion, science, and magic; love, fear, lust, and hate; literacy and education; family, kin, community, class, and race; ritual, symbol, and custom; crime and punishment; deference and egalitarianism; classes, status groups, and social mobility; popular protest and millenarian hope; and nature, ecology and disease. Were not these subjects more pertinent and interesting than the deeds of dead monarchs and warriors?

Yet the new history, however relevant to contemporary concerns it may appear in theory, has in practice only further alienated the general reader from professional scholarship. This is in part a result of its quasi-scientific methodology and hieratic language. The attitude of many new historians has been that what they have to say is so important that it does not matter whether the layman understands it or not. Do we ask the physicist, chemist, or biologist to communicate his findings in polished literary style? The historians too should be judged by the quality of his research, not of his writing. Indeed, the reconditeness of what he does is a measure of its originality. As for the task of popularization, that can be left to journalists and litterateurs.

Equally alienating has been the tacit assumption of the new history that the deeds of those who possess power, wealth, and status are no more important — indeed, they may be less important — than the deeds of those who do not possess them. Yet in everyday experience we accept, almost instinctively, as a matter of common sense, clear gradations in the importance ascribable to the activities of various groups and classes in the community. Even a historian absorbed in the study of folk festivals and village riots in seventeenth-century France is more interested, when he reads his morning newspaper, in what is happening in the White House or the Kremlin than in the manifestations of popular culture appearing on the sports page, in the entertainment section, the comic strip, or the column of advice to the lovelorn. There is a compelling logic which insists that the policies and decisions of masters of politics or captains of industry affect society's vital interests more profoundly than the folkways and mores of hewers of wood and drawers of water. And if that is the case, then it would be premature to write off the old history with its narrative account of the *res gestae* of the powerful and affluent. Rather, a revival of biographical, political, diplomatic, and military historiography appears highly likely in the long run. It has never disappeared from the work of amateur historians, and its renewed acceptance by professional scholarship as well as in all probability only a matter of time.[13]

Indeed, the new history of the postwar era can now be seen as only the latest in a series of recurrent new histories which have characterized the development of the discipline in the last hundred years. There was the new history of the 1880s, by which the founders of the American Historical Association hoped to achieve a greater degree of professionalism and a higher standard of scholarship. Some thirty years later came the new history taught by James Harvey Robinson and his followers, who believed that the study of the past should help improve American society in the present. A generation later there was still another new history, cultural and psychological in emphasis, which the economic historian Herbert Heaton dismissed as only a penchant for novelty: "In December 1939, a mighty wooden horse was pulled into the Mayflower Hotel, Washington, D.C., where the American Historical Association was holding its annual meeting. Out of its capacious interior popped a crowd of evangelists to preach a new way to salvation, called 'The Cultural Approach.' Conversion apparently involved complete immersion in cultural anthropology and social psychology." Ten years and a world war later came the most recent new history, based on quantification, social-science methodology, and psychoanalytic insight. Thus the rejection of tradition in historical scholarship is itself something of a tradition.

Each of these new histories began by promising to liberate the discipline, to give it new significance, to tear down the bars within which historical understanding is imprisoned, to rejuvenate and regenerate. But after about two decades of innovation, each tended to rigidify into a traditionality or orthodoxy of its own. Pierre Goubert, professor of history at the Sorbonne, has aptly described this process of conventionalization: "All success brings with it excess. As historical work . . . is carried out mainly within universities, it tends to reproduce the faults of the universities. Soon, a servile imitation of innovation establishes a new tradition, or a negative and violent contestation which often ends in reinforcing the thing originally disputed."

13. L. Stone, *Past and Present*, p. xi; idem, "History and the Social Sciences," p. 40; Robert Darnton, "Intellectual and Cultural History," in *Past before Us*, ed. M. Kammen, p. 353; L. Stone, "Revival of Narrative," p. 15.

The cyclical succession of iconoclasticism and consolidation is seemingly a normal characteristic of the evolution of historical learning.

There can be no doubt, of course, that the new history of the postwar era has made an important contribution to our understanding of the past, widening the range and technique of scholarly research. But it has also suffered from an overweening pride, the capital sin of all new histories. It has overestimated the ability of methodology to re-create a living reality out of inanimate documents and statistics. It has been reluctant to acknowledge that even the best work of the historian, whatever his subject or technique, must by its nature prove flawed and imperfect.

A recognition of this fallibility, which is admittedly hard to accept, has led some scholars to emphasize the existential limitations of historical knowledge. In his presidential address to the American Historical Association in 1936, Charles Howard McIlwain admonished: "Each [historian] must also see that his answer can never be more than a tentative one. He must realize how very narrow the range of his vision must be; how infinitely small a part of the whole varied experience of our race, which is history, can be mastered in one short span of life or even in many. All history should be a lesson in humility to us historians." Some twenty years later Allan Nevins repeated this admonition in his presidential address: "We are all amateurs, we are all professionals. Perhaps what we all most need is a dual sense of humility; humility because we know that however hard we search for Truth we shall not quite find it, humility because we are in the last analysis servants of the democratic public. . . . This is a time not for arrogance, disdain, or rivalry, but for union in a common and exalted effort." Even Lawrence Stone warned the new historians in 1977 against methodological doctrinairism: "If the profession does indeed begin to narrow its viewpoint and closes off its intellectual options, . . . it runs the risk either of growing sterility or of factional fragmentation. Only if the two principles of methodological diversity and ideological pluralism are vigorously defended will the necessary intellectual interchange between the historian and the social scientist continue to be a fruitful one."

Indeed, the very distinction between the new history and the old appears largely artificial. The only real difference is between good and bad history or rather between good and bad historians. For it is not subject matter or scholarly viewpoint or research technique which produces enduring works of historical learning, but imaginativeness and creativity. A talented, exciting historian can make the most familiar and conventional topic appear new and interesting. A dull, uninspired pedant, on the other hand, will make even an original and important subject seem only pedantic. History is written by men and women, not by formulas and methodologies. That is what Handlin meant in reminding us that "the historian . . . will find something to say as a historian only through the creative tension that arises from exercising the full power of his imagination and understanding against the unyielding evidence that survives the past. He can continue to do so as an individual even if the crisis in the discipline should leave him without a community of investigators of which to be part." In the present winter of their discontent, historians would do well to ponder that.[14]

14. Herbert Heaton, "The Economic Impact on History," in *The Interpretation of History*, ed. Joseph R. Strayer (Princeton, N.J., 1943), p. 104; Pierre Goubert, "Local History," *Daedalus* 100 (1971): 122–23; C. H. McIlwain, "The Historian's Part in a Changing World," *American Historical Review* 42 (1936–37): 207; A. Nevins, "Not Capulets, Not Montagus," p. 270; L. Stone, "History and the Social Sciences," p. 40; O. Handlin, *Truth in History*, p. 22.

CHAPTER VI

What Is the Use of History?

The present crisis in historical learning has forced historians to deal with a question which most of them find awkward. They prefer as a rule to avoid any rigorous philosophical examination of their discipline, assuming that its justification is either self-evident or inexplicable. Their inclination is to write history, not analyze it. They agree with the advice of Goethe's Mephistopheles to the student who had come seeking knowledge: *Grau, teurer Freund, ist alle Theorie,/Und grün des Lebens goldner Baum.*

Resolute evasion of a systematic inquiry into the nature of their craft is especially characteristic of historians in America and Great Britain. Those on the Continent have been more willing to deal with the underlying principles and assumptions of historical knowledge, although this has not helped them achieve superiority in scholarship. There seems to be little correlation between analysis and creativity, between the ability to describe what the historian tries to do and doing it. Most members of the profession do not concern themselves with theory, and those who do are generally no better historians than those who do not. If anything, the reverse may be true. The philosophy of history has therefore usually been left to philosophers, and the few historians who have tried their hand at it, like Charles A. Beard or Carl Becker, have done so late in life, their practical experience shaping their theoretical insight, not the other way around.

The spontaneous, almost instinctive nature of historical learning has been recognized by most writers dealing with the nature of the discipline. Robin George Collingwood, a rare combination of philosopher and historian, though more the former than the latter, maintained that a scholar qualified to answer such questions as "what history is, what it is about, how it proceeds, and what it is for" should not only have the experience of historical thinking, but should have reflected on that experience. He should be not only a historian but also a philosopher. His philosophical thought, moreover, should include special attention to the problems of historical thought. Yet Collingwood also conceded that "it is possible to be a quite good historian (though not an historian of the highest order) without thus reflecting upon one's own historical thinking. It is even easier to be quite a good teacher of history (though not the very best kind of teacher) without such reflection." The important thing to remember is that experience comes first and reflection on that experience second. "Even the least reflective historian has the first qualification. He possesses the experience on which to reflect; and when he is asked to reflect on it his reflections have a good chance of being to the point. An historian who has never worked much at philosophy will probably answer . . . questions [about the nature of historical knowledge] in a more intelligent and valuable way than a philosopher who has never worked much at history."

In this indifference to formal theory, historians are unlike most scholars in the social sciences or even the humanities. The recent tendency has been in the direction of a more systematic examination of the forms and functions of higher learning. The institutionalization, bureaucratization, and professionalization of knowledge has forced all disciplines to define their scope and technique more rigidly. As history has moved closer to the methods and purposes of the social sciences, it too has become more explicit regarding its basic principles. Yet despite that, it remains far less rigorous or structured than most fields of organized study.

The lack of a clearly articulated theoretical foundation has been deplored by some historians who would like to see historical learning become more social-scientific in nature. "Undergraduate education in history consists almost exclusively in the introduction of the student to the substantive knowledge of history itself," complained the History Panel of the Behavioral and Social Sciences Survey. This was the case even with graduate education. "Indeed, it is no exaggeration to say that of all the social sciences, none is less introspective about the way it does its work. There are some historians, even, who look upon a concern with methodology as a kind of intellectual 'cop-out'—a refuge for those who cannot write good history." The charge is not altogether unjustified. For the majority of historians practice is more important than theory, doing is more important than reflecting on what is being done. They tend to feel that those who can, write about history; those who can't, write about the philosophy of history. Most of the work on the epistemological basis of historiography is therefore published in highly specialized scholarly journals with a philosophical rather than historical orientation.

This deliberate avoidance of theoretical speculation is cheerfully acknowledged by many historians. Far from trying to disguise it, they maintain that a preoccupation with the principles of historical study can actually prove an obstacle to scholarly creativity. In his Raleigh Lecture on History read before the British Academy in 1950, Ernest Llewellyn Woodward declared at the outset that "I am not approaching the fundamental problem of the nature of history knowledge." There was no need to do so, he maintained. "I am in good company if I evade a master problem of this kind, since nearly all English historians have evaded it. They may have been wise to do so; hitherto we have had no satisfactory solution propounded to the problem either by the few trained philosophers who have also been historians or by the smaller number of trained historians who have also been philosophers." He conceded that few questions were answered merely by deciding not to take notice of them, and that he was in fact making important assumptions about the nature of historical knowledge generally when he spoke of the particular difficulties confronting historians at the present time. "Nevertheless, it is possible to follow up an inquiry to a point short of first principles."

The most spirited rejection of formal theorizing, however, has come from the American medievalist Joseph R. Strayer. In a book dealing with the problem of interpretation in historical learning, he defended the traditional indifference of historians to epistemology:

> The ordinary historian has always been somewhat embarassed when asked to justify his devotion to his subject. Interest in history seems to him natural and inevitable; it no more needs explanation than the act of breathing. If he is completely honest with himself, he will wonder if his original decision to concentrate on the study of history was not due more to the fact that it gave him pleasure than to any profound conviction of its value and significance. When under attack, he may develop elaborate arguments to prove the social usefulness of his work, but these bursts of enthusiasm are apt to leave him with the uneasy feeling that he has yielded to the common human failing of inventing good reasons for doing what he would have done in any case. Nagging by scientists and social scientists may drive him to formulate laws of historical research, but the next day he will be wondering if he has not invented a complicated terminology to discuss a method which must be based more on instinct and common sense than on the principles of the physical

sciences. History, at least in its final stages, is more of an art than a science, and historians, like artists, have seldom been able to describe their work in purely intellectual terms. In both cases there is a belief that a certain arrangement of carefully selected facts will illustrate some aspect of universal truth, and a feeling that this belief can never be fully justified by purely rational argument.

No one has described more charmingly or perceptively the casual attitude of the average historian toward the theoretical underpinnings of his discipline.[1]

How long the historical profession will be able to go on dodging problems of epistemology, however, is an open question. For one thing, the increasing scientism of historiography, the growing tendency toward precision in the methods and procedures of scholarly research, is likely to lead to a greater preoccupation with the theoretical attributes and limitations of knowledge about the past. Even more important, rising doubts about the usefulness of historical learning, about the reliability of collective experience as a guide to collective action, will probably force more and more historians to ask themselves how they can justify what they do to a skeptical world. Until recently this problem had not been acute. There had been general agreement that the study of history could provide practical direction for the solution of political and social questions with which the community was grappling. But this faith in the utility of historical knowledge has now largely eroded. It has been replaced by a feeling that the lessons of the past are no longer applicable to the problems of the present.

The world has become so different from what it had been, according to this view, it faces such extraordinary dilemmas and dangers, that the experience of earlier generations is irrelevant to the crisis of contemporary society. "The turn from history toward myth is to be observed in some of the important creative works of [the twentieth century]," warned Philip Rahv in the *Partisan Review* shortly after the Second World War. "The craze for myth is the fear of history. It is feared because modern life is above all an historical life producing changes with vertiginous speed, changes difficult to understand and even more difficult to control. And to some people it ap-

---

1. R. G. Collingwood, *The Idea of History* (New York, 1956), pp. 8–9; *History as Social Science*, ed. D. S. Landes and C. Tilly, p. 82; E. L. Woodward, "Some Considerations on the Present State of Historical Studies," *Proceedings of the British Academy* (1950): 95; Joseph R. Strayer, "Introduction," in *Interpretation of History*, ed. J. R. Strayer, pp. 3–4.

pears as though the past, all of it together with its gods and sacred books, were being ground to pieces in the powerhouse of change, senselessly used up as so much raw material in the fabrication of an unthinkable future."[2]

To nonintellectuals this way of describing the growing distrust of historical knowledge may sound a little portentous, but the decline in history enrollments in institutions of higher learning and the drop in sales of history books suggest that the general public, even the educated general public, may indeed be turning "from history toward myth." Some scholars have therefore begun to search more systematically for the values which might be derived from an understanding of history and for the justifications which might be found for the study of the past. Their concern with the uses and benefits of historical learning, to be sure, is not the same as an examination of its principles and assumptions. But it does suggest an awareness that the customary indifference of historians toward theoretical speculation has become risky in an age grown dubious regarding the experience of history.

The most common argument advanced in defense of historical learning has been that it can teach society to make more rational decisions about actions to be taken or policies to be pursued. The contention that there is a certain repetitiveness, a certain parallelism in human experience has often appeared in writings on the nature of history, but it has received special emphasis in works on historical theory and methodology published in the twentieth century. On the eve of the Second World War, for example, Nevins spoke of the didactic or pedagogical value of knowledge about the past. "Mankind is always more or less storm-driven," he declared, "and history is the sextant and compass of states which, tossed by wind and current, would be lost in confusion if they could not fix their position. It enables communities to grasp their relationship with the past, and to chart on general lines their immediate forward course."

A few years later Strayer, after first asserting that the belief in history was instinctive or spontaneous, proceeded to offer very logical and calculated reasons for its study: "As soon as a community substitutes conscious decisions and rational choices for the automatic responses of custom it finds that its memories of the past must be kept distinct and arranged in some sort of order. Every deliberate modification of an existing type of activity must be based on a study of individual precedents. Every plan for the future is dependent on a pattern which has been found in the past." History

2. Philip Rahv, "The Myth and the Powerhouse," *Partisan Review* 20 (1953): 642.

is a guide to life, but too often the indications which it gives are vague, incomplete, or even misleading. "The task of the professional historian is to remedy these defects as far as he can."

Strayer then lapsed briefly into the ineffability of any justification for historical learning: "The value of history, like the existence of free will, cannot be proved—it is simply a basic fact of human experience." But he concluded with a ringing reaffirmation of the practical importance of studying the recorded experience of mankind:

> We all believe that the past explains the present and forecasts the future—not in the crude sense of an absolute duplication of events, but in the sense that there will always be familiar elements in a new situation which will aid us in making decisions and in judging what the results of those decisions will be. The wider and deeper our experience the greater our chances of recognizing these familiar elements, and history, properly written, can increase our stock of experiences many fold. We may go wrong in following the clues which it offers, but we would be lost without them. No one could stand the strain of beginning each day in a new world in which there was no rational basis for any decision and no way of predicting the results of any action. History, even at its worst, gives us the comforting and necessary feeling that the world is stable and intelligible. History at its best gives us a real chance of reacting sensibly to a new situation. It does not guarantee the correctness of our response, but it should improve the quality of our judgment.

The contention that a study of the past can prove useful in the determination of public policy, that it can provide guidance to a nation facing the problems of peacemaking and reconstruction, was heard even more frequently after the Second World War, as the place of history in the system of education and learning began to be questioned. In a paper which he presented in 1947, Garrett Mattingly, author of important works on Catherine of Aragon, the Spanish Armada, and Renaissance diplomacy, maintained that once we recognize that every human situation contains some elements of uniformity as well as of uniqueness, we can begin to examine each new one and to compare it with everything we are able to learn about similar situations in the past. We can try to assign values to constants and to isolate the variables. We can seek to determine what factors are significant, what choices are actually available, and "what the probable consequences are of choosing course A and rejecting B." The suggestion that historical learning could provide a more rational solution to the problems of the postwar era was bound to appeal to an America which had suddenly become the greatest power in the world.

This same argument, though hedged in with provisos and qualifications, was advanced a decade later in a popular primer on historical method by Louis Gottschalk, a prominent scholar on the French Revolution. History, he conceded, was no open sesame to successful statecraft; it was no substitute for native intelligence or sound judgment. But used with discernment, it could prove helpful in the shaping of public policy. On the premise that like consequences were derived from like antecedents, the historian might deduce that comparable circumstances in the future might be followed by comparable consequences. "In less academic circles, such deductions would be called 'the lessons of history.'" The trouble with historical parallels as a means of prognostication, however, was that, although it was reasonably clear that human beings could learn from history, they could not be counted upon either to do so or not to do so. "If they should learn, the chances of their doing the same thing over if it is desirable, or avoiding doing it if it is undesirable, are good. But since they cannot be counted upon, historical analogies present us most often with clues to *possible* rather than *probable* behavior, with the ability only to *anticipate* rather than to *predict*, to *take precautions* rather than to *control*." Gottschalk was too good a scholar to indulge in glib generalizations about what the present might learn from the past or about the reliability of forecasts based on historical evidence. But he did maintain that, combined with practical experience and sound judgment, a knowledge of history could turn out to have considerable utilitarian value.

The most systematic analysis of the predictive capability of historical learning, however, appeared right after the Second World War in a report of the Committee on Historiography of the Social Science Research Council. Composed of several leading historians — Charles A. Beard, Shepard B. Clough, Thomas C. Cochran, Merle Curti, Louis Gottschalk, Jeannette P. Nichols, Richard H. Shryock, and Alfred Vagts — the committee dealt with such problems as the nature of historiography, the controlling assumptions of American historians, and the terminology employed in historical scholarship. Its report concluded with a series of propositions regarding the premises, principles, and limitations of historical knowledge. Here the members sought to determine the extent to which the experience of history could be used for prognostication. They warned that "the so-called 'constants' or 'repetitions' derived from the study of history" — war, tyranny, revolution, dictatorship, or democracy, for example — "are not exact repetitions nor do they afford proof of 'laws' in history." Action based on such an assumption was likely to prove erroneous. Yet antecedents found through a study of the past might be used as "furnishing analogous situations." They were valuable as "serving analytical, comparative and descriptive purposes and as supplying guidance in the search for approximate historical patterns and for future probabilities, a search capable of much social usefulness."

To be sure, the committee cautioned, many important questions of public interest cannot be answered conclusively on the basis of historical knowledge. "Historians true to the scientific spirit will avoid encouraging the pretensions that they can be so answered." But in certain limited cases, by the use of historical knowledge and analogy, "the historian may, in respect of given situations, indicate various contingencies, one or more of which may be anticipated with a high degree of probability." The wording was so careful, so full of caveats and qualifications, that even the fastidious were not likely to object. And yet it left the distinct impression that, used with prudence, intelligence, and perspicacity, history could prove helpful in the solution of political, social, and economic problems.[3]

This increasing frequency of the contention that historical learning has practical value may look a little suspicious. Its reiteration seems to protest too much. It is almost as if, by saying the same thing over and over again, historians were hoping to drown out a growing skepticism about their discipline. Truths which are secure do not require constant repetition. Yet the belief that historical experience has an important prognosticative usefulness is almost as old as history itself. Even in the ancient world there were writers who maintained that what had happened in the past was a key to what would happen in the future. In his account of the Peloponnesian War, Thucydides argued that there was a parallelism in human affairs which historical study could discover and use for the purpose of prediction. "The absence of romance in my history will, I fear, detract somewhat from its interest," he declared in the opening chapter. "But if it be judged useful by those inquirers who desire an exact knowledge of the past as an aid to the interpretation of the future, which in the course of human things must re-

3. A. Nevins, *Gateway to History*, p. 3; J. R. Strayer, "Introduction," pp. 10, 14–15; J. Barzun and H. F. Graff, *Modern Researcher*, p. 151, n. 25; Louis Gottschalk, *Understanding History: A Primer of Historical Method* (New York, 1950), pp. 265–69; "Theory and Practice in Historical Study," *Social Science Research Council Bulletin* 54 (1946): 137, 139.

semble if it does not reflect it, I shall be content." His intention was to instruct rather than please or entertain. "I have written my work, not as an essay which is to win the applause of the moment, but as a possession for all time." Its enduring value would lie in its utility.

Cicero was also convinced that historical study had practical importance. In his treatise on the making of an orator, he suggested that the collective experience of mankind was the only reliable guide to the future. "And as History," he wrote, "which bears witness to the passing of the ages, sheds light upon reality, gives life to recollection and guidance to human existence, and brings tidings of ancient days, whose voice, but the orator's, can entrust her to immortality?" To him, as to other classical writers, it seemed clear that there was a repetitiveness in the fortunes of mankind which could be discovered and used to anticipate coming events. Accordingly, the function of historical learning was to discern the recurrent patterns or configurations in seemingly discrete and unrelated happenings.

The perceived value in the study of history changed during the Middle Ages. To many medieval historians, the past revealed above all the gradual unfolding of the divine plan on earth. Historical learning was important as a testimony to faith rather than as a means of prognostication. It was useful not in the formulation of public policy but in the reinforcement of religious belief. The deeds of monarchs and saints, the favorite theme of pious chroniclers, were taken to reflect in some mysterious way the inscrutable will of God. Only with the revival of secularism in the early modern period did history come to be regarded once again as not only a branch of theology or moral philosophy, but as a useful civic discipline. Languishing in the Tower of London, Sir Walter Raleigh sought consolation in contemplating the past. Historical study can teach us, he declared in the preface to his *History of the World*, "How Kings and Kingdomes have florished and fallen; and for what vertue and piety GOD made prosperous; and for what vice and deformity he made wretched, both the one and the other." So far he was only repeating the accepted medieval view. But then he went on: "History . . . hath made us acquainted with our dead Ancestors; and, out of the depth and darkenesse of the earth, delivered us their memory and fame." Finally, there was the argument advanced by Thucydides and Cicero more than fifteen hundred years before: "Wee may gather out of History a policy no lesse wise than eternall; by the comparison and application of other mens fore-passed miseries, with our owne like errours and ill deservings."

But the full emergence of historical learning as a discipline justified primarily by practical utility did not come until the eighteenth century, the Age of Enlightenment. That was when political thinkers on both sides of the Atlantic, many of them men prominent in public life, began to revive the belief of the ancients that the study of the past was a key to understanding the future. In his *Reflections on the Revolution in France*, Edmund Burke maintained that "in history a great volume is unrolled for our instruction, drawing the materials of future wisdom from the past errors and infirmities of mankind." Those who know how to read it "will stand upon that elevation of reason which places centuries under our eye and brings things to the true point of comparison, which obscures little names and effaces the colors of little parties, and to which nothing can ascend but the spirit and moral quality of human actions." In the future, history, "better understood and better employed, will, I trust, teach a civilized posterity to abhor the misdeeds of . . . these barbarous ages" of the past.

While for Burke historical learning was a weapon in the struggle against revolution, for the founding fathers of the American republic it was a vindication of the right to revolution. As they embarked on their great political experiment, they consulted and invoked it repeatedly. In his famous "liberty or death" speech before the second Virginia Convention in 1775, Patrick Henry emphasized the importance of history. He declared, according to the testimony of his listeners, that "he had but one lamp by which his feet were guided; and that was the lamp of experience. He knew of no way of judging the future but by the past." That past, he declared, had taught him not to trust Great Britain.

In Thomas Jefferson's *Notes on the State of Virginia*, published a decade later, historical learning was important not as a justification of national independence, which had by then been secured, but as the guardian of civil liberty. "History, by apprising [the people] of the past," he felt confident, "will enable them to judge of the future; it will avail them of the experience of other times and other nations; it will qualify them as judges of the actions and designs of men; it will enable them to know ambition under every guise it may assume; and knowing it, to defeat its views." A knowledge of history was the palladium of democracy.

Alexander Hamilton, on the other hand, had doubts about the usefulness of collective experience. He spoke a little disparagingly about "the dim light of historical research," preferring to rely on "the dictates of reason and good sense." And yet when he contended in the seventieth *Federalist* that the establishment of a single executive was not inconsistent with the spirit of republican government, he too relied on the teachings of history. After first declaring that "the experience of other nations will afford little instruction on this head," he proceeded to invoke that experience: "As far however as it teaches any thing, it teaches us not to be inamoured of plurality in the executive." He pointed out that the ancient Achaeans, after experimenting with two praetors, decided to abolish one. Similarly, "the Roman history records many instances of mischiefs to the republic from the dissentions between the consuls, and between the military tribunes, who were at times substituted to the consuls." Even for him history contained useful lessons on how the constitution of a new nation should be framed.

It was during the nineteenth century, however, the golden age of historiography, that historical learning came to be accepted as the most reliable guide to diplomacy and statecraft. At a time when faith in religious dogma and philosophic doctrine was waning, before the social sciences began to offer what appeared to be more precise and dependable solutions, the study of history was regarded as essential for the conduct of public affairs. Not only publicists and scholars, but political leaders turned to it for help. Upon his return to Paris after the disastrous campaign in Russia in 1812, Napoleon declared that the misfortunes of France were the fault of "ideology," of "that gloomy metaphysic" which sought to base legislation on ultimate causes, instead of shaping laws in accordance with "a knowledge of the human heart and the lessons of history." Those who are called to regenerate a state must follow entirely different principles, he told his state councilors. "History portrays the human heart. It is in history that we must look for the advantages and drawbacks of different kinds of legislation. Those are the principles of which the council of state of a great empire should never lose sight."

Some eighty years later another leading statesman spoke of the role of historical experience in the formulation of public policy. Shortly after his dismissal from office, Bismarck declared in a newspaper interview that "for me history was there above all so that we could learn something from it. Even though events do not recur, situations and characters do; by observing and studying them we can stimulate and improve our minds." He had learned from the mistakes of his predecessors in statecraft, formulating his own "theory", although it would be a mistake to speak of one in the strict sense of the word. "For there is no clearly defined science of politics, any more than there is a clearly defined science of national economy. Only pro-

fessors manage to compartmentalize the changing needs of civilized mankind into scientific laws." For the fallen German chancellor, as for the de-
feated French emperor, history embodied not the abstract categories of
political theory but the vital experiences of life itself.[4]

The defenders of historical learning as a guide to state policy have generally admitted that the study of the past does not yield hard-and-fast rules
or foolproof predictions. A knowledge of history can only make it a little
easier to guess right, to assess what the consequences of a particular course
of action are likely to be. Used with intelligence and judgment, supported
by favorable circumstances and good luck, it may prove helpful in making
sound political decisions. But it cannot be applied mechanically or automatically, independent of the personal capacities and talents of those seeking its assistance.

Gaetano Salvemini, well-known in both Europe and America as scholar,
publicist, and politician, maintained that the historian differed from the scientist in precisely this dependence on individual or private insight. All his
reasonings could be reduced to the common denominator of analogy with
our inward experience, whereas the scientist, being concerned with physical
phenomena, lacked the help of such an analogy. "It follows that the broader
the experience of the historian the better he will be able to understand the
past. One who has a wide experience of economic facts will be more successful as an interpreter of the economic life of a thousand years ago than
one who lacks all experience in that field. One who has a wide experience
of military facts will be more successful in studies of military history than
one whose training has been exclusively literary." Hence the practical utility
of historical learning depends on a subjective ability to make use of it.

Strayer provided a homely but graphic illustration of the role which history could be expected to play in political decisions:

A rough parallel may be found in certain card games. There is almost no
chance that one distribution of cards will be repeated in a subsequent deal

---

4. Thucydides, *The Peloponnesian War*, trans. Richard Crawley (New York, 1951), pp. 14–
15; Cicero, *De Oratore*, trans. E. W. Sutton and H. Rackham, (2 vols., London and Cambridge, Mass., 1942–48), I, 225; Walter Ralegh, *The History of the World*, ed. C. A. Patrides
(Philadelphia, 1971), p. 48; *The Works of the Right Honorable Edmund Burke*, 4th ed. (12
vols., Boston, 1871), III, 418, 421; William Wirt Henry, *Patrick Henry: Life, Correspondence
and Speeches* (3 vols., New York, 1891), I, 262; *Basic Writings of Thomas Jefferson*, ed. Philip S.
Foner (Garden City, N.Y., 1944), p. 151; *The Federalist*, ed. Jacob E. Cooke (Cleveland and
New York, 1961), pp. 473–74; *Le Moniteur universel*, December 21, 1812, p. 1408; Otto von
Bismarck, *Die gesammelten Werke* (15 vols., Berlin, 1924–35), IX, 90.

in bridge. Yet a man who has played several thousand hands of bridge should be able to make intelligent decisions and predictions even though every deal presents a new situation. He should be able to use his high cards and long suits effectively; he should be able to make some shrewd guesses about the location of cards in other hands. Not every experienced player will develop these skills. Some men are unable to generalize from their past experience, and others cannot see analogies between the present and the past. But, generally speaking, the experienced player will make better use of his cards than the man who has played only ten hands. There is such a thing as card sense, developed from long experience. There is also such a thing as a sense of the realities and possibilities of social activity, which can be developed from a study of the proper sort of history.

It is in acquiring, or seeking to acquire, this sense of social realities that the historian ceases to be a scientist and becomes an artist.

But the most systematic attempt to analyze the subjective qualities which the historian must possess in order to gain a true insight into the past appeared in an article on the theory of history by Isaiah Berlin. The kind of knowledge which the student of history seeks, he wrote, is neither deductive, nor inductive, nor founded on direct inspection. It is neither the "knowing that" which is provided by the natural sciences, nor the "knowing how" which is the result of a disposition or skill, nor the knowledge derived from direct perception, acquaintance, or memory. It is rather the knowledge which an administrator or a politician must have regarding the people with whom he deals. "If the historian is endowed with this too poorly, if he can fall back only on inductive techniques, then, however accurate his discoveries of fact, they remain those of an antiquarian, a chronicler, at best an archeologist, but not those of an historian."

Some light might be cast on this point, Berlin suggested, by comparing the historical method with the method of linguistic or literary scholarship. A scholar cannot emend a text without a capacity, which no technique is able to impart, for "entering into the mind" of another society and age. Electronic brains are unable to perform this task. They may offer alternative combinations of letters, but they cannot choose between them successfully. How then do gifted scholars actually arrive at their emendations?

> They do all that the most exacting natural science would demand; they steep themselves in the material of their authors; they compare, contrast, manipulate combinations like the most accomplished cypher breakers, they may find it useful to apply statistical and quantitative methods, they formulate hypotheses and test them; all this may be indispensable but it is not enough.

In the end what guides them is a sense of what a given author could, and what he could not, have said; of what fits and what does not fit, into the general pattern of his thought. This, let me say again, is not the way in which we demonstrate that penicillin cures pneumonia.

The successful application of historical experience to the problems of state and society depends accordingly on individual discernment and perceptiveness, on an almost intuitive sense of the feasible or probable on the part of those seeking to understand the past.[5]

In the heyday of scientific methodology and positivistic philosophy, however, the concept of history as a useful though inexact discipline began to seem inadequate to many scholars. Why should not historical evidence be analyzed with the same precise, rigorous techniques as the data of physics, chemistry, or biology? Why should it not yield results equally exact and conclusive? Why should it not reveal to the historian the same repetitiveness of patterns and configurations which the scientist finds in his data? And why should it not enable him to formulate laws and make predictions which are just as valid? What these scholars sought was a history independent of the historian, beyond the reach of subjective explication, a history which did not have to be created or interpreted but simply discovered. Here was a concept of historical study in which the task of the scholar was merely to find the facts, examine them, arrange them in their proper chronological or topical order, and let the results speak for themselves. Such a history, they believed, would be more than the handmaid of statecraft, suggesting solutions to political or social questions on the basis of past experience. It would be a beacon of light in the darkness which surrounds mankind, imparting the confidence and courage which only systematic, organized knowledge can inspire.

Among the pioneers of this positivistic or scientific history was the French scholar Numa Denis Fustel de Coulanges, author of important books on *The Ancient City* and *The Political Institutions of Early France*. According to his obituarist Gabriel Monod, founder of the *Revue historique* and a distinguished historian in his own right, he firmly believed that history was "a positive science," able to guide those who study the texts conscientiously

---

5. Gaetano Salvemini, *Historian and Scientist: An Essay on the Nature of History and the Social Sciences*, (Cambridge, Mass., 1939), p. 71; J. R. Strayer, "Introduction," p. 15; I. Berlin, "History and Theory," p. 27.

and critically to "a truly scientific certainty." Although "a great artist and a great writer," Fustel had rejected all praise of his talent or style, almost as if perceiving in it a malicious intent. "He had . . . such a deep conviction of the reliability of his method and his research that the conclusions he reached no longer seemed to him personal opinions subject to error and open to discussion, but absolute truths, independent of him, for which he merely acted as interpreter and servant." He regarded criticism as an attack on his convictions, as blasphemy against what he believed to be the truth. Hence the mixture of modesty regarding his person and pride regarding his ideas. "Do not applaud me," Monod quoted him as saying one day to his students. "It is not I who am speaking to you; it is history which is speaking through my mouth."

The high tide of positivism and scientism in historical learning, based on the assumption that nature and history were essentially similar in structure, came in the early decades of the twentieth century. The great achievements of the natural sciences had encouraged the belief that their methods and principles could be applied with equal effectiveness to other fields of learning. Not only did they hasten the emergence of the social sciences as independent disciplines, but they fostered the hope that a rigorous, exact, scientific form of history would soon prove attainable.

Albert J. Beveridge was only one of many scholars whose work reflected this confident expectation. A prominent American politician who had embraced the doctrines of imperialism and Progressivism with equal zeal, he belonged to that now vanished breed of amateur historians successfully combining a career in public life with a keen interest in learning. To him historical scholarship was a vast jigsaw puzzle made up of countless little pieces, some of them hidden in obscure or out-of-the-way places. The primary task of the scholar was to find the scattered fragments and fit them together in their natural pattern, for once that had been done, the picture as a whole would immediately become recognizable.

This was the reason for Beveridge's tireless search for facts and details, for all the particulars, however minute. He conducted his own investigations, recalled the editor of his Lincoln biography, questioning what had been published by other authors and trusting no assistant without verifying his work. He sifted the many traditions which had grown up around the martyred president; he tried to determine for himself to what extent the physical environment had shaped the man. He was inexhaustible in reading collections of unpublished documents and going through files of old newspapers. "A little fact is as important as what is called a big fact," he declared. "The picture may be well-nigh finished, but it remains vague for want of one more fact. When that missing fact is discovered all others become clear and distinct; it is like turning a light, properly shaded, upon a painting which but a moment before was a blur in the dimness." His basic conviction regarding the nature of historical research was similar to that which Fustel had expressed to his students. "Facts when justly arranged interpret themselves. They tell the story."

If the most important task of the scholar is to gather data, however, if the facts do indeed tell the story, then it follows that the highest form of history is the most comprehensive. For the greater the volume of evidence, the greater the trustworthiness of the narrative and the soundness of the conclusion. This was in part at least the reasoning behind the plan for a great collective history of the world which appeared in Great Britain in the decade before the First World War under the title *The Cambridge Modern History*. The distinguished historian Lord Acton, who initiated the project, described its underlying purpose in a report to the syndics of the Cambridge University Press in 1896: "It is a unique opportunity of recording, in the way most useful to the greatest number, the fullness of the knowledge which the nineteenth century is about to bequeath." The venture would prove not only feasible but highly beneficial, he predicted. "By the judicious division of labour, we should be able to do it, and to bring home to every man the last document, and the ripest conclusions of international research." The work would represent a major step toward a true historical science. "Ultimate history we cannot have in this generation; but we can dispose of conventional history, and show the point we have reached on the road from one to the other, now that all information is within reach, and every problem has become capable of solution." Almost a century later this faith in the attainability of certitude in historical learning seems artless and yet appealing.

The boldest champion of scientific historiography, however, was John Bagnell Bury, whose field was the ancient and medieval world, although he also ventured from time to time into less conventional areas of scholarship. He wrote about freedom of thought, for example, and about the idea of progress. But nothing he published attracted more attention or aroused greater controversy than his inaugural lecture on "The Science of History," given in 1903 at Cambridge University on the occasion of his appointment as regius professor of modern history.

He opened by reminding his listeners how recently it was, within only three short generations, that "history began to forsake her old irresponsible ways and prepared to enter into her kingdom." In any account of the nineteenth century, which had witnessed so many far-reaching changes "in the geography of thought and in the apparatus of research," the transformation and expansion of history would occupy an important place. "That transformation, however, is not yet universally or unreservedly acknowledged. It is rejected in many places, or ignored, or unrealised." Therefore it had not yet become superfluous to insist that "history is a science, no less and no more." Those who were beginning their historical studies should realize that the alteration which those studies were undergoing was a great event in the history of mankind. "We are ourselves in the very middle of it; . . . we are witnessing and may share in the accomplishment of a change which will have a vast influence on future cycles of the world." History had been enthroned at last among the sciences, and yet "the particular nature of her influence, her time-honoured association with literature, and other circumstances have acted as a sort of vague cloud, half concealing from men's eyes her new position in the heavens."

By becoming more scientific, Bury continued, history would become more reliable and useful, for as long as it was regarded as only an art, the "sanctions of truth and accuracy" could not be very severe. The historians of ancient Rome had shown what historiography was likely to become when associated with rhetoric. There might have been individual scholars in various ages who had a high standard of accuracy, but "it was not till the scientific period began that laxity in representing facts came to be branded criminal." Even at the present time, in a period of rapid scientific advance, it was necessary to remind the world of learning that history was not merely a branch of literature. "The facts of history, like the facts of geology or astronomy, can supply material for literary art; for manifest reasons they lend themselves to artistic representation far more readily than those of the natural sciences; but to clothe the story of human society in literary dress is no more the part of a historian as a historian, than it is the part of an astronomer to present in an artistic shape the story of the stars."

Bury concluded by asserting that just as the student of science whose mental attitude has been determined by a large grasp of cosmic problems will have the best prospect of becoming a successful researcher of nature's secrets, so the student of history should learn to view the human story *sub specie perennitatis:*

If, year by year, history is to become a more and more powerful force for stripping the bandages of error from the eyes of men, for shaping public opinion and advancing the cause of intellectual and political liberty, she will best prepare her disciples for the performance of that task, not by considering the immediate utility of next week or next year or next century, not by accommodating her ideal or limiting her range, but by remembering always that, though she may supply material for literary art or philosophical speculation, she is herself simply a science, no less and no more.

For Bury there was no doubt that the same principles and procedures which had uncovered the laws of matter, energy, and space would also uncover the laws of historical experience.[6]

The rise of scientism in historiography exerted a profound influence on the development of the discipline. It led directly to the emergence of the new history after the Second World War, with its emphasis on the measurable, quantifiable, classifiable, and comparable. Cliometrics and social-science history, even psychohistory, reflected to a large extent the positivistic faith that historical learning must become more scientific and less literary or artistic, if it is to realize its predictive capabilities. But the conviction of an Acton or a Bury that history is or can become a science was even more apparent in the work of the great historical system builders of the twentieth century — writers like Oswald Spengler, Pitirim A. Sorokin, and Arnold J. Toynbee — who claimed to have found the fundamental laws of growth and decay in human society. Many of them were not professional historians; they were not inhibited by the caution and sense of fallibility which a lifelong preoccupation with historical data often engenders. But they were profoundly influenced by the vision of a new scientific history in which a study of basic patterns or processes would lead to valid generalizations about the nature of mankind's development. The laws of change in society which they thought they discovered derived variously from the life cycle of living organisms, or from a perceived oscillation between idealistic and materialistic collective values, or from the challenge of a physical environment and the community's response to it. They all shared the belief,

6. G. Monod, "M. Fustel de Coulanges," *Revue historique* 41 (1889): 278; Albert J. Beveridge, *Abraham Lincoln, 1809-1858* (2 vols., Boston and New York, 1928), I, v; Lord Acton, *Longitude 30 West: A Confidential Report to the Syndics of the Cambridge University Press* (New York, 1969), pp. 4, 8; *Selected Essays of J. B. Bury,* ed. Harold Temperley (Cambridge, 1930), pp. 3–7, 9, 22.

however, that since there is regularity or repetitiveness in human affairs, history is "simply a science, no less and no more."

Yet from its beginning the argument in support of scientific historiography encountered more critics than defenders. They maintained generally that there was a fundamental distinction between inanimate nature and living society, that human beings behave in ways which are inherently different from particles of matter. To study them both by the same methodology is bound to destroy the sensitivity and imaginativeness which are essential for an understanding of social experience. Hence the transformation of history into a science would not enrich but impoverish historical learning; it would not broaden but narrow historical vision. It must be resisted.

Indeed, within a year after Bury had given his inaugural lecture on the science of history, a young Cambridge don published a vigorous rebuttal of the new regius professor's views. George Macaulay Trevelyan was only in his twenties, still an unknown, just beginning a brilliant career which would culminate in his appointment to the same chair which Bury had occupied. But he was already prepared to assume the role of defender of the literary tradition in historiography. Who had a better right to it than a grand-nephew of the great Macaulay? He conceded that "the present writer . . . has produced no work which he can call either literary or scientific," yet he did not hesitate to express his firm belief in "a few of the many proper functions of history which Professor Bury hopes to see suppressed." The question was not whether history was a science as well as an art, "for that has been long decided in the affirmative," but whether history was an art as well as a science. "If Professor Bury has his way that will be decided in the negative." Yet both approaches to historical learning, the artistic no less than the scientific, were necessary for the full development of the discipline. "It is not a question of recognition for the collectors of facts, which in our country was never denied to them; but of toleration for those who wish to apply the art of literature to the comment on the facts collected."

The function of the historian was to study the past not merely in order to find patterns and repetitions, but to protect cultural values against the materialism of an acquisitive society. "History keeps alive the spirit of rest and beauty, so alien from the spirit of our age," Trevelyan maintained. "Our industrial civilisation has been half redeemed from the uniformity of its outward appearance, at once so vast and squalid, by new knowledge and repentant love of that past upon which it has laid such violent hands, and which, externally at least, it has not mended but marred. The man who carries some history in his heart, has a constant resource against the worry of *ennui,* and an ever-present antidote to visions of ugliness." The threat of scientism to historical learning was especially acute now. "History is still young. In a few thousand years it may have developed into a study and art, embracing a thousand schools of thought, feeling and opinion, as multiform as the human mind." But the twentieth century would prove a period of grave peril to its natural development. "For in our age, when the emotional and spiritual qualities of the race are everywhere yielding before scientific method and materialistic commercialism, it will be an added danger to the course of civilisation, if we allow the common ground of history to be enclosed as the preserve of science." Historiography, like literature, music, and art, was a guardian of the cultural values of society against materialism.

Most critics of the scientific approach to history, however, based their opposition on logical or philosophical rather than esthetic grounds. They argued that the differences between the processes of nature and the experiences of society were too great to be overcome or reconciled. To Carl Becker, the scientific historian was a technician who presented the bare facts without injecting into them any extraneous meaning. He was the "objective man" whom Nietzsche had once described as "a mirror: accustomed to prostration before something that wants to be known." He deliberately renounced philosophy only to submit to it without awareness that he was doing so. His philosophy appeared to be that by not taking thought a cubit would be added to his stature. He believed, according to Becker, that, with no preconception other than the will to know, a historian could capture in his work the "order of events throughout past times in all places," so that eventually, in the fullness of time, after countless expert scholars, by "exhausting the sources," had reflected without refracting the truth of all the facts, the ultimate and definitive meaning of human experience would emerge of its own accord to enlighten and liberate mankind. "Hoping to find something without looking for it, expecting to obtain final answers to life's riddle by resolutely refusing to ask questions — it was surely the most romantic species of realism yet invented, the oddest attempt ever made to get something for nothing!" The very concept of such a scientific history was absurd.

Isaiah Berlin's analysis of the problem was not as trenchant or eloquent, but it was even more compelling. The talents which historians need, he maintained, are basically different from those required of natural scientists. The latter have to be able to "abstract, generalize, idealize, quantify, dissociate normally associated ideas (for nature is full of strange surprises, and as little as possible must be taken for granted), deduce, establish with certainty, reduce everything to the maximum degree of regularity, uniformity, and, so far as possible, to timeless repetitive patterns." Historians, to be sure, also have to possess a considerable capacity for thinking in general terms in order to practice their craft. But in addition they need special attributes of their own: "a capacity for integration, for perceiving qualitative similarities and differences, a sense of the unique fashion in which various factors combine in the particular concrete situation, which must at once be neither so unlike any other situation as to constitute a total break with the continuous flow of human experience, [nor] yet so stylized and uniform as to be the obvious creature of theory and not of flesh and blood."

That was why sound judgment of the sort useful in everyday life was more important to the student of history than to the student of science. "A man who lacks common intelligence can be a physicist of genius, but not even a mediocre historian." The essential characteristics of the historian were more closely related to those needed in "active human intercourse" than in "the study or the laboratory or the cloister." What gave concreteness and plausibility to historical accounts, what gave them the breath of life, was the capacity for associating the fruits of experience in a way which enabled its possessor to distinguish, without the benefit of rules, what was central, permanent, or universal from what was local, peripheral, or transient.

In Berlin's opinion, the ability to verify facts by means of observation, memory, or inductive procedure, though admittedly indispensable for the discovery of all truth about the world, is not the rarest quality required by a historian, nor is the desire to find recurrences and laws a mark of historical talent. Rather, if we were to ask ourselves which historians have commanded the most lasting admiration, we would find that they were neither the most ingenious nor the most precise nor even the most successful in discovering new facts or causal connections, but "those who (like imaginative writers) present men or societies or situations in many dimensions, at many intersecting levels simultaneously, writers in whose accounts human lives, and their relations both to each other and to the external world, are what (at our most lucid and imaginative) we know that they can be." The talents which scientists need, on the other hand, are altogether different. They have to be prepared to question everything, to formulate bold hypotheses unrelated to empirical procedures, and to push their logical implications as far as they will go, free from control by common sense or by ordinary fear of departing from what is normal or possible in the world. For the discovery of new truths, and of the relations between those truths, in disciplines such as physics or mathematics does not depend on the peculiarities of human nature and its activity. "In this sense, to say of history that it should approximate to the condition of a science is to ask it to contradict its essence." The behavior of matter and the experience of mankind are too different, too disparate to be studied by the same methodology.[7]

The belief in historical scientism, in the ability of history to discover laws and make predictions comparable in reliability to those in the natural sciences, reached its peak around the beginning of the twentieth century and continued to flourish for the next three or four decades. Since the Second World War, however, it has been abandoned by almost all historians. There is agreement now that while the collection and examination of historical data should be conducted in accordance with the methodology of science, generalizations based on that data represent probabilities or approximations rather than certainties. Even the cliometricians, social-science historians, and psychohistorians lay claim to scientific procedure, not to scientific knowledge. History appears at present to be a science in technique but an art in interpretation, objective in analysis, subjective in perception, logical or systematic in structure, but intuitive or imaginative in outlook.

In the view of the philosopher Morton White, however, the indeterminate position of historical knowledge between the humanities and the sciences need not be a source of weakness. There is no basic incompatibility between its diverse elements. "The complexity and variety of narrative," he wrote in 1965, "the fact that one story seems so different in structure from another, may give both the romantically minded historian and the classically minded logician pause." Yet although human beings also exhibit vast differences, that does not prevent us from X-raying them in an attempt to see the skeletal structure which each of them possesses. If a roentgenologist, upon discovering this structure, were to reach the absurd conclusion that people are nothing but skeletons, we would naturally regard him as mad. Similarly, if a logician of narrative, upon discovering its structure, concluded that narratives are nothing but logical conjunctions of certain kinds of statements, we would regard him also as mad. The point is that

7. G. M. Trevelyan, "The Latest View of History," *Independent Review* 1 (1903- 4): 396, 407, 413; C. Becker, "Everyman His Own Historian," pp. 232–33; I. Berlin, "History and Theory," pp. 30–31.

the objective and the subjective elements in our perception of the past are not mutually exclusive, though sometimes they may appear so. "History is literary art as well as a discipline aimed at discovering and ordering truth, and if we neglect some of the narrative's literary qualities in order to clarify certain epistemological problems connected with it, our procedure is like that of the sane roentgenologist, who searches for the skull without denying that the skin exists and without denying that the skin may vary enormously in color, texture, and beauty." Science and art intermingle in the study of history, their combination giving the discipline its unique character.

This position is not really very different from that which Trevelyan had taken sixty years before. It seeks to reconcile the artistic and the scientific aspects of historical learning, the objective process of research with the subjective process of interpretation. It concedes by implication the impossibility of achieving certainty or predictability through a systematic study of the past. History is now generally perceived as a heuristic rather than scientific discipline, offering precedents, choices, and probabilities rather than reliable forecasts. It may complement native intelligence and practical judgment with the wisdom of experience, but it cannot yield scientific laws, universal formulas, or positive predictions. It is no substitute for such personal qualities as leadership, insight, imaginativeness, and sensitivity. It offers no protection against collective calamities like wars, depressions, epidemics, and famines. It can only help make the vital decisions which society faces a little less risky.[8]

Even this modest assessment of the usefulness of historical learning is more than some writers are prepared to concede. There have always been those who maintain that history cannot provide any guidance in the conduct of human affairs. The evidence on which it rests is incomplete and contradictory; the situation confronting each succeeding generation is unprecedented and incomparable; the capacity of the historian to interpret the materials he studies is limited and inadequate. To rely on history is to trust in the staff of a broken reed.

Even during the Age of Enlightenment, while Burke was describing historical knowledge as a great volume unrolled for our instruction, while Jefferson was predicting that it would enable the people to judge the future, Voltaire insisted that it was only a hodgepodge of rumors, guesses, distor-

8. Morton White, *Foundations of Historical Knowledge* (New York and London, 1965), pp. 220–21.

tions, and downright falsehoods. Why should anyone trust such an unreliable guide? Though the author of a number of important historical works, he remained as skeptical toward the conventional truths of history as toward those of religion or philosophy. In the *Fragment on General History*, describing what he had been able to learn about the struggle between Christianity and Mohammedanism in the eighth century, he complained that "it was a grand spectacle but a laborious piece of research. I had to squeeze five hundred pounds of lies in order to extract one ounce of truth. The multitude of old chroniclers who wrote only to deceived us is appalling."

The evidence for what had happened in the more recent past was equally untrustworthy. In *The Pyrrhonism of History*, in a chapter entitled "Mistakes and Doubts," Voltaire maintained that even our knowledge of the seventeenth century was bound to be faulty and incomplete. "All the great events of this globe," he sighed, "are like this globe itself, half of which is seen in broad daylight, while the other half is immersed in darkness." And a few months before his death, in a letter to Frederick the Great of Prussia, he repeated the view that historiography was little more than storytelling and rumormongering: "As for history, it is, after all, only gossip. Even the truest is full of falsehoods, and the only merit it can have is that of style." Behind the casual disparagement was a profound doubt whether human understanding is ever capable of solving the riddles and mysteries of historical experience.

According to Voltaire, then, the past cannot guide the present because we do not know enough about it. According to Hegel, on the other hand, even if we knew enough, that would not really matter, because the past is fundamentally different from the present. Each period is unique; each has its special problems; each faces particular needs. Hence to rely on the experience of one generation in dealing with the issues challenging another is futile. Hegel was emphatic on this point in his *Lectures on the Philosophy of History:*

> Even though we agree that examples of virtue elevate the spirit, and would be applicable in the moral instruction of children for impressing excellence on their minds, yet the destinies of peoples and states as well as their interests, conditions, and problems are a different matter. We refer rulers, statesmen, and nations for instruction to the experience of history above all else. But what experience and history teach is that nations and governments have never learned anything from history, and have never acted on the teachings which might have been derived from it. Each period confronts such special circum-

stances, it represents such a unique situation, that within that situation decisions must be and can be determined solely by its particular nature. Amid the pressure of world events, neither a general principle nor the remembrance of similar circumstances is of any help, for something like pale recollection has no power against the vitality and freedom of the present. In this regard, nothing is more insipid than the frequently recurring invocation of Greek and Roman examples, which occurred so often among the French during the period of the revolution. Nothing is more unlike than the nature of those nations and the nature of our own times.

History, in short, may teach moral lessons and illustrate spiritual truths, but it is too fragmented, too incoherent to guide civic conduct or public policy.

A generation later John Lothrop Motley expressed still deeper pessimism in his lecture on "Historic Progress and American Democracy." For him there was no such thing as human history, because an accurate, comprehensive account of the development of mankind had never been written and, indeed, could never be written. Even if it had been written, our mind would be unable to grasp its significance. This was a sad but unalterable truth. All we can ever see is a page or two torn from "the great book of human fate," fluttering in the stormy wind which is always sweeping across the world. We may try to make out their meaning with our feeble vision; we may try to learn their secret as we drift ever closer to the abyss. "But it is all confused babble, hieroglyphics of which the key is lost." History is by its nature bound to remain incomprehensible.[9]

These theoretical doubts regarding the utility of historical knowledge were intensified during the twentieth century by new and bewildering experiences: total wars, world depressions, social revolutions, and armaments races. The present began to seem so different, so unprecedented that the past could offer little guidance for dealing with its complexities. Social science now appeared more useful than historical experience as an instrument of public policy. Some writers therefore sought to bolster the traditional argument that history had a predictive value with the further contention that it performed an essential psychological function. What mattered more than its objective accuracy was its ability to create a network of emotional connections between past and present by which the individual could be made to

---

9. *Oeuvres complètes de Voltaire* (52 vols., Paris, 1877–85), XXVII, 297; XXIX, 236; L, 339; Georg Wilhelm Friedrich Hegel, *Sämtliche Werke*, ed. Herman Glockner (26 vols. Stuttgart, 1949–59), XI, 31; J. L. Motley, *Historic Progress*, p. 3.

feel part of an organic community. It helped establish a pattern of beliefs, ideals, loyalties, and aspirations capable of transforming a random aggregation of human beings into a coherent society. Thus the historian was not a scientist seeking to discover external truths independent of inner consciousness, but a priest or bard creating socially necessary myths whose importance was not contingent on the exactness with which they reflected factual reality. The true significance of what he said about the past had to be measured by its implications for the present. In this sense, all history, regardless of the period with which it dealt, was contemporary history.

As early as the 1860s, after historiography had already begun to move in the direction of scientism, James Anthony Froude, the author of a well-known work on Tudor England, expressed a surprisingly relativistic view of historical knowledge. "It often seems to me as if History was like a child's box of letters, with which we can spell any word we please," he admitted. "We have only to pick out such letters as we want, arrange them as we like, and say nothing about those which do not suit our purpose."

Thus the historian, according to Froude, could make his discipline teach whatever lessons he wanted it to teach: "You may have your Hegel's philosophy of history, or you may have your Schlegel's philosophy of history; you may prove from history that the world is governed in detail by a special Providence; you may prove that there is no sign of any moral agent in the universe except man; you may believe, if you like it, in the old theory of the wisdom of antiquity." You may talk, as was common in the fifteenth century, about "our fathers, who had more wit and wisdom than we," or you may talk about "our barbarian ancestors," whose wars were merely the scuffling of kites and crows. "You may maintain that the evolution of humanity has been an unbroken progress towards perfection; you may maintain that there has been no progress at all, and that man remains the same poor creature he was." You may even agree with Rousseau that people were purest and best in primeval simplicity. "In all or any of these views, history will stand your friend. History, in its passive irony, will make no objection." For historical learning was no oracle revealing the purpose of the gods, but a ventriloquist's dummy appearing to express ideas of its own, while in fact only mouthing someone else's words.

Such skepticism remained rare as long as there was hope that history could provide direction to social action. But seventy years later, after the experience of a world war and the great depression had undermined faith in a scientific historiography, assertions of its relativity became more frequent and overt. They generally emphasized the emotional or inspirational importance of a subjectively determined interpretation of the past. Their inescapable corollary, however, was that the main function of history was not to discover factual truths, but to provide the community with shared beliefs and collective myths.

Nevins, for example, writing "in defence of history," first mentioned its usefulness as the guide to an unknown future. Since mankind is always "storm-driven," beset by doubts and dangers, he declared, it must look to historical experience for some sense of direction, for some landmark in determining which road to follow. Only with its help can states arrive at reasonable decisions. Having studied what happened in the past, they are in a better position "to chart on general lines their immediate forward course." But then Nevins shifted to the mythmaking function of historical learning, to its sacerdotal or thaumaturgical qualities: "By giving peoples a sense of continuity in all their efforts, and by chronicling immortal worth, it confers upon them both a consciousness of their unity, and a feeling of the importance of human achievement." History is more than a guide to nations, he maintained. It is their creator and inspirer. "Without [history] this world, a brilliant arena of human action canopied by fretted fire, would indeed become stale, flat, and unprofitable, a congregation of pestilent vapors." The role of the historian is thus closer to that of tribal prophet or religious teacher than of scholar or scientist.

Strayer was more cautious in affirming the subjectivity of historical knowledge, but what he had to say was by implication just as relativistic: "We are ruled by precedents fully as much as by laws, which is to say that we are ruled by collective memory of the past. It is the memory of common experiences which makes individuals into a community, just as it is the memory of his own experiences which makes a child into a man." This was essentially the same point Nevins had made.

The remembrance of a common past did not always reach the level of history, Strayer conceded, because primitive peoples had little sense of chronology and were likely to reduce all their collective experiences to a timeless brew of custom. "But as soon as a community substitutes conscious decisions and rational choices for the automatic responses of custom it finds that its memories of the past must be kept distinct and arranged in some sort of order. Every deliberate modification of an existing type of activity must be based on a study of individual precedents. Every plan for the future is dependent on a pattern which has been found in the past." Since history constituted a vital part of civilized human existence, it was futile to debate whether we should or should not devote attention to it. Yet though it was undeniably a guide to life, "too often the indications which it gives are vague, incomplete, or actually misleading." Accordingly, "the task of the historian is to remedy these defects as far as he can." Strayer's argument rested on a combination of the advisory and inspirational functions of history. The past instructs the present, he seemed to say, but the present shapes the past.

The frankest and boldest avowal of the relativity of historical knowledge, however, came from Becker, who made an enduring contribution to the debate concerning the nature of our knowledge about the past in his presidential address to the American Historical Association in 1931. Here he argued that the scholar must adapt his learning to the needs and interests of "Mr. Everyman," the broad general public, whose support is essential for the continuing vitality of historiography:

> The history that lies inert in unread books does no work in the world. The history that does work in the world, the history that influences the course of history, is living history, that pattern of remembered events, whether true or false, that enlarges and enriches the collective specious present, the specious present of Mr. Everyman. It is for this reason that the history of history is a record of the "new history" that in every age rises to confound and supplant the old. It should be a relief to us to renounce omniscience, to recognize that every generation, our own included, will, must inevitably play on the dead whatever tricks it finds necessary for its own peace of mind. The appropriate trick for any age is not a malicious invention designed to take anyone in, but an unconscious and necessary effort on the part of 'society' to understand what it is doing in the light of what it has done and what it hopes to do. We, historians by profession, share in this necessary effort. But we do not impose our version of the human story on Mr. Everyman; in the end it is rather Mr. Everyman who imposes his version on us — compelling us, in an age of political revolution, to see that history is past politics, in an age of social stress and conflict to search for the economic interpretation. If we remain too long recalcitrant Mr. Everyman will ignore us, shelving our recondite works behind glass doors rarely opened. Our proper function is not to repeat the past but to make use of it, to correct and rationalize for common use Mr. Everyman's mythological adaptation of what actually happened. We are surely under bond to be as honest and as intelligent as human frailty permits; but the secret of our success in the long run is in conforming to the temper of Mr. Everyman, which we seem to guide only because we are so sure, eventually, to follow it.

Becker's defense of relativism in historical knowledge was in no way incompatible with scientism in historical methodology. It conceded that the historian should gather his data with patience and discrimination, that he should carefully weigh its validity and reliability, that he should analyze it statistically, comparatively, social-scientifically, psychohistorically, or by any other appropriate scholarly technique. But he should also realize that the recognition his work receives depends primarily not on its objective conformity to past realities, but on its subjective significance for present realities. The great and influential historians, the masters of the craft—Macaulay celebrating the triumph of true religion and parliamentary government in England in the Glorious Revolution; Michelet idealizing the common people as the bearers of the national destiny of France; Treitschke glorifying the historic mission of the Hohenzollerns to achieve the unification of Germany; Pokrovsky showing how property relations and class conflicts determined the structure of Russian society; Beard examining the economic and social forces behind the rise of American civilizations—all achieved their importance by weaving disparate historical materials into a pattern which had meaning for contemporary society. The accounts they wrote of what had happened in an earlier time were not only logically consistent with the ascertainable facts; they made the accepted values, customs, beliefs, and institutions of the present time seem more coherent and intelligible. They combined the scientist's rigor with the artist's vision, the scholar's judgment with the prophet's passion. They explained to the eager multitude the meaning of the Delphic oracle.[10]

This conception of the historian's role had the advantage of placing him beyond the reach of mounting doubts about the predictive value of historical knowledge. For now it did not really matter whether history was an art or a science, whether it was subject to law or chance, whether it could prognosticate or merely guess. What mattered was that it satisfied a profound emotional, psychological, and social need, regardless of its factual accuracy. But while the relativistic position protected the historian against some forms of criticism, it left him exposed to others. It deprived him of the claim to enduring truth, to objective validity, to the portrayal of historic experience *wie es eigentlich gewesen*. It implied the successive or even simultane-

10. James Anthony Froude, *Short Studies on Great Subjects* (New York, 1868), pp. 7, 22; A. Nevins, *Gateway to History*, p. 3; J. R. Strayer, "Introduction," pp. 9–10; C. Becker, "Everyman His Own Historian," pp. 234–35.

ous existence of several different kinds of history, each appropriate to a distinct society and ideology — liberal, democratic, socialist, communist, conservative, authoritarian, or fascist — all of them equally useful. If, as Becker put it, every generation "must inevitably play on the dead whatever tricks it finds necessary for its own peace of mind," then it followed that histories written from opposing political perspectives or social viewpoints could not be described as better or worse, only different. For they all used the same raw materials to weave their fabric of epics, legends, pieties, and myths custom-made for a particular nation, class, community, or culture.

Such an uncompromising avowal of subjectivism in historiography, however, was more than most historians were prepared to accept. They continued to cling to the belief in a form of historical learning which could be objectively true, which could remain immune to changing times and circumstances. They conceded that history must meet the needs of Mr. Everyman, but they insisted that it must reflect an enduring, independent reality as well. Only a Becker was bold enough to embrace all the implications of his defiant, unbending relativism.

That is why the inspirational argument for historical learning has always remained overshadowed by the pedagogical argument. Both emerged at about the same time in response to the same skepticism about the value of history. But whereas the inspirational argument maintained that a knowledge of the past was essential for the development of collective civic consciousness, the pedagogical argument asserted that it was important for the achievement of individual self-fulfillment. This new conception of the function of historical learning was part of a general redefinition of the role and purpose of higher education. Until the time of the industrial revolution, the accepted view had been that the function of colleges and universities should be practical: to prepare students, usually of middle-class background, for one of the learned professions such as law, administration, medicine, or the ministry. Members of the patriciate, on the other hand, men destined to occupy the leading positions in state and society, were not expected to go through a period of formal, institutionalized study. They generally received their training at court, in the diplomatic service, in the armed forces, or on the family estate.

That changed, beginning in the late eighteenth century, as a new ideal of higher education emerged. The main purpose of learning, it was now argued, should not be to train men for an occupation, but to teach them to become better human beings. The gentleman-scholar replaced the skilled professional as the epitome of what a university ought to produce. In a society undergoing economic rationalization, in which wealth and leisure were rapidly spreading, the aristocratic standard of education and conduct was challenged by the more sober and moralistic outlook of the middle class. Learning came to be seen as a means of self-fulfillment and self-perfection rather than as an instrument of professional competence or effective statecraft. The ultimate objective of education became not action but wisdom, not success but culture and virtue.

The highest expression of this new view appeared in the 1850s in a series of lectures by Cardinal Newman on the idea of a university. "It is more correct, as well as more usual, to speak of a University as a place of education, than of instruction," he declared, "though, when knowledge is concerned, instruction would at first sight have seemed the more appropriate word." Instruction was what we received in manual exercises, in the useful arts, in the trades, and in the various ways of doing business. It consisted of imparting methods and techniques which had little effect on the mind, which were contained in rules committed to memory, tradition, or use, and which sought to attain an external goal. "But education is a higher word; it implies an action upon our mental nature, and the formation of a character; it is something individual and permanent, and is commonly spoken of in connection with religion and virtue." Thus when we described the communication of knowledge as being education, we implied that knowledge was a state or condition of mind. Since cultivation of the mind was worth seeking for its own sake, however, we were brought to the conclusion which such words as "liberal" and "philosophy" suggested. "There is a Knowledge, which is desirable, though nothing come of it, as being of itself a treasure, and a sufficient remuneration of years of labour."

Accordingly, the business of a university was to make intellectual culture its immediate object, to become employed in the education of the intellect. Its purpose was not moral impression or mechanical production. "It professes to exercise the mind neither in art nor in duty; its function is intellectual culture; here it may leave its scholars, and it has done its work when it has done as much as this. It educates the intellect to reason well in all matters, to reach out towards truth, and to grasp it."

In America there was another prominent educator, like Newman a moralist at heart, who argued that learning should not provide practical training but cultivate a liberal outlook and broad vision. In his inaugural address as president of Princeton in 1902, Woodrow Wilson spoke of two ways to prepare a young man for his life work. "One is to give him the skill and special knowledge which shall make a good tool, an excellent bread-winning tool of him; and for thousands of young men that way must be followed." It was a good way, honorable and indispensable, but it was not and could never be the way which an institution of higher education ought to follow. "The college should seek to make the men whom it receives something more than excellent servants of a trade or skilled practitioners of a profession. It should give them elasticity of faculty and breadth of vision, so that they shall have a surplus of mind to expend, not upon their profession only, for its liberalization and enlargement, but also upon the broader interests which lie about them, in the spheres in which they are to be, not breadwinners merely, but citizens as well, and in their own hearts, where they are to grow to the stature of real nobility." What the world needed most was the "free capital of mind . . . that awaits investment in undertakings, spiritual as well as material, which advance the race and help all men to a better life."

This ideal of the gentleman-scholar, of the well-rounded personality — generous in outlook, liberal in spirit, cultivated in manner — was appropriate to a social order dominated by a successful bourgeoisie. To the preindustrial community, whose cultural attitudes had been shaped by a hereditary landed nobility, the chief object of education was practical: the acquisition of a skill, the performance of a service, the practice of a profession, the earning of a livelihood. This utilitarian view, in which the textbook instruction offered in the classroom was regarded as inferior to the direct experience of court life or military service, gave way during the industrial revolution to the concept of learning as a quest for wisdom and virtue. The basic purpose of education, according to the new doctrine, was not leadership or skill or efficiency, and certainly not livelihood, but self-perfection.[11]

The role of history in this changing perception of learning was to assist the process of individual cultural refinement. Although it might also contribute to wiser public policy or greater civic awareness, its main function was the cultivation and enrichment of the mind. It thus served primarily a didactic purpose. There was disagreement about precisely how historical learning could improve character and intellect, but the common assumption was that knowledge about the past helped make students better, wiser, kinder, and more discerning human beings. To Lord Acton, it provided a

11. John Henry Newman, *The Idea of a University Defined and Illustrated* (London, 1910), pp. 113-14, 125-26; *Papers of Wilson*, ed. A. S. Link, XIV, 177.

sense of perspective, a lofty standpoint from which to view the present with greater objectivity. "History must be our deliverer not only from the undue influence of other times," he declared in 1899 in one of his lectures at Cambridge, "but from the undue influence of our own, from the tyranny of environment and the pressure of the air we breathe. It requires all historic forces to produce their record and submit to judgment, and it promotes the faculty of resistance to contemporary surroundings by familiarity with other ages and other orbits of thought." Historical learning broadened the intellectual horizon, enabling us to see others as well as ourselves free from the interests and preoccupations of everyday life.

Becker, on the other hand, emphasized the ethical character of history, its capacity to refine intellect and improve behavior. Long before describing the study of the past as socially useful mythologizing, he spoke of it as a force for morality, guiding conduct and shaping character. In words which could have come from Wilson or even Acton, he emphasized the connection between an understanding of historical experience and the attainment of personal virtue. "The value of history is, indeed, not scientific but moral," he wrote in 1915. "By liberalizing the mind, by deepening the sympathies, by fortifying the will, it enables us to control, not society, but ourselves,—a much more important thing; it prepares us to live more humanely in the present and to meet rather than foretell the future." This was a far cry from the Becker who declared in 1931 that historians are "of that ancient and honorable company of wise men of the tribe, of bards and storytellers and minstrels, of soothsayers and priests, to whom in successive ages has been entrusted the keeping of the useful myths."

His transformation during the interwar period from a historical moralist to a historical relativist reflected the diminishing cogency of the pedagogical argument in defense of history. The ideal of the gentleman-scholar in quest of knowledge, culture, and wisdom became increasingly anachronistic with the democratization of the social base of higher education. Yet as late as the 1940s Collingwood was still arguing that the ultimate purpose of historical learning was to achieve personal growth and insight. In reply to the question constantly asked of historians—What is history for?—he wrote:

My answer is that history is "for" human self-knowledge. It is generally thought to be of importance to man that he should know himself: where knowing himself means knowing not his merely personal peculiarities, the things that distinguish him from other men, but his nature as man. Knowing yourself means knowing, first, what it is to be a man; secondly, knowing what it is to be the kind of man you are; and thirdly, knowing what it is to be the man *you* are and nobody else is. Knowing yourself means knowing what you can do; and since nobody knows what he can do until he tries, the only clue to what man can do is what man has done. The value of history, then, is that it teaches us what man has done and thus what man is.

The importance attached to historical learning lies accordingly in its ability to provide a perception of what we are or at least what we are capable of being.[12]

The most enduring and persuasive argument for the study of history, however, has been neither the predictive nor the inspirational nor the pedagogical. The belief that the past holds the key to the future has been eroded, partly by the challenge from the social sciences, partly by a sense of the uniqueness of historical experiences. The view of history, moreover, as a fabric of myths and fictions, woven out of actual but disparate events, serving primarily to maintain the cohesiveness of society, has proved too stark and uncompromising for most historians. It has failed to satisfy their need to feel that what they do is not only socially useful but objectively valid. The contention, finally, that historical knowledge can uphold private virtue has lost its persuasiveness for a generation which considers collective progress more important than individual perfectibility. We are thus left with the ontological argument, with the assertion that history by its nature, by its being, appeals to the human intellect and spirit. It does not have to justify its existence; it simply is, indigenous and instinctive, as spontaneous as art, music, or literature. It is an essential and distinctive characteristic of all mankind.

This argument disposes of the question of the utility of historical learning by declaring it to be irrelevant. We should not ask what is the use of history, any more than we ask what is the use of painting or singing or storytelling. We should rather respond naturally and spontaneously to the deep-seated interest in the past which all of us share. This is a position which many contemporary historians have taken. Strayer, writing with characteristic urbaneness, dismissed the entire debate regarding the usefulness of historical learning as largely academic. "History is an essential part of civilized human life," he insisted, "and it is futile to argue whether we shall or shall

12. John Emerich Edward Dalberg-Acton, *Lectures on Modern History* (London, 1906), p. 33; Carl Becker, "A New Philosophy of History," *Dial* 49 (1915): 148; idem, "Everyman His Own Historian," p. 231; R. G. Collingwood, *Idea of History*, p. 10.

not devote some attention to it. . . . The value of history, like the existence of free will, cannot be proved — it is simply a basic fact of human experience." Therefore, since the importance of knowledge about the past does not have to be demonstrated but can be simply assumed, "the real problem . . . is to improve the quality of the history which we use."

To Handlin, an interest in historical learning was also indigenous and spontaneous, but it was scientific rather than artistic in nature. That is, it expressed a fundamental human need for clearer insight into objective reality. It resembled in this respect the study of pure mathematics, physics, or astronomy, intellectual pursuits which have no practical applicability, but which bring us closer to an understanding of the universe of which we are part. "The uses of history," he argued, "arise neither from its relevance nor from its help in preparing for careers — nor from its availability as a subject which teachers pass on to students who become teachers and in turn teach others to teach." Nevertheless, many of those who had studied it in school testified long afterward that by locating them in time and space, it had helped them know themselves as human beings. But how could knowledge about the past enable men and women to gain a deeper understanding of what they are? "Not by relevance," Handlin explained, "in the competition for which the other, more pliable, social sciences can always outbid history. Nor by the power of myth, in the peddling of which the advantage lies with the novelists. . . . The use of history lies in its capacity for advancing the approach to truth."

The historian's vocation thus depends on an article of faith: "Truth is absolute; it is as absolute as the world is real. It does not exist because individuals wish it to anymore than the world exists for their convenience. Although observers have more or less partial views of the truth, its actuality is unrelated to the desires or the particular angles of vision of the viewers. Truth is knowable and will out if earnestly pursued; and science is the procedure or set of procedures for approximating it." To Handlin the reason for studying historical experiences is essentially the same as the reason for studying galactic patterns or subatomic particles or the topological properties of geometric configurations: because they are there, because they are part of objective reality, and because the human mind has an innate desire to explore and understand that reality.

At first glance this position may seem an admission of defeat, an escape from doubt regarding the value of history. It appears to signal withdrawal from an intellectual battle which the other side is winning into a citadel of axioms and dogmas, impregnable to rational assault. It suggests a discipline at bay, struggling against criticisms and misgivings. Yet the ontological argument is in fact the oldest justification for the study of history, outdating the various other attempts to demonstrate its utility or value. Even before Thucydides wrote that a knowledge of the past was helpful in anticipating the future, "which in the course of human things must resemble if it does not reflect it," Herodotus maintained that historical learning did not have to be vindicated by its predictive or pedagogical usefulness. Its only function was to preserve for posterity the memory of what had once happened. Hence his purpose in writing a history of the Persian Wars, he said at the outset, was simply that "the things wrought of men be not blotted out by time, neither works great and marvellous performed of Greeks and barbarians be without fame."

Aristotle too saw in history nothing more than a factual record of human experience. Indeed, that is why he regarded it as inferior to poetry. It was self-contained, it reflected no extraneous reality or truth. "The distinction between historian and poet is not in the one writing prose and the other verse," he argued in the *Poetics*. "You might put the work of Herodotus into verse, and it would still be a species of history." The distinction consisted rather in the fact that "the one describes the thing that has been and the other a kind of thing that might be." Poetry was more philosophical and important than history, because its statements were of the nature of universals, whereas those of history were merely singulars. "By a universal statement I mean one as to what such or such a kind of man will probably or necessarily say or do — which is the aim of poetry, though it affixes proper names to the characters; by a singular statement, one as to what, say, Alcibiades did or had done to him." The historian's commitment to a literal truth, in Aristotle's view, had the effect of inhibiting the originality and inventiveness requisite for the highest forms of human creativity.

To Sir Walter Raleigh, on the other hand, factual accuracy was essential to the vital function which historical learning performed. By providing an objectively valid account of the past, he maintained in his preface to *The History of the World*, it enables us to rise above the narrow scope and limited experience of everyday life:

> Among many other benefits, for which it hath beene honored; in this one [history] triumpheth over all humane knowledge, That it hath given us life in our understanding, since the world it selfe had life and beginning, even to this day; yea it hath triumphed over time, which besides it, nothing but

eternity hath triumphed over: for it hath carried our knowledge over the vast
& devouring space of so many thousands of yeares, and given so faire and
peircing eies to our minde; that we plainely behould living now, as if we have
lived then, that great World, . . . as it was then, when but new to it selfe.
By it I say it is, that we live in the very time when it was created: we behold
how it was governed: how it was covered with waters, and again repeopled.

He concluded with a statement almost identical with that which Herodotus
had made twenty centuries earlier: "It is not the least debt which we owe
unto History, that it hath made us acquainted with our dead Ancestors; and,
out of the depth and darkenesse of the earth, delivered us their memory
and fame."

Though the view of the importance of history as inherent rather than ex-
trinsic is thus as old as history itself, never has it seemed more cogent than
at the present time, when the various utilitarian justifications of the study
of the past are under attack. It is heartening to reflect that, even if society
decides that historical experience is irrelevant to the unprecedented problems which it must face, even if historical study is gradually dropped from
the school curriculum, even if the historical profession dwindles as rapidly
as it had once grown, the writing and reading of history will go on, as they
have always done, because they are essential for the sense of identity of
a civilized community. The acceptance of this position requires greater humility than historians have been accustomed to display. It means the abandonment of cherished illusions and pretensions, the renunciation of inspired
wisdom and prophetic vision. Inflated ambitions have to give way to a sober,
realistic assessment of what knowledge about the past is capable of achieving. But in return historians will gain the satisfaction of performing an important cultural function without the need to compete in the marketplace
of ephemeral academic fashions. A more modest appraisal of what history
can do has inspired great works of learning in the past; it will surely be
able to do so again in the future.[13]

The ontological argument, to be sure, does not preclude the various utilitarian justifications of historical learning. Many of those who agree with
Aristotle that history is essentially what Alcibiades did or had done to him
will go on hoping that a knowledge of the past can also occasionally, in

13. J. R. Strayer, "Introduction," pp. 10, 14; O. Handlin, *Truth in History*, pp. 404–5; Thucydides, *Peloponnesian War*, trans. R. Crawley; Herodotus, trans. J. E. Powell, I, 1; Aristotle,
On the Art of Poetry, trans. Ingram Bywater (Oxford, 1920), p. 43; W. Ralegh, *History of
the World*, ed. C. A. Patrides, p. 48.

some obscure way, provide a glimpse of the future. During the 1860s Motley maintained that although our understanding of historical experience must necessarily remain imperfect, "neither fools nor sages; neither individuals nor nations; have any other light to guide them along the track which all must tread, save that long glimmering vista of yesterdays which grows so swiftly fainter and fainter as the present fades off into the past." A hundred years later Arthur M. Schlesinger, Jr., made the same point even more poignantly. History should lead us, he wrote, "to a profound and humbling sense of human frailty." It should lead us to the perception, "so insistently demonstrated by experience and so tragically destructive of our most cherished certitudes," that "the possibilities of history are far richer and more various than the human intellect is likely to conceive." And yet, since "the tragedy of history implicates us all in the common plight of humanity, we are never relieved, despite the limits of our knowledge and the darkness of our understanding, from the necessity of meeting our obligations." Responsible, thoughtful men and women will continue to study history in order to meet those obligations.

Many of them, morever, will go on believing that a knowledge of the past, thought always relative or subjective, is of great social importance, providing the basis for a collective sense of direction and purpose. They will agree with Becker that "neither the value nor the dignity of history need suffer by regarding it as a foreshortened and incomplete representation of the reality that once was, an unstable pattern of remembered things redesigned and newly colored to suit the convenience of those who make use of it." The historian's function, according to this view, should not be less highly prized because his task is limited or his contribution of incidental and temporary significance. "History is an indispensable even though not the highest form of intellectual endeavor." For the genetic approach to human experience can only transform the problems with which it deals; it can never solve them. "However accurately we may determine the 'facts' of history, the facts themselves and our interpretations of them, and our interpretations of our own interpretations, will be seen in a different perspective or a less vivid light as mankind moves into the unknown future. Regarded historically, as a process of learning, man and his world can obviously be understood only tentatively, since it is by definition something still in the making, something as yet unfinished."

Finally, there will be those who will study history because it is a vital part of the cultural heritage of mankind, teaching wisdom and fostering virtue, making us into better human beings. Their position has been defended most persuasively by John Stuart Mill, who argued that universities were intended to teach students something other than how to earn a livelihood. "Their object is not to make skillful lawyers, or physicians, or engineers, but capable and cultivated human beings." Men are men before they are lawyers, physicians, merchants, or manufacturers, "and if you make them capable and sensible men, they will make themselves capable and sensible lawyers or physicians." What students should carry away with them from a university is not professional knowledge, but that which can direct the use of professional knowledge, bringing "the light of general culture to illuminate the technicalities of a special pursuit." Men may become competent lawyers without general education, but only general education can make them thinking lawyers, "who demand, and are capable of apprehending, principles, instead of merely cramming their memory with details." The same is true of all useful pursuits, even the most menial. "Education makes a man a more intelligent shoemaker, if that be his occupation, but not by teaching him how to make shoes; it does so by the mental exercise it gives, and the habits it impresses." Many people will continue to pursue historical learning as part of that general education which is the chief source of personal cultivation.

Yet while reading and writing history for its predictive or inspirational or pedagogical qualities, we must remember that it is above all a self-sufficient and self-contained discipline, important for its own sake. By providing a coherent, intelligible account of the past, it satisfies a profound human yearning for knowledge about our roots. It requires no justification other than that. We will go on studying history, whether it is taught in the classroom or not, whether it is supported or neglected by government agencies and philanthropic foundations, whether it ranks high or low on the constantly shifting scale of values on which the various branches of knowledge are weighed. We will study it because we must, because it broadens the cultural vision of mankind, because it expresses some essential quality of our existence as human beings. Our ultimate purpose in studying it, however, will remain the one expressed long ago at the first dawning of historical consciousness: that the deeds performed by men shall not be blotted out by time, and that the great and marvelous works of Greeks and barbarians shall not be without fame.[14]

14. J. L. Motley, *Historic Progress*, p. 5; Arthur Schlesinger, Jr., "On the Inscrutability of History," *Encounter*, November 1966, p. 17; C. Becker, "Everyman His Own Historian," pp. 235–36; J. S. Mill, *Inaugural Address*, pp. 5–7.

Appendices
Index

The Philanthropic Foundations
and Historical Scholarship

I n the summer of 1983, hoping to gain a better understanding of the role which philanthrophy has played in shaping the study of history, I interviewed seven current or recent administrators of the six foundations which have been most active in supporting historical research: the American Council of Learned Societies, the Ford Foundation, the Guggenheim Memorial Foundation, the National Endowment for the Humanities, the Rockefeller Foundation, and the Social Science Research Council. Five of the people I talked to were in senior positions, one was a middle-level administrator, and one a junior executive. Each interview lasted between an hour and an hour and a half. In order to focus the discussion, I had prepared a list of twenty-nine questions, which dealt broadly with the background of the interviewee, the process of applying for support, the evaluation of the applications, and the criteria for making awards. These questions, however, served only as a point of departure, the interviewees being urged to digress, reflect, and expand on any subject which seemed to them important for an assessment of the work done by the foundations.

To encourage candor, I assured them that I would not reveal their names or even their institutional affiliations. After all, it did not make a great deal of difference which administrator from which foundation said what. It was the general thrust of what they had to say which mattered, at least for my purposes. To what extent they were in fact frank is hard to judge. They were all pleasant and courteous, although two seemed a little cagey, wondering perhaps why I wanted to know what I was asking and what use I would make of it once I found out. But most appeared quite forthright, and a few were surprisingly outspoken. On the whole, I was left with the impression that the people I talked to were open in describing their work and in analyzing the function it performed.

All of the administrators had started out as academics. This was true of the great majority of the people employed by the foundations, I was told, although one interviewee said that in his institution academics were no more than "a sizable fraction." The others, he explained, came from government or business. The academics, moreover, were in his opinion not always very good in dealing with technical details, while the nonacademics, especially the lawyers, tended to be "too narrow." The people I interviewed had generally gone into foundation work fairly early in their careers. Even those who had done so at a later stage had acquired considerable administrative experience at the school where they had taught. As scholars they had typically been active and productive rather than outstanding. Indeed, one interviewee, a junior executive who was returning to teaching at the end of the year, confided that, with some notable exceptions, the foundation administrators she knew had not been "very effective" in their scholarship.

According to their own testimony, they had usually made the shift from campus to foundation through contacts they had established as advisers, referees, panel members, or fellowship holders. In talking about what had led them to make the move, none mentioned money, prestige, or power. For the two youngest the reason was simple: they had been unable to find teaching jobs. Of the rest, one found "the idea of encouraging individuals and programs" very satisfying, while another spoke of the challenge of trying to "broaden and globalize" scholarship. A third insisted that he had not really abandoned academic life, since his foundation encouraged him to continue doing research and writing, and he even taught an occasional course at Columbia.

As they looked back at the decision to make the change, most of the interviewees were reasonably satisfied, although the two youngest were a little ambivalent—both spoke of "mixed feelings"—and one of the senior administrators admitted that he missed teaching and research, indeed, that sometimes he felt "like a fish out of water." For all of them, however, the work was challenging and often gratifying. "You learn how difficult it is to give away money," according to one. They each believed, moreover, that the foundation which employed them performed reasonably well the function it was supposed to perform. There were comments, for example, about a "very sincere effort to support scholarship" and about the work "being done effectively and efficiently."

As for the question whether foundations should merely support and encourage scholarship or whether they should also shape and guide it, the answers differed widely. Two of the respondents said without hesitation that foundations should reflect rather than direct the development of learning, and that this indeed was the policy followed by their own institutions. "We are just a referee" is how another put it. But there were also differing views. One interviewee was equivocal. The foundations should both lead and follow, he said, but more the latter than the former. Although the opinions of professional scholars ought to play a major role, the foundations should not simply respond to popular or academic pressures. "We must use our heads about what is important and what is a fad." Others expressed even stronger convictions. The junior executive, after routinely declaring that foundations should both lead and follow, which she described as the generally accepted view, went on to say that recent discoveries in scholarship must be explored and expanded. Foundation funds ought to encourage new lines of research. "Contemporary political or intellectual developments" were especially important. A senior administrator spoke of the need to enlarge the scope of learning, adding that there was some pressure in his organization toward "contemporaneous issues." Another explained that he always had to fight for the budget for his programs by emphasizing their usefulness and practicality. The directors were interested primarily in proposals which could contribute to the "quality of life." In short, most of the interviewees, though not all, felt in varying degrees that foundations should not merely finance but also strengthen, broaden, and improve scholarly research.

The process of applying for support was roughly the same in all six foundations. The applicant submitted a detailed form or outline accompanied by letters of recommendation or by the names of referees able to provide an evaluation of his qualifications. The foundations soliciting evaluations directly maintained that they often received more candid and critical responses than if the applicant himself had requested them. In all the foundations except one the applications were then reviewed by panels of outside experts. Only the Ford Foundation, which typically awards grants to programs rather than individuals, left the decision almost entirely to its staff and board. The others relied primarily on the opinions of the panels, sometimes guided also by a preliminary evaluation or screening through outside referees.

The panels consist usually of between five and ten voting members, all or most of them academics, and one representative of the foundation serving ex officio as chairman without a vote. In the majority of cases they are

made up of people in a variety of disciplines and they deal with all applications, whatever their field. The National Endowment for the Humanities,
however, submits applications from historians to panels consisting of historians, while applications from other disciplines are reviewed by panels
made up of experts in those disciplines. In all the foundations using this
system, the recommendations of the panels, though theoretically subject to
approval by a board of directors or trustees, are almost invariably accepted.
Finally, the interviewees were in agreement that on the whole historians have
done at least as well as scholars in other fields, indeed, often they have done
better.

The process by which awards are made thus depends heavily on "peer
review," on the opinions of scholars regarded as experts in the applicant's
discipline. I therefore asked the interviewees how the names of potential
panelists were obtained and what qualities were sought in those invited to
serve. The answer to the first question was simple. Each foundation had
a pool of names, some provided by members of the staff who knew the field,
others suggested by former panel members or outside referees. A few administrators even relied occasionally on computerized lists of experts. The
final choice was made as a rule through consultation among the permanent
staff, although one interviewee, recently retired, smiled a little when I questioned him about this and said dryly: "I myself would ask them to serve."

Since the supply of names far exceeded the need, how did the administrators decide whom to invite? That is, what were the traits they looked for
in the people asked to provide expert opinions? Here it proved surprisingly
difficult to get at anything concrete. The initial reaction from almost all the
interviewees was a flow of cosmic nouns and adjectives. "Quality" was the
most common, but it was frequently replaced or reinforced by "distinction,"
"excellence," "judgment," "knowledge," "breadth," "outstanding," or "first-rate."
When I tried to press them to describe more precisely what they meant by
"quality" or "excellence" and how they measured those attributes, the response
was usually real or feigned incomprehension. They could not or would not
see that behind the high-sounding phrases was an implicit system of values
central to what they were trying to achieve. The more I pressed, the more
they resisted, so that I would soon shift the conversation to other issues.
Thereby I frequently succeeded in obtaining information which I had been
unable to elicit through direct questioning. Casual comments or opinions
expressed in the course of a discussion of some minor point were at times
highly illuminating regarding the way the entire "peer review" process works.

To begin with, it became clear that the attributes of "quality" or "excellence," considered so important in panel members, were often modified by or combined with other, more practical considerations. There was the need, for example, for geographical balance, so that no single region of the country would be too heavily represented. It was also desirable that scholars from both large and small schools and from both private and public institutions serve. One administrator added, with what seemed a slightly studied casualness, that, while a "first-rate mentality" was the most important thing, panels ought to have a "fair distribution of men and women," all other things being equal, of course. Another spoke vaguely about the desirability of having members of ethnic or racial minorities. And then there were some talents and aptitudes only remotely connected with scholarly distinction. A panelist should be "a committee man of sorts," that is, he should be "fair," "tolerant," and "articulate," he should possess "good judgment," and he should be able "to hold his own in discussion."

Even more important, the implicit definition of "quality" or "excellence" guiding the appointment of panel members leaned subtly but unmistakably in the direction of scholarly innovation. All the interviewees agreed that the volume of publication, though of some importance, was not the decisive factor in the choice of consultants. As one of them put it, a panelist should have "at least one book," but the prime consideration must be "quality." The others agreed that what really mattered was not any objective measure of how much a scholar had written but the subjective evaluation of its merit.

How was that merit determined, however? Specifically, was the new and different more likely to be regarded as meritorious than the old and traditional? On this point there was wide though not unanimous agreement. One administrator insisted a little indignantly that in his foundation only the excellence of a panelist's academic work counted. There was no preference for innovators over traditionalists, although of course consultants should be people of broad scope. Another hedged a bit, talking vaguely about "innovation" and "originality," but concluding that the emphasis was primarily on "distinction." The others all felt in varying degrees that "peer review" favored innovative research, and for good reasons.

After first dwelling on the importance of the "quality of mind," one of them said: "Yes, there is some tendency toward innovation. . . . Scholars have their preferences and views on what is important and new in the profession." But he maintained that the administrative staff stayed out of controversies regarding innovation. Another spoke of the need for "sensitivity to new ways of dealing with the field," so that panelists should be "sympathetic to innovative techniques, but not necessarily practitioners" of those techniques. A third interviewee observed that since "originality counts" in panelists, preference seemed to be given to scholars in the new fields of history. Besides, since many of the senior historians were unwilling to serve on panels, the members tended to be the younger and "more innovative" people. A similar point was made by the junior executive, who was the one most sympathetic to scholarly experimentation. She too spoke at first about "stature" and "excellence," but soon shifted to "originality" and "innovativeness," which seemed to her even more important than prominence in the profession. Indeed, she had detected a trend away from "visibility" in choosing panelists toward "less well-known, up-and-coming Young Turks."

The tilt of the "peer review" process in the direction of innovation, exploration, and experimentation was equally apparent in the replies I received to the last and most important set of questions, those dealing with the criteria by which the foundations awarded grants. Their measure of merit was clearly subjective, relying on what one administrator called "creative judgment." The volume of publication by the applicant, though not unimportant, did not constitute the major consideration. But what did? Here there was first the usual recital of impeccable scholarly attributes. A senior executive, the same one who had insisted that only academic excellence counted in the selection of panelists, maintained that the approval of a request for support depended entirely on "excellence in history" and a "good proposal," nothing more. Another interviewee was equally insistent that in his foundation all that mattered was "quality." The applicant's specialty and interest or the proposal's timeliness and "visibility" were of little importance. The middle-level administrator offered similar assurances that in his organization the only test was the "quality of the applicant's work or the promise of quality," although he did feel that familiar fields provided less opportunity for scholarly originality than new areas.

The other four suggested, however, that at least some of the foundations play a more active role in directing historical research. One conceded that he had felt pressure from the higher-ups in his organization to support proposals with some significance for contemporary problems. The junior executive explained that "you start with the nature of the proposal," that was the most important thing. But she did not necessarily mean "visibility"; there was also the need to "plow unknown fields." Asked whether such subdisciplines as women's history, ethnic history, urban history, or family history had a better chance than diplomatic, constitutional, national, or local history, she acknowledged that it was "probably true," although there were no explicit criteria or instructions on this point. A senior administrator also agreed that, other things being equal, an applicant's specialty or interest was important. The newer fields of history had an edge, not independently or separately, but as reflections of a "quality of mind" or an "overall excellence." The timeliness and "visibility" of a proposal, moreover, often affected the judgment of the selection committees. There was a common view, for example, that women's history "is a field which should be opened up," although some members of a panel might disagree with this opinion.

The recently retired foundation executive was the most outspoken of the interviewees, probably because he now felt free to talk quite openly. In his opinion, the American Council of Learned Societies and the Guggenheim Memorial Foundation tended to support pure scholarship; the Ford Foundation, the Rockefeller Foundation, and the Social Science Research Council preferred projects of some practical or utilitarian value; and the National Endowment for the Humanities was ambivalent. He complained that the officers of his own organization "tried to nudge history into women's history, ethnic history, and other new fields [such as] oral history [or] public history programs." The timeliness of a proposal was important. "It had to illuminate an issue of contemporary significance." Did innovative approaches such as cliometrics, social-science history, or psychohistory have a better chance than traditional forms of historiography like biographical studies, military accounts, or political narratives? "Yes, I think so" was the answer. The "big shots" in his foundation would often tell him pointedly: "This is what historians say is new." There was "no doubt" in his mind, therefore, that the more recent historical subdisciplines had an advantage over the old and traditional ones. The officers he dealt with, moreover, often had to be convinced of the usefulness of history. You could never get by with "scholarship for the sake of scholarship." Yet on the whole he seemed to look back with pride and satisfaction at what he had been able to accomplish as an administrator.

Although it became clearer to me in the course of the interviews that the foundations have indeed exercised an important influence over the recent development of historical learning, my opinion of them became progressively more favorable. For one thing, I found the people I talked to intelligent and dedicated, less self-assured or self-important than I had expected, more sensitive to the pitfalls as well as benefits of academic philanthropy. They were sincerely committed to the encouragement of creative scholarship. Second, their claim that they were followers rather than leaders in determining the direction of historical research appeared to a considerable extent valid. Almost all the innovations they promoted had originated within the profession, the foundations in their eagerness to pioneer had then fostered those innovations, and their support in turn had further encouraged the transformation of the discipline. In this process of reciprocal influence and reinforcement between scholars and administrators, the former had usually taken the initiative.

Would the major works of historical scholarship in the last fifty years, the really important books, have been written without the foundations? Probably, although some might have taken considerably longer. But there is also a large body of solid and useful even if not outstanding research which only scholarly philanthropy has made possible. Was this accomplishment worth the psychological tensions and pressures generated or aggravated by the sudden transformation of an old and established profession? Was it worth the invidious division of historians into "bold pioneers" on one side and "stodgy traditionalists" on the other? Was it worth the rush to novelty in which common sense, good judgment, and even intelligibility were sometimes sacrificed for "originality" at any cost? The answers are bound to be as subjective as the procedures by which the foundations have exercised their influence over historical learning in America.

The World of
Nonacademic History

arly in 1984 I conducted interviews with seven distinguished nonacademic historians: George Dangerfield, James Thomas Flexner, Paul
Horgan, George F. Kennan, David McCullough, Edmund Morris, and
Barbara Tuchman. In addition, I talked to Arthur Schlesinger, Jr., because,
as a scholar who has written important works of history both within and
outside the academic environment, he might have some special insight into
the problems of nonacademic historiography. My purpose in meeting with
them was to determine in what way historians who are not affiliated with
an institution of higher learning differ from those who are. Do they bring
a richer experience or broader perspective to the study of the past? Does
their freedom from the burdens of teaching and administration enable them
to reflect more deeply on problems of scholarship? Does their dependence
on the literary marketplace shape in any way how they write about historical events? Do their wider contacts with the world beyond the college
campus provide them with a richer comprehension of public life or human
character? Does their independence from institutional and professional con-
straints make possible a more spontaneous or creative form of historiography? Such questions seemed to me important for an understanding of the
historical profession today.

The nonacademic historians had dominated the discipline for two millennia; indeed, they had long been the only historians. As recently as fifty years
ago they still played an important role in organized historical scholarship.
Almost half of the distinguished writers of history in the 1920s and 1930s
earned their living in occupations other than teaching. Today they are reduced to a handful. My aim, then, in interviewing them was to determine
the differences between the practitioners of institutionalized history and the
remaining adherents to an older nonacademic tradition. I did not concern

myself with the much larger number of historical popularizers who present in interesting and readable form the results of scholarly research to which they themselves make little contribution. Rather, I wanted to study a representative sample of leading nonacademic historians who differ from the academics not in the quality of their scholarship but in their source of livelihood and their way of life.

Looking back at the interviews, I recall most vividly the graciousness I encountered. Although several of the people I talked to lead very busy lives, closer to that of a business executive than an academic scholar, they readily agreed, with one or two exceptions, to find time in their schedules to meet with me. The interviews, moreover, were invariably cordial and friendly. I soon felt that I was discussing common interests and problems with a group of professional colleagues. Some of them offered to assist me by helping to arrange other interviews. I remember one historian who talked to me, with passion and eloquence, at eight in the morning, while finishing his breakfast, answering the telephone, and packing for a flight to New York to prepare a television program. Another made me a snack of chicken pâté and a cup of coffee before rushing off to his publisher for an autographing party. There were lunches and drinks and good, stimulating conversation. It was captivating.

I was impressed, moreover, by the opulence, cultural even more than material, of the nonacademic historians' life-style. Although some of my meetings with them took place in an office, most were in the home of the interviewee. There was the comfortable nineteenth-century town house in Georgetown on a street that looked the way it must have during the Civil War; the tastefully furnished apartment on Fifth Avenue in New York, across from the Metropolitan Museum of Art, overlooking Central Park; the gleaming structure on a California hilltop, all glass and polished wood, the Pacific on one side and mountains on the other, with orange trees luxuriating in the yard. This was quite a contrast to the faculty homes in a typical college community. But even more striking was the difference in the social and intellectual milieu of the nonacademic historians. There were casual references to prominent writers, poets, artists, musicians, theater people, and political leaders with whom my interviewees mingled. They would mention in passing the prestigious scholarly or literary organizations to which they belonged, the elite clubs, societies, and academies. Here and there I even heard talk about luncheon or dinner in the White House. To a university professor accustomed to the humdrum of the campus, it all seemed dazzling.

Each of the interviews lasted about an hour and fifteen minutes. I sought to encourage my respondents to speak freely by assuring them that while I would mention in my book the names of the people I had talked with, I would not identify any opinion with any individual. I'm not sure that this precaution was really necessary, because, except for comments about academic historians, they displayed little hesitation in expressing their views. In preparing for my meetings with them, I had drafted a questionnaire of thirty items dealing with four major subjects: the background of the interviewee, the method or procedure he followed in writing history, the distinctive qualities or values of nonacademic historiography, and the personal and professional relationship between academic and nonacademic historians. These questions were not designed to restrict the discussion in any way, but simply to get it going. I urged the respondents to expatiate or digress whenever they liked, and in fact many of their most interesting observations came in the form of casual reflections rather than formal replies. All in all, I have the impression that they spoke quite freely, without trying to disguise their thoughts and feelings.

To begin with, the nonacademics I talked to usually developed an interest in history early in life. Though a few had been history majors in college, they had generally been drawn to the past by something they had experienced in childhood or adolescence, by some books they had read, stories they had heard, or places they had visited. What attracted them was the thought that there had once been men and women whose experiences had been as exciting or challenging as those of people today. One of the interviewees traced his interest to the realization that what had happened a long time ago could be "as dramatic, colorful, and wonderful as anything alive now." He spoke of the "falseness of time," that is, the erroneous perception that what had formerly occurred was somehow more predetermined and therefore less exciting than what is occurring now. "People in the past are closer to us than we think." Another interviewee talked about his childhood recognition that "history is the story of real events." A third said that in studying the past, he tried to "recapture the total effect of what once happened." In short, quite early in life they all developed, spontaneously or instinctively, without any external direction, an intense interest in historical experience.

For most of them this interest is closely associated with the study of human nature and conduct. Hence the history they write is almost without exception narrative in form, emphasizing the role of individual personality in shaping or reflecting the social environment. One of the interviewees told me that essentially he dealt with "character and its effect on behavior," and that in this sense the historian carried on the tradition of the novelist. Another spoke of his desire "to recapture the distant dimension of people's lives." Still another said point-blank that "if there's no story, I'm not interested." And one even declared: "I'm really a writer by profession who happens to write history." It is clear that although the early experiences which aroused their interest in the discipline are similar to those of academic historians, the nonacademics differ in their much greater emphasis on the literary and dramatic qualities of historiography. As one of them put it, "narrative is the spine or bloodstream of history." He added, a little self-consciously perhaps, that historical writing is "a work of art."

An even more striking difference is that none of the nonacademic historians had received advanced training in the discipline, and that all of them had turned to it after earlier employment in another field. Some had been in government work, others in journalism. One had worked as a copywriter, another as a librarian, a third as an art critic, a fourth as an editor. A few had become historians while still in their twenties, but one not until after he was fifty. All of them had thus had experience in occupations other than history, and none had spent any time in academic life.

Did they wish they had received more instruction in historical methodology? Did they feel a lack of professional training in their research and writing? A few said, though without strong conviction, that it might have been better if they had spent some time in graduate work. Yet when asked what they thought they would have gotten out of it, they seemed vague and undecided. "I might have saved time in going through my materials," one of them told me. "Maybe I missed something." Another wished he had learned more history; besides, perhaps he would have gotten to know his teachers better. A third thought he might have become more fluent in foreign languages, but then added after some reflection that the requirements for a Ph.D. could be "stifling." In general, none of the interviewees sounded sorry or apologetic about his lack of formal instruction. One said that though he wished he had acquired "more knowledge of history," he really felt "no need for methodology." His experience in journalism had provided him with excellent training. Another agreed that "the mechanics are learnable on one's own"; indeed, they then have "the shock of newness or freshness."

I concluded my inquiry into their background by asking whether the writing of history provided them with an adequate livelihood, or did they have to supplement it with other sources of income. The replies varied, but all of the interviewees seemed to enjoy a standard of living superior to that of the average academic historian. Some had in fact done exceedingly well in the literary marketplace. One had inherited money; another's wife had independent means, I surmised. Two were associated with research institutes which provided them with some support. Several improved their earnings by free-lance writing, television work, or service on literary boards and committees. A few, however, lived almost entirely on royalties from their historical writings and on advances from their publishers which, as one of them put it, might seem "very generous" or even "incredible" to an outsider. But there were the expenses of paying for the house, he pointed out, sending the children through college, and maintaining a comfortable life-style. Another confessed that he felt under considerable financial strain. He had received a substantial advance on his next book, but that would have to last several years. Besides, he was behind schedule, a chapter which should have taken two months was now in its sixth month, the end was still not in sight, and so on. Nevertheless, none of them appeared greatly troubled by the economic uncertainties of an author's existence, and none expressed a wish to exchange the independence of a free-lance historian for the constraining security of an academic appointment.

My next series of questions sought to examine the process by which non-academics write history. It was clear, to begin with, that they dealt with a far greater variety of subjects than academic historians usually do. They were unrestrained by the inhibitions which specialization and profession-alization breed, by fears of trespassing on someone else's scholarly property, of being branded interlopers. They ranged from the Johnstown Flood to the Brooklyn Bridge to the Panama Canal to the young Theodore Roosevelt; from liberal England at the opening of the twentieth century to the Era of Good Feelings in the United States ninety years earlier to the awakening of American nationalism in the 1820s to the timeless Irish Question; from the Zimmerman Telegram to the outbreak of the First World War to European society at the *fin de siècle* to General Stilwell in China to the Black Death. Very few academic historians would dare to be so venturesome.

How did the interviewees decide on a subject? A few maintained that there was usually some element of congruity or coherence behind their decision. An interest in the nature of liberalism had led one of them from Herbert Asquith's England to James Monroe's America. Another had decided to move back in time gradually from an important incident in the First World

War to the military beginning of the conflict and then to its social background. One interviewee liked to deal with topics "where judgment can be enriched by my own experience and knowledge; where the subject matter is close to my own interests." But most simply dealt with whatever happened to capture their fancy. Sometimes a personal memory or family experience was the decisive factor; sometimes it was the picturesqueness of an age or an environment. "I wrote from nostalgia, I suppose," as interviewee told me. "I wrote about my own childhood." One said that something interesting would "just pop into my head." Another would find some topic or milieu irresistible. "I was always seized by the subject, just as in writing fiction." To the author of an important biography his protagonist had seemed "of limitless interest." The best summary of the selection process, however, came from the interviewee who maintained that he always had anywhere from twenty to fifty topics in mind. The decision which to pick was "instinctive," a "gut reaction"; it was "like falling in love." The procedure by which nonacademics choose their subjects appears unplanned and spontaneous, sometimes even haphazard.

Despite their lack of training in historical method or a clearly defined area of specialization, the research on which the nonacademic historians base their writing is of a very high order; indeed, it is as a rule indistinguishable from that which academic historians pursue. To be sure, since what they write is narrative history—primarily biographical, political, or social in content—they do not need the more recondite techniques of quantification, social-science analysis, or psychohistorical investigation. But for the sort of historiography they do, their methodology, though self-taught, is unimpeachable. Not only do they read the important secondary works on the subject, but they examine the published primary materials and the unpublished archival records as well. A careful scrutiny of their notes and bibliographies reveals in most cases no significant difference between the scholarly apparatus they employ and that of the academics. In short, though they compete in the literary marketplace for the patronage of a broad reading public, their technical expertise is quite comparable to what is generally found in specialized professional historiography.

But does their dependence on the sale of their books help shape the way they write? Do they consciously try to appeal to popular taste, to emphasize the colorful, simplify the complex, or dramatize the drab? When I asked my interviewees whether they aimed their writings at the general reader, the history buff, or the professional scholar, a few mentioned the general reader, and one even said that he was now more conscious of the opinion of professional scholars, something he found slightly inhibiting. Most of them, however, said that they wrote only for themselves, though in the hope that others would find it interesting. "Let the seeds fall where they may" was one reply. "I simply want to increase the general fund of historical knowledge." They all denied, moreover, that their approach to history, their way of viewing and portraying the past, was in any way influenced by popular taste or literary fashion. But since their perceptions and interests were closer to those of the general reading public, what they wrote had a wider appeal than the works of academic historians. This accounted for their success, though it was not the result of a conscious decision, they maintained.

The most important category of questions I asked dealt with the distinctive qualities which the nonacademic historians bring to historiography. How did they differ from the academics in their writing, and how did they explain that difference? All of the interviewees felt that the work of the nonacademics was by and large more subtle and perceptive, more sensitive to the diversity of life. As one of them expressed it, "academic historians, in interacting with one another, often lose contact with what they're writing about." They become addicted to "fads," they are "less free to pursue their interests," they find themselves imprisoned in "the formalities of footnotes." Another added that nonacademics are better at "re-creating the atmosphere in which events occur." They emphasize "character delineation," because they recognize that "plot derives from character." They are also generally "more tolerant of human frailty." Because of their independent position, moreover, "they can afford to be big." According to another interviewee, creative writing has to be "richly fertilized," it has to "feed on experience." In other words, the nonacademics perceive in the breadth of their vision the basic difference between them and academic historians.

And how did they acquire that vision? Here the answers almost invariably touched on the restrictive nature of the academic environment. The institutionalization of scholarship, to give a few examples, has the effect of "keeping the younger historians from flying." Academics are too often "constricted by worries about their colleagues"; they soon develop "tunnel vision." And yet "it is important for historians to know how nonhistorians behave." That is where the free-lancers, who "live in the world," have an edge. Their employment in pursuits other than the writing of history has sharpened their perception and understanding. As "lone wolves," they have a richer opportunity to meet a variety of people and situations than the college campus can provide. Even their greater mobility is an important asset. "Living in New York has considerable advantages over living in Sauk City." The nonacademics see themselves as more interested in the art of writing, the delineation of character, and the motivation of behavior than the average academic historian. They feel that they are closer to the realities of life, the ultimate source of historical understanding, than the cloistered university scholars.

Yet although all the interviewees recognized fundamental differences between them and the academic historians, they seemed puzzled when I asked them why there had been such a sharp decline in the relative number of nonacademics in the last fifty years. They hadn't thought about it and weren't even aware that it had occurred. Was I quite sure that a decline had in fact taken place? some asked. In any case, while the idea may have been surprising, it did not appear to disturb them. They were confident that their kind of historiography was in no danger. Asked whether there was a future for the nonacademic historian in America, they replied with a unanimous yes. Since "the professionals generally fail to meet the popular interest in history," the free-lancers would always have an important function to perform. "Of course there is a future. Everybody wants to hear a story, and the nonacademics know how to tell it." But the most affecting reply was simply: "It is important to have historians who are not obligated to anybody." The nonacademics, unlike academic scholars, remain untroubled by serious doubts about their prospects.

My last set of questions dealt with their relationship to the academic historians. Did they have any regular contacts, either professionally or socially? Did they exchange ideas and insights? Did they feel any sense of common participation in an exciting intellectual pursuit? The answers I received suggested that the two are separated by profound differences in interest and outlook. By and large, the nonacademics are outsiders in the network of organizations and publications which play such an important role in the lives of academic historians. Some are members of the American Historical Association, although they rarely go to its meetings or participate in its politics. While several belong to the Society of American Historians, that is an honorific rather than professional organization — membership is by invitation only — which emphasizes literary skill as much as technical expertise.

The nonacademic historians, moreover, do not follow the scholarly periodical and monographic literature with the same assiduity or regularity as academics. They read the things pertaining to the subject on which they happen to be working, but they are much less interested in what is being done in other fields or what is occurring in the profession at large. Indeed, they are often put off by the occupational chitchat which is a staple of conversation among academics. One of them, recalling a year he had spent with university scholars at a research institute, described it as on the whole an unpleasant experience. He had been a complete outsider. "I felt like the new kid on the block."

This undercurrent of tension is generally not apparent in the personal contacts between academic and nonacademic historians. Some of my interviewees complained, however, that they knew academics with whom they got along quite well on informal occasions, but in a professional setting the atmosphere became entirely different. "When you meet them face to face, they are very pleasant, but at conventions they can be most uncordial." A number of the nonacademics felt, moreover, that they were sometimes treated by academic scholars with superiority or condescension. One remembered that when he had given a course at a neighboring university, some of the faculty members had been supportive, but others had sneered behind his back that "he is just a stylist." When he once read a paper at a meeting of the American Historical Association, he was made to feel "amateurish." Another interviewee complained that there is great resentment by Ph.D's of successful non-Ph.D's. "They really protect their turf." When he had objected to a patronizing review of his book by some academic scholar, the only response was a wisecrack about "crying all the way to the bank." A third insisted that there was a "mind-set" among academics against those who had not "gone through the mill" or were not familiar with "professional jargon." One of the interviewees was especially critical of "computerizers," of those "who do nothing with people, with the human heart." They refuse to recognize that "history is not a science."

In view of such comments, I expected that they would all answer no to my last question: "On the whole, has the professionalization and institutionalization of historical learning had a beneficial effect on the discipline?" In fact the opposite occurred. Those who had thought about it agreed that the more systematic study of the past during the last hundred years had made possible a sounder and deeper understanding of historical experience. Indeed, despite its emphasis on technique at the expense of creativity, institutionalized scholarship had enabled the nonacademics to improve the quality of their own work. Academic historians had made the discipline "more solid"; they had forced it "to dig its feet into the facts." They had helped create "broader interest and productivity in the field." Without them there would be "much less primary material available for historical writing." All in all, "their weaknesses notwithstanding," they had done a great deal of "substantial work." Yet here and there I heard mild reservations. Professionalization had admittedly been "of great benefit" to historiography; it had led to "an immense increase in research." But "there is not as much fun now" as in the days of the independent hit-and-miss historians.

In short, my glimpse into the world of nonacademic history proved far more heartening than my earlier contemplation of the state of academic scholarship. Here is an area of the discipline which, though small, remains confident and hopeful. The optimism displayed by nonacademics reflects not only a sense of personal accomplishment, but their conviction that what they do is successful because it is indispensable. They believe that there will always be people interested in learning about the past from books which tell a good story, which portray human character, political vicissitude, social interaction, or armed conflict, which examine the vast collective experience of mankind. They are not troubled by the decline of history on the college compus; most of them are not even aware of it. They do not worry about the steady drift of students to competing fields like sociology, psychology, or economics. Their way of life, to be sure, as one of them told me, can produce "great anxiety" resulting from "financial pressure." For them it is "sink or swim." But there are also "important rewards, both material and intellectual." They feel that they have greater freedom, richer experience, and deeper insight than most university scholars. They are convinced that whatever happens to history as an academic discipline, they will continue to do what nonacademic historians have always done. All in all, I think they are right.

Index

DESIGNED BY JOANNA HILL
COMPOSED BY METRICOMP, GRUNDY CENTER, IOWA
MANUFACTURED BY INTER-COLLEGIATE PRESS, INC., SHAWNEE MISSION, KANSAS
TEXT AND DISPLAY LINES ARE SET IN PALATINO

Library of Congress Cataloging-in-Publication Data
Hamerow, Theodore S.
Reflections on history and historians.
Includes bibliographical references and index.
1. History — Study and teaching.   2. Hamerow,
Theodore S.   I. Title.
D16.2.H19   1987   907′.202   86-22451
ISBN 0-299-10930-5